PLAY FOR ALL Guidelines

PLAY FOR ALL Guidelines

Planning, Design and Management of
Outdoor Play Settings for All Children

Second Edition

Editors:
Robin C. Moore
Susan M. Goltsman
Daniel S. Iacofano

Contributors:
Sally McIntyre
Lynda Schneekloth
Jay Beckwith
Larry Bruya

Illustrators:
Yoshiharu Asanoumi
Nana Kirk

Project Director:
Susan Goltsman

Communications

Berkeley, California

MIG Communications, 1802 Fifth Street, Berkeley, CA 94710, USA, (510) 845–0953

Library of Congress Catalog Card Number: 92-064424
Main Entry Under Title:

*Play For All Guidelines: Planning, Design and Management of
Outdoor Play Settings for All Children*

   1.   Play and Playgrounds   2.   Environmental Design   3.   Child Development
   I.   Moore, Robin C.   II.   Goltsman, Susan M.   III.   Iacofano, Daniel S.

ISBN 0–944661–17-3

Second Edition coordinated by David Driskell and Anne Endrusick.
Cover design by Tim Lehane.

When using these guidelines . . .

The authors, editors, publishers, contributors, PFA participants and others involved in the preparation of this document assume no risk or liability for incidents arising from the application of this information in any way whatsoever.

This document should not be construed as a substitute for guidelines and requirements regarding play environments as set forth by the Consumer Product Safety Commission, the Americans With Disabilities Act, local codes and ordinances, or any other jurisdiction, nor should it be considered as a replacement for an independent agency's own guideline-setting process. It is expressly intended by the editors that the material contained in this book be used by communities and agencies in the process of developing their own guidelines which, ultimately, must be adapted to local conditions.

ABOUT THE EDITORS

The editors are partners in the planning and design firm of Moore Iacofano Goltsman, Inc., with many years experience in the field of children's environments. Together they founded PLAE, Inc. (Play and Learning in Adaptable Environments) in Berkeley, California, in 1980, through which projects related to children, environment and integration of children with disabilities continue to be sponsored—including Play For All.

Robin Moore holds degrees in Architecture (London University) and City Planning (MIT). His design research and development work with children's play environments began in Boston with the Lenox–Camden Experiment in Playground Design (1966); this was followed by his major work, the Environmental Yard (1971–81), in Berkeley, California. In 1984, the Environmental Yard was recognized by the National Endowment for the Arts as an Exemplary Design Research Project. Robin served as the principal investigator for the Accessibility Standards for Children's Environments project at the Center for Accessible Housing (where he is Director of Training and Dissemination), North Carolina State University. He has authored numerous articles and books, including *Childhood's Domain: Play and Place in Child Development* (Croom Helm, 1986; MIG Communications, 1990). He is Professor of Landscape Architecture at North Carolina State University, Raleigh; president of the International Association for the Child's Right to Play; and former chair of the Environmental Design Research Association.

Susan Goltsman, ASLA, holds degrees in Landscape Architecture (North Carolina State University), Environmental Psychology (University of Surrey, U.K.) and Environmental Design (Parsons School of Design, New York City). Susan is Director of PLAE, Inc. For the past twenty years, she has been creating programs and environments that promote the development of all children. She has been recognized by the National Endowment for the Arts and the American Planning Association for her work with children and youth, and received the 1986 California Park and Recreation Merit Award for PLAE's contribution to the field of recreation therapy. Recently, she has been the principal-in-charge for development of Standard Designs of Outdoor Play Areas for the U.S. Army's Child Development Centers. She currently serves on the ASTM Subcommittee on Accessibility Standards for Playground Equipment and is working with the Department of the Interior on the Accessible Design Guide for Outdoor Recreation Environments. Susan has taught at Stanford University in the Program on Urban Studies, has served as president of the California Council of the American Society of Landscape Architects (ASLA), and is a member of the board of the Northern California Chapter of ASLA.

Daniel Iacofano, Ph.D., AICP, holds degrees in Environmental Planning (University of California, Berkeley), Environmental Psychology (University of Surrey, U.K.) and Urban Planning (University of Cincinnati). For more than fifteen years, Daniel has applied his planning and design background to projects in community design, organizational planning and development, physical planning, strategic planning, and public involvement program design. He has been a Visiting Lecturer at Stanford University and the University of California at Davis, and has consulted and lectured throughout the U.S. and Europe, pioneering many innovative techniques for community participation and interagency collaboration. His work has won awards from the National League of Cities, the American Society of Landscape Architects, and the American Planning Association. He is also a former executive officer of the Environmental Design Research Association.

CONTENTS

Acknowledgments viii

Preface xi

PART A: SITE PLANNING AND DESIGN

1. Child Development Objectives 3

2. Site Analysis 5

3. Site Design Criteria 9

PART B: SETTING DESIGN AND MANAGEMENT

4. Management Criteria for Play Settings 29

5. Entrances 34

6. Pathways 38

7. Signage 54

8. Fences/Enclosures 60

9. Manufactured Play Equipment Settings 64

10. Multipurpose Games Settings 110

11. Ground Covers/Surfacing 114

12. Landforms/Topography 128

13. Trees/Vegetation 132

14. Garden Settings 142

15. Animal Settings 145

16. Water Settings 150

17. Sand Settings 160

18. Play Props and Manipulative Settings 166

19. Stage Settings 176

20. Gathering, Meeting and Working Places 179

21. Storage Settings 193

PART C: PFA GUIDELINES IN ACTION

22. Flood Park, San Mateo County, California . . 199

PART D: PROGRAMMING AND MANAGEMENT

23. Play Programming 229

24. Risk Management Strategies 233

APPENDICES

A. About Disability and Integration 247

B. Organizations and Institutions Involved 261
    in Play For All

BIBLIOGRAPHY 267

INDEX 283

ACKNOWLEDGMENTS

Publication of the first edition of the *Play For All Guidelines* represented the cumulative result of the efforts of many. First, the U.S. National Endowment for the Arts and the San Francisco Foundation, who were crucial in getting initial funding for Play For All.

Second, the members of the Play For All Task Force who were instrumental in mapping the scope of the program and setting its direction. The members were: **Jay Beckwith,** Playground Designer; **Kim Blakley,** Associate Director of Play Environments Research at the Graduate School of the City University of New York (CUNY); **Phyllis Cangemi,** Director, Whole Access; **Susan Goltsman,** ASLA, Director, PLAE, Inc.; **Roger Hart**, Ph.D., Director of the Center for Human Environments, CUNY; **Daniel Iacofano,** Ph.D., AICP, Principal in the planning and design firm of Moore Iacofano Goltsman; **Richard Klink,** ASLA, landscape architect with the Los Angeles Department of Parks and Recreation; **Sally McIntyre,** RTR, recreation therapist, PLAE, Inc.; **Clare Cooper Marcus,** Professor in the Departments of Architecture and Landscape Architecture, University of California at Berkeley; **Robin Moore,** President of the International Association for the Child's Right to Play (IPA); **Elaine Ostroff,** Director of the Adaptive Environments Center in Boston, Massachusetts; **Barry Ryan,** Compliance Division, Office of the California State Architect; **Lynda Schneekloth,** Associate Professor in the Department of Architecture, State University of New York at Buffalo; **Kevin Stoops,** Associate Park Planner for Seattle's Department of Parks and Recreation; and **Fred Etzel,** AICP, of Henn, Etzel & Mellon, Attorneys at Law, counsel to the PLAY FOR ALL Conference and PLAE, Inc.

Third, the working group facilitators, recorders and participants who conducted the review of the draft of the guidelines at the Stanford Conference, held in September, 1986: **Susan Goltsman,** ASLA, Project Coordinator; **Daniel Iacofano,** AICP, Process Manager; **Robin Moore,** Director of Research; **Sally McIntyre,** RTR, Administrator; **Yoshiharu Asanoumi,** Design Research; **Kerri Glover,** Clerical; **Carolyn Francis,** Recorder; **Mark Francis,** ASLA, Facilitator; **Joe Frost,** Ph.D., Facilitator; **Sharyl Green,** Facilitator; **Louis Hexter,** Recorder; **Clare Cooper Marcus,** Facilitator; **Jim Oswald,** Recorder; **Mary Jo Porter,** Recorder; **Lynda Schneekloth,** Facilitator; and **Leland Shaw,** Facilitator.

The following people participated in the development and review of the guidelines:

Suzanne Alexandra	Andrea Angelo	Karen Bagelatos
Jeanette Anders	Yoshiharu Asanoumi	James Barnard
Don Anderson	Jerry Bagelatos	Jay Beckwith

Joan Bergy
John Blackburn
Kim Blakely
Rae Blasquez
Judy Boshoven
Daniel Brenman
Larry Bruya, PhD
Shirley Bulpe, EdD
Karen Bult
John Busch
Don Cadman
Phyllis Cangemi
Rodney V. Castro
Ed Chandler
Rod Corbett
F. Clayton Dade
Charles O. Davis
Harry Dean, Jr.
Edith Dowley
J. Frederick Druck
Felix Drury
Stan Edmister
Jim D. Edwards
Sandra Edwards
Fred Etzel
Morgan Jasper
Susan Ferreyra
Carolyn Francis
Mark Francis
Joe Frost, PhD
Dick Gannon
Marilyn Golden
Selwyn Goldstein
Seymour M. Gold, PhD
Gabriel Goulart
Sharyl Green
Patricia Hadley

Goran Hag
Gary Harrison
Roger Hart, PhD
Horst Henke
Peter Heseltine
Chris Heusser
Louis Hexter
Paul Hogan
John Holborn
Eileen Hooker
Jeff Johnson
Susan Jurgenson
Susan Kaplan
Jennifer King
Steve King
Richard N. Klink
Walter Kocian
Gary Koenig
Susan Landry
Elaine Day LaTourelle
A. Ann Lovell
Deborah Learner
Louis Leff
Mary Lincoln
Denise J. Lynch
Rob Lynch
Dennis Maloney
Clare Cooper Marcus
Lauren Martelli
Kim McAdams
Sally McIntyre
Bill Michaelis, PhD
Robert Morrissey
Ann A. Nathan
Lindsay Nee
James E. Niskanen

Helge B. Olsen
Elaine Ostroff
Jim Oswald
Marlyn Perritt
Ewing Philbin
Dr. William Robert Pitt
Alice Poggi
Mary Jo Porter
Sally Reese
Christine Russell
William Russo
Greg Sagen
Jill Sager
Barbara Sampson, PhD
Lynda Schneekloth
Leland Shaw
Dannette Shoemaker
Amita Sinha
Fran Smith
Laurene Smith, PhD
Troy Squires
Sharon Stine
Kevin B. Stoops
Theodora Briggs Sweeney
Donna Thompson, PhD
Louis Torelli
Tod. W. Turriff
Michael J. Waite
Curt Wear
Cathy Weissberg
Rosemary Wills
Winifred Yen Wood
Marshal R. Wortham, PhD
Sue Wortham, PhD
Connie Zimmerman
Nicholas J. Zirpolo, PhD

Fourth, the almost 200 organizations and institutions (Appendix B) involved in Play For All who continue to lend support to the program in many ways.

Fifth, the following manufacturers of play equipment and surfacing who provided financial as well as informational support: Iron Mountain Forge; Big Toys; Creative Playgrounds, Inc.; Landscape Structures; Wooden Environments; Hags Play (Sweden); Airspace USA; Kompan; Log Rhythms; Playscapes; Tiger Hug Toys; Reese Industries; and Cam-Turf.

From the supporting cast of hundreds, special contributions by several individuals must be recognized: Peter Heseltine for his careful review of the manuscript with respect to European experience and literature; Lynda Schneekloth for generously allowing us to adapt sections of her manuscript for *Play Environments for Disabled Children*; Jay Beckwith for his draft of Chapter 9 in the first edition and the many other ideas he contributed during the development of the text; James Tuomey and James Donovan for their thoughtful critique from the manufacturing perspective and Phyllis Cangemi from the access perspective; Larry Bruya for his thorough review, critique and contributions to Chapter 9; and Sally McIntyre, for her thorough review of safety and accessibility issues and contributions to Chapters 9 and 11.

Thank you also to: Cheryl Barton, President, American Society of Landscape Architects; Barbara Sampson, Ed.D., Executive Director, The American Alliance for Health, Physical Education, Recreation and Dance; and Charles Davis, President, California Parks and Recreation Society. Their time and support was invaluable in promoting the work of Play For All.

Last but not least, a special garland of recognition goes to the staff at PLAE, Inc.: Yoshiharu Asanoumi, Ann Cuthbertson, Louis Hexter, Keri Glover, Erika Jenssen, Sally McIntyre, Jim Oswald, and Lowell Kline for his organizing, computer and desktop publishing skills. To these names must be added David Driskell and Anne Endrusick of MIG Communications for their painstaking coordination of the many revisions to the second edition. Without their tireless shouldering of responsibility none of this would have been possible.

PREFACE

Although five years have passed since Play For All Guidelines *was first released, much of what was said in the preface to the first edition in 1987 remains relevant (perhaps even more relevant) in 1992. Passage of the Americans With Disabilities Act and revisions to the Consumer Product Safety Commission Guidelines have given a strong legal mandate to the goal that the Play For All effort set out to accomplish in 1986 and 1987: to promote children's play areas as places where all children can play and learn together, without being exposed to unnecessary risks. We are therefore reprinting the preface from the first edition in near entirety, with the addition of a description of the Universal Design concept and two paragraphs to summarize the changes that were made in updating the* Play For All Guidelines *for 1992.*

A children's play environment of quality is more than a piece of play equipment set neatly into a circle of sand in a park, schoolyard or residential development.

Play is the child's way of learning. It is an intricate, intimate process which helps children develop and become socialized. Play is learning in its most experiential sense, but it is only as rich as the supporting social and physical environment. The *Play for All Guidelines* focus attention on the physical environment, where choice and diversity are the keys to success. A good play and learning environment must be designed as a range of settings carefully layered on the landscape. The design of a good play environment requires an interdisciplinary understanding of human development, and how that development can be stimulated by both natural and manufactured settings.

The *Play For All Guidelines* are a tool to help professional designers, park and recreation managers, and community groups make informed decisions about the planning, design, and ongoing management of children's play environments.

The *Guidelines* are based on six principal assumptions:

a. All children have a right to play. Play is a process by which children learn. Good quality play opportunities have a significant impact on child development.

b. The type, quality, and diversity of children's physical settings (play value) directly affect the type, quality, and diversity of children's play.

c. The type, quality, and diversity of the social setting (play leadership and program-ming) directly affects play value. Play leadership (or animation, as it is sometimes called), refers to the critical role of trained staff, or play leaders, engaging children in creative interaction with each other and their surroundings.

d. Children with physical, mental, emotional and social disabilities have an equal right to play opportunities.

e. Integration of children with different abilities is based on the concept of accessibility which relates to both the physical and social environments (e.g., the attitudes and awareness of staff towards children with disabilities will greatly affect the rate and depth of integration).

f. The quality of settings and their play value are severely threatened by liability costs and the threat of suit. Risk management strategies and management policies should be developed to protect the quality and value of children's settings.

Addressing the Safety and Liability Crisis

Today, safety, security, and liability have become major factors in determining the quality of children's outdoor play environments and play programs. While the safety and security of our children, whether in supervised or unsupervised play environments, justifiably deserves careful attention, the goals of safety and security must be balanced with the goal of providing stimulating and challenging environments for children's play and development. The concept of a healthy, safe environment need not be at odds with child development objectives.

Without taking risks, children cannot learn to their full potential. Settings must challenge them to take risks without being hazardous.

The difference between "hazard" and "challenge" must be understood when creating play settings. Children will use equipment and parts of the environment in all possible ways, regardless of design intentions. Since the idea of play is to explore and maximize the potential of any play setting, children will test its use to the limits of their abilities.

Such testing should present a challenge. It teaches children new skills. Children will run up slides, jump out of swings, and climb trees. Well-designed play settings reflect an understanding of children's behavior and provide for risk-taking without introducing hazards or unforeseen consequences.

Universal Design

Universal Design is the concept most readily applied to the design of environments for all people. This concept is directly counter to the idea of designing special facilities for people with special needs. In the past, the "special needs" approach has resulted in users with disabilities being segregated from their peers, relatives, colleagues, and friends as they navigate the physical environment. Universal Design is an attitude towards design that broadens the scope of accessibility to create environments that are usable by most people regardless of their level of ability or disability (Mace et al., 1990). In the design of integrated environments for children and their families, Universal Design is a critically important concept. It is achieved by thoughtful planning and design focused on user needs at all stages of the project.

The Purpose of Play For All

Play For All is a national program to develop design guidelines and criteria for children's play environments. The program has an added focus on the needs of children with disabilities, and their integration into the community of all children.

The guidelines are concerned primarily with public play environments. Other sectors of play environment development (daycare and child development centers, community-built settings, etc.), while recognized as important, are not explicitly addressed. The editors encourage professionals in these sectors to use these guidelines as a springboard.

In January 1986, PLAE, Inc., with support from the National Endowment for the Arts (an agency of the United States Government), convened a national task force of child development specialists, designers, and representatives of the disability field, in Berkeley, California. They proposed a National Working Conference which was held at Stanford University, California, in the fall of that same year. The main task of the conference was to review and critique a draft version of these guidelines, prepared by PLAE, Inc., based on an outline developed by the task force. This version of the *Play For All Guidelines* is based on the results of the conference review and additional reviews by experts in the field.

Play For All has been funded by the National Endowment for the Arts, the San Francisco Foundation, play equipment manufacturers, and other sources. The effort has been endorsed by nearly 200 organizations and universities.

In preparing the *Play For All Guidelines*, the editors drew heavily on a number of research publications and other guideline documents (published and unpublished) as referenced in the text. Permission to extract from these documents is gratefully acknowledged. A major source of information, from which the concept of play settings was derived, was the ten-year archive of research material (1971–80) from the Environmental Yard, Berkeley, California. Several chapters of this book are based on an earlier manuscript prepared by Robin Moore. A further invaluable source has been the archives of PLAE, Inc., from 1981–87, documenting the operation of a summer play program based at a number of park sites in the city of Berkeley, California.

As much as possible, these guidelines are based on empirical research findings and post-occupancy evaluations of children's settings.   In other cases where empirical research is weak or nonexistent, the guidelines are supported by arguments that stem from child development theories, especially those which emphasize the child's interaction with physical settings (Björklid, 1986).

In cases where PFA experts could not reach agreement on any aspect of a guideline, it has been omitted from the text and earmarked for further discussion. Issues requiring further research are also noted in the text.   In 1989, the issues and topics requiring further research were published elsewhere in a chapter titled "Playgrounds at the Crossroads" (Moore, 1989b).

About The Second Edition

The *Play For All Guidelines, Second Edition* has been updated to meet or exceed the requirements of the Americans With Disabilities Act (ADA) Guidelines (*Federal Register*, July 26, 1991) and the revised Consumer Product Safety Commission (CPSC) guidelines (*Handbook for Public Playground Safety*, 1991).   The reader should also refer to the background technical report (Ratté et al., 1990) to the revised CPSC guidelines. Because of the special accessibility needs of children, the *Play For All Guidelines, Second Edition* has also drawn upon the *Recommendations for Accessibility Standards for Children's Environments* (1992) developed by the Center for Accessible Housing (CAH) at North Carolina State University. These invaluable recommendations were developed through an extensive study commissioned by the Architectural and Transportation Barriers Compliance Board. They are in the process of being incorporated as a supplement to the Uniform Federal Accessibility Standards (UFAS).

Most of the changes between the first and second editions have been in chapters with detailed guidelines for safety and accessibility issues. These chapters are: Chapter 5, Entrances; Chapter 6, Pathways; Chapter 7, Signage; Chapter 9, Manufactured Play Equipment Settings; and Chapter 20, Gathering, Meeting and Working Places.

Berkeley, California
December 1987; July 1992

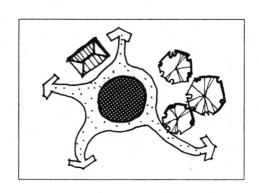

PART A :

Site Planning and Design

I. CHILD DEVELOPMENT OBJECTIVES

A well-designed, well-managed play environment should provide children with the following developmental opportunities (adapted from Schneekloth, 1985; Frost & Klein, 1983):

a. **Opportunities for motor skill development.** Large and fine muscle development, eye-hand-foot coordination, and balancing and locomotion skills must be supported. A range of opportunities to practice and test limits of abilities is required.

Regardless of the abilities of the children playing, they should have opportunities to practice and extend whatever skills they have. There should always be something further to reach. When children accomplish one skill, they can test themselves in new ways.

b. **Opportunities for decision making.** Any environment in which children live should allow them to make decisions about their own activities (Moore, 1989a). For this to happen:

1) The child must be in control of some or all of the environment.

2) The experiences provided by the environment must not be "dead-ends." They must have decision points that allow the child options for continuing a current activity, terminating it, or initiating a new one.

3) Decision points must be appropriate to different age and skill levels and present a sufficient range of choices so that forced repetition is avoided.

c. **Opportunities for learning.** Properties and relationships among physical objects, space, and self can be demonstrated in play settings. With appropriate supervision, children will solve problems, actively manipulate the environment, transform it, dismantle it, and re-create it in order to learn about the nature of the world.

Children need opportunities to change their relationship to the world and see it from new perspectives: from high and low places; through energy and motion; in time and space.

Programs must help children appreciate ecological relationships, the natural order of things, and the need for peaceful coexistence with each other, their surroundings, and ultimately, the planet.

1   Every type of child, no matter what level of ability, needs play opportunities.

2   Play settings should offer opportunities to learn about the physical world.

3   Play settings must be accessible to children with all forms of disability.

d.   **Opportunities for dramatic play**. The environment is a resource for imaginative and cooperative play; it provides the props and stage. The richness of physical elements in the setting and their relationship to each other should arouse curiosity and trigger imaginative associations (Moore, 1989a). If the environment is too literal, imagination will be limited; if too abstract, imagination will not be fully stimulated.

e.   **Opportunities for social development**. Settings must support positive interpersonal interaction and socialization between children with different abilities, between different ethnic groups, between girls and boys, and between children and adults (Moore & Wong, in press).

Children need opportunities for role playing, development of self-esteem, emotional development, and social skills development. Protected spaces must be available where small groups can withdraw from highly active equipment areas for quiet social play.

f.   **Playing should be fun**. Smiling faces and laughter are the clearest indicators of a successful play setting.

These behavioral goals and objectives apply to all environments used by all children.

2. SITE ANALYSIS

Every site is a special situation—in its own unique location in a particular community. External aspects (location, access, visibility, etc.) and internal aspects (size, shape, configuration, etc.) all influence site development, program administration, play opportunities, and integration.

Every site should be analyzed for its appropriateness as a children's play area. Levels of analysis should expand from site, to neighborhood, to regional context.

The park planner and designer may face the task of evaluating an existing site or portion of a site for rehabilitation; a pre-selected site for new construction; or, several sites for selection and eventual development. In each case the process is the same: site features are inventoried and evaluated; climatic, biophysical, and social contexts are assessed (Cunningham, 1984; Lynch & Hack, 1984; Moore & Wong, in press; Flood Park case example, Chapter 22; Rutledge & Molnar, 1986).

2.1 Design Programming and Analysis

Site analysis should occur at the same time that the design program is being prepared because each impacts the other with constraints and opportunities. An early analysis of the site will indicate its appropriateness for the proposed uses and indicate adjustments to the design program.

If the site designer or landscape architect is involved in the design programming, continuous reconciliation of the program will be required with site constraints, recreation program support, and the available budget for development (Moore & Wong, in press).

2.2 Existing Conditions

A thorough inventory of the characteristics of each site should include, but not be limited to (Lynch & Hack, 1984; Rutledge & Molnar, 1986):

a. **Location.** Is the site located so as to serve the population of the neighborhood? Is it visible and attractive? Is it easy to get to by foot, by bike, by car, by transit?

b. **Site Function.** Each site must be judged for its fitness to accommodate the intended programs and facilities. The site must have ample space for the planned use and be amenable to development. The site should not require extensive, expensive reworking to function as a play environment.

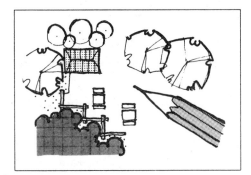

4   *Both external and internal aspects are important considerations in the site planning of play environments.*

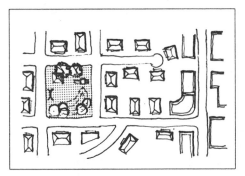

5   *What planning issues are raised by site location?*

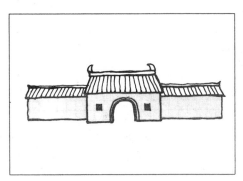

6   *Does the site have an existing use pattern which should be taken into account?*

c.   **Natural Features.**   What are the characteristics of the topography? Vegetation? Are there any especially valuable amenities such as water or views? Are there any potential hazards such as bluffs or swamps? Are there toxic compounds in the soil? (Freeberg, 1983)

Children have a strong interest in playing in and learning from nature: streams (natural or created), hillsides, climbing trees, dirt mounds, leaf piles, and so forth. Imported climbing rocks, wooded areas with trails, meadows, groves of trees, and amphitheaters can be natural extensions of more formal play areas.

d.   **Utilities.**   Is the site served by all utilities? Storm sewers?

e.   **Human and Cultural Features.**   Is the site in an area that is frequently traveled? Are there areas nearby where people congregate? How have people traditionally used the site, how is it used now, especially by children? Are there particular features that are well-used and valued by existing users?

What is the character, scale, and history of the neighborhood? Are there unusual design determinants such as special cultural or ethnic features to consider?

f.   **Existing Park Features.**   If sited within a park, how does the proposed playground relate to the entire park area with its trees, bushes, paths, walls, and drinking fountains? These must all be recognized as part of the child's play environment.

1)   **Topography** in or near the playground can provide active play space on slopes.

2)   **Landscaping and plantings** can provide screening, wind breaks, shade, shelter for retreat, and protective barriers.

3)   **Shelters** located close to the playground area can facilitate observation of children from covered seating areas.

4)   **Storage** [close by] for equipment and play props is an asset.

5)   **Sports fields** are an asset, if located where the sideline activity will not interfere with the play area.

6)   **Restrooms** and **drinking fountains** located adjacent to the play area are essential. If possible, they should be for play area users only.

7)   **Medical facilities** information should be provided close at hand, especially in unsupervised areas.

8)   **Public telephones** are needed as an extra measure of security and as a service to users.

2.3   Community Context (Adapted from Canadian Council on Children and Youth, hereafter CCCY, 1980*).

The opportunities and constraints of the local community should be fully recognized and used to advantage in the planning, design, and management of play settings. The following strategies will help:

a.   **Adapting to local conditions.** This document should be used as a set of guidelines, not prescriptions. Adjustments in how the guidelines should be applied and to what settings will vary to suit local conditions, demographic and social factors, legal requirements, and economic resources.

b.   **Involving other programs.** While these guidelines focus primarily on playspace design, the physical aspect is only one part of the total provision for play opportunities. In any situation, physical planning should be undertaken in concert with other play programs to provide maximum support of child development.

c.   **Integrating with open space planning.** The planning of local play spaces must be integrated into comprehensive planning strategies for the whole community. Collaboration with departments such as public works, housing, education, and recreation will avoid duplication of effort as well as enhance opportunities for supporting child development.

d.   **Collaborating with all agencies working on behalf of children.** No individual, organization, government department, or level of government is likely to have all the resources and expertise to plan effectively for the full range of children's play opportunities. Efforts must be coordinated.

e.   **Encouraging community participation.** Consultation and participation by community organizations, families, and individuals contribute to successful planning for children's play. Local residents, child development experts, and children should be included as members of the planning team. Incorporation of the ideas,

* A full listing of reference abbreviations is given at the beginning of the Bibliography.

suggestions, and criticisms of citizens makes the planning, design and management of the play space a community effort. For children, it can become a significant learning experience. It is also an effective risk management strategy because it helps citizens understand and support children's developmental needs, including the need to take risks.

f.   **Facilitating children's involvement.** Children and youth are important contributors to the planning process, and active participation by young people in community projects can help reduce their sense of alienation. Techniques are available to facilitate the genuine participation of young people (Hart, 1987). However, adult commitment to participation by young people in the planning and management of play spaces is the first critical step towards involvement.

3. SITE DESIGN CRITERIA

Because each site, community, and planning process is different from the next, a wide margin of choice, interpretation, and a combination of physical settings is needed to fit many different circumstances. The designer must be familiar with the particular characteristics of each situation.

The following criteria can help, but are not sufficient by themselves to produce a design solution. They provide a framework for the designer's imagination and skill.

There are five key design criteria for a good play environment (AEC, 1980; CCCY, 1980; CMHC, 1980; Cooper Marcus, 1986; Los Angeles, 1987; Schneekloth, 1985; Seattle, 1986): accessibility; safe challenge; diversity and clarity; graduated challenge; and flexibility. But there are many others of almost equal importance as described below.

a. **Accessibility**. Good places must be accessible to the intended users. This term implies that children can first of all get there safely; that it is integrated into the daily life of a child; that it is "barrier free" (i.e., it has no or few physical barriers to its use) and, further, that it is "psychologically accessible" (i.e., attractive and secure) and understandable to the children who use it.

Entrances mark the interface between site and community and should be designed to entice children into the site. A primary entrance should be designated and highly visible while secondary entrances may be less visible so children can "discover" them. Following are general considerations regarding site access. More specific guidelines are provided under "Setting Design and Management."

1) Play areas should be located to minimize potential contact between children and traffic (Beamish, 1980; Sandels, 1968).

2) Entrances to the park or playground should be clearly identified, visible from nearby housing, and used to direct young pedestrians along safe routes to the park.

3) Parking areas and driving aisles must be separated from play areas by barriers. Parking area perimeters should be open and unobstructed to view.

4) Play areas should be accessible from main pathways through the park and routes to other use areas such as ballfields and picnic facilities.

5) Main pathways should be connected with main entrances, exits, meeting areas, and working places to provide users with a clear mental image of the facility, especially children with orientation impairments.

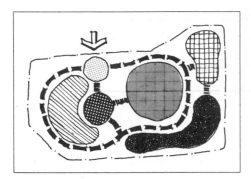

7 *Circulation is a critical aspect of site planning.*

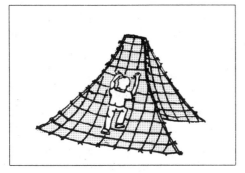

8 *Play settings should include challenging environments and play elements.*

6) Fences, berms, plantings, or other devices should be used to define playground areas, but not so strongly that they seem separated from the rest of the park.

7) Hard surface paths and bike paths should be separated from play areas.

8) Paths leading to restrooms and drinking fountains will inevitably carry bicycle traffic and must be separated from children's play areas.

9) Maintenance vehicles must have access to playground areas. Access ways must be at least 10 feet wide and be capable of supporting service vehicles.

b. **Safe Challenge** (Moore, G.T., et al., 1979; Seattle, 1986). Play areas should provide highly challenging settings with many different events for the physical development of the upper body, balance, and coordination without exposing children to unnecessary hazards. This function is important because of the correlation between learning disorders and balance deficits. Coordination affects judgement about taking risks—the ability to visualize a movement before making it. Activities requiring full coordination should be supported.

A hazard is something a child does not see; a challenge is a risk the child can see and chooses to undertake or not. Children need to take risks to challenge their skills and courage. A risk-free play area is neither possible nor desirable.

Injuries can and do occur from many different types of activities on playgrounds; falls cause the majority. Any fall can injure, particularly if the child strikes a hard surface (Boyce et al., 1984; Langley et al., 1981, 1982; Langley, 1984; Ratté et al., 1990). Far more research is needed in order to understand the relationships between accidents and environment—both physical and social aspects.

To provide safe challenges, the following should be considered:

1) Settings which stimulate upper body strength like rings, turning bars, horizontal bars, climbing trees, swinging ropes, and things to lift should be designed and positioned to promote mixed use by children with and without disabilities. Designs that protect children from common hazards, especially falling and collision, reduce the possibility of severe injury.

2) Balance settings which stimulate the inner ear, such as tire swings, climbing surfaces, bridges, narrow rails, or walls.

3) Coordination and judgement settings, such as horizontal ladders, stepping logs, climbers, tunnels, banister slides.

9 *Use of the natural environment adds more sensory variety.*

c. **Diversity and Clarity**. To meet their wide-ranging, ever-changing needs, children need access to a diversity of play settings. To stimulate curiosity and exploration, environments should be novel and complex. Some aspects should change continually. Other aspects should be predictable to foster feelings of security.

Novelty and predictability will be balanced in an environment that presents a clear overall image to the user. Major areas, main access routes, and principal play opportunities should be easily seen (which may differ for children with disabilities because of sensory or mobility limitations). Many minor "backwaters" should be designed to be discovered over time.

Diverse play settings can liberate creative energy from children. A breadth of action and interaction distinguishes a play environment that is well-designed and well-managed; that always has something new to offer, but at the same time is thought of as a familiar friend, a comfortable secure haven.

An aim of site design is to locate and juxtapose settings in such a way that the greatest variety of play activity patterns will be generated, producing the greatest possible range of interactions and relationships while meeting the requirements of different ages, abilities, and development stages.

d. **Graduated Challenges** (Moore, G.T., et al., 1979; Seattle, 1986). Play settings should provide activities with a broad range of challenges and graduated levels of safe risk-taking to children of different ages and abilities.

Children should be invited to test their skills and build self-confidence. They should be able to reach, jump, climb, or slide to the level of their ability without frustration and should be able to withdraw from the activity without the risk of failure and humiliation.

1) Provide several levels of difficulty for each activity: steep, steeper and steepest.

2) Provide several levels of accomplishment for each activity: high, higher and highest.

3) Provide places to enter and exit a setting at intermediate levels.

4) Arrange settings so that the next level of challenge is apparent.

5) Do not relate challenges to heights, hazards and danger, but to increasingly more difficult mastery of the body.

Settings do not have to be dangerous to be challenging. The important aspect of graduated challenges is that the challenge be "perceived" (Schneekloth, 1985). Therefore, construct physically challenging settings so that children read them as challenges, but in such a way that if they fail, they are not injured. For example:

1) Balance beams of varying widths are just as challenging one foot off the ground as six feet off the ground; it is their width that is critical. (The same is true of cargo nets and similar devices.)

2) High places are perceived as challenging regardless of the safety of their enclosure: the smaller the high place, the more dangerous it is perceived, even if well-protected by edges and railings.

e.   **Flexibility.**   Physical elements that can be changed and moved around are needed. Children develop continuously, so their needs change as they learn and grow. To accommodate these changes, spaces must also have the ability to change. With careful planning, a space can allow for continual "tailoring" without requiring costly or time-consuming renovations. Care must be taken to design flexible structures.

Play leaders should be trained to manage flexible spaces. The environment should allow for easy rearrangement of elements for different programs and the addition or removal of special equipment for particular activities.

The needs of children with disabilities develop just as the needs of children without disabilities. Disabilities may be associated with other predictable conditions in individual children. A disease may be degenerative, a disabling condition may improve, or a child's physical and mental abilities may develop at different rates. The physical environment for all children must be planned with present and future adaptations in mind. Methods of supporting flexibility include:

1) Modular systems that can be moved around.

2) Mobile equipment, such as inflatables, hoses, buckets, pulleys, and ropes.

3) Play bases that can be set up, taken down and moved to a new location periodically.

4) Add-ons such as sheets that can be used to transform a play structure into a fire truck, spaceship, house, storefront, etc.

5) All manner of natural objects and materials.

f. **Defensible Space.** Play areas should be visible to both parents and children, although local values vary on this issue and should be assessed. There must be no area hidden from view which could encourage or harbor deviant or criminal behavior. This is especially important in unsupervised or partly supervised areas and less important in fully supervised areas (Cooper Marcus & Sarkissian, 1986).

1) Boundaries of the play area should be defined, but transparent. There should be no high, continuous, opaque barriers between nearby houses and the play area.

2) Nearby housing or other places where adults gather should be used as the "eyes" of the neighborhood. Children's areas should be both visible and accessible (Cooper Marcus & Sarkissian, 1986).

3) Large pieces of equipment might be placed toward the back of the site; other equipment might be either slightly recessed or raised to maintain visibility throughout the area.

4) Spaces and equipment must be designed and placed to allow views over, under and around. Private play spaces should be semi-enclosed with enough openings to see a child from any angle.

5) Adults should have two directions of visibility into all play spaces: from the surrounding area and from the play area itself.

6) Structures or vegetative barriers should be open for two-thirds of their enclosure.

7) Care must be taken to balance defensible space requirements with play value. At times, it is valuable for children to have at least an illusion of privacy.

8) Tunnels, openings into or under a play space should be large enough for an adult and should have at least two means of egress.

g. **Supervision.** The presence of adult playground supervisors allows for a much greater range of activities than at unsupervised areas. Activities which would be too hazardous, too difficult to maintain, or too difficult to organize and equip without supervision can be planned if there are to be active recreational programs at the park. Play area designers should be aware of this potential and provide programmable spaces and facilities (Westland & Knight, 1982).

10 *Program support is a critical consideration in site planning and design.*

11 *Supervision is a critical aspect of site planning.*

h. **Permanence.** Elements that remain fixed provide familiarity, security, and identity (e.g., entrance features, benches, specimen trees, large rocks, play structures).

i. **Change.** Elements that indicate changes in season (e.g., deciduous trees), weather (e.g., plants like bamboo that move in the wind, materials like sand that gets wet when it rains) and the life of the community (e.g., bulletin boards).

j. **Open-endedness.** One way to provide flexibility is with elements that users can manipulate and build onto for their own reasons (e.g., a corner of a play structure that can be draped with a blanket to make a "house," a low shelf where "mixtures" can be made from plant parts) (Moore, 1986 a,b).

k. **Manipulability.** Some aspects of settings should allow children to manually change them to serve their own purposes (e.g., sand, dirt, water, vegetation, and small toys) (Moore, 1989a).

l. **Multisensory Stimulation.** Settings should expose users to the greatest range of colors, smells, textures, shapes, sizes, sounds, objects, materials, interactions, people, climate, time, space, movement, and change. (See also Multisensory Cues, item **w.** below.)

m. **Ambient Microclimate/Year-round Use.** Settings should protect users from excessive wind, rain, sun, shade, and noise (protection from smog is also necessary in some locations), and provide for year-round bodily comfort. Trees, walls, and shrubberies are important modifiers of climate (Moore & Wong, in press).

The play season for many play areas could be expanded to year-round use by consciously creating favorable microclimates and providing protection from adverse weather conditions. It is important to provide sunny areas, shady areas, wind buffers, and dry spots. Cold climate play settings of snow and ice need careful consideration (Björklid, 1984/85; Thompsen & Borowieka, 1980). The features most appreciated by children are slopes suitable for sliding and sledding activities. Such features should be located to avoid potential conflict with other users. Flat areas that can be flooded and used for skating and other sliding games are also desirable.

All play areas should be capable of year-round use. While some special features, such as wading pools, might not be used during the winter (although they may be flooded for skating and sledding activity in cold climates), other play elements will be. The special features that may be built with the supervised play area

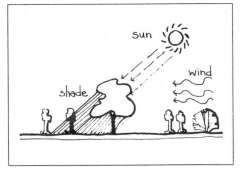

12 *Microclimate modification is a critical aspect of site planning.*

13 *Play settings should be sunny.*

14 *Play settings should provide shade.*

15 *Play settings should protect children from cold winds.*

must be designed to withstand weather, vandalism, and deterioration which can occur during the off-season and when supervisors are not present.

1)   Local climatic conditions should be taken into account when designing play areas. Best local climates for play area sites are usually on south or southeast slopes, near water, and on upper or middle slopes rather than at their foot or crest.

2)   Wind is generally quieter on the leeward rather than the windward side of a slope.

3)   Wind speeds on the crest of a ridge may be 20% greater than on flat ground. Wind also tends to speed up around the sides of buildings.

4)   Thick belts of shrubs or trees are effective wind breaks. They reduce wind velocities by more than 50% for a distance downwind of ten times their height and by 35% for twice that distance.

5)   Structures can block winds, channel winds, or create unpleasant, gusty, "wind tunnel" effects.

6)   Depending on climatic conditions, play areas and activities should be located to either avoid or take advantage of the shading effects of buildings and evergreen tree clusters.

7)   Deciduous trees provide summer shade and sun in winter.

8)   Proper drainage should help to dry play areas quickly after rain.

n.   **Shelter.** There should be some shelter at every playground even though it might only be a place to get out of the rain, like a covered picnic table.

Ideally, there should be a shelter house containing indoor play space combined with storage for equipment and play props.

1)   **Location.** A shelter should be located near the center of action: a wading pool, playing fields or special play feature. It should be highly visible and have clear sight lines to all areas of the play setting; however, space for quiet activities should also be available, perhaps on the nonactive side of the shelter.

2)   **Storage.** The shelter can be used to store maintenance equipment, chlorine and pool-cleaning equipment, sports equipment, mobile play things, and play props.

3)   **Use.** The shelter may be used as a place for children to "hang out" and play indoor games or for special events, such as plays, dances, and community activities. In this sense it would function as a "clubhouse."

o.   **Social Interaction.** Settings that stimulate social development and support social relationships for different-sized groups should be provided (e.g., bench and platform groupings, enclosed sitting areas, small shelters, play houses, domes, multi-person slides).

p.   **Design for All Ages.** Wherever possible, play areas should be designed for users of all age groups, although some separation may be necessary because of incompatible activities. Often, children's play areas lack facilities or accommodations for teenagers, parents, or other adults. Providing facilities and accommodations for adults will encourage family use. Barrier-free design and good maintenance will encourage use by everyone. Facilities should include:

1)   Hard surfaced areas for court games and bike riding.

2)   Challenging equipment, especially if there is a supporting recreation program at the park.

3)   Picnic tables, barbecue stands, comfortable seating, lawn game areas, and checkerboard tables.

4)   Specially designed areas for preschool children.

q.   **Variety of Social Spaces** (Moore & Wong, in press; Seattle, 1986). A variety of spaces, from small to large, are necessary to support different-sized groups of children engaged in different social activities:

1)   Small spaces for quiet play by one to five children.

     These spaces can serve as "refuges" that allow individuals and small groups to withdraw from social interaction when desired (Kirkby, 1989).

2)   Private places supporting quiet exploration, that children can get into but adults cannot, such as under low platforms, spaces on different levels, and areas screened by vegetation.

     Children, like adults, need time and space to be alone or in small groups. Make sure active, noisy areas are separated from quiet spaces.

3)   Age-specific places as well as places where several age groups can play together.

Preschool children like to play in their own groups but in the company of older children; therefore, preschool areas should be included in spaces for older children.

4)   Semi-enclosed spaces for group play led by adults.

5)   Large grassy spaces for large group play.

6)   Large group areas designed to facilitate gatherings of an entire class, a whole family, or a complete neighborhood for a wide range of activities.

7)   Child-sized tables and benches.

By providing a variety of spatial settings—private, semiprivate, and public—the stage is set for a spectrum of personal and social experiences that together can contribute to full child development (AEC, 1980).

Children with disabilities often have limited opportunities for large group experiences. Environments which allow the experience of solitude as well as group activity can help children develop social skills and positive self-identities.

Where possible, leave space for wheelchairs to pull up for peer interaction, or for a hearing-impaired child to be close to a speaker or interpreter. Note: the idea is not to make a "parking space" for wheelchairs, but to provide enough space so that a person in a wheelchair can move about easily.

r.   **Variety of Spatial Experiences** (Moore, 1966, 1974; Seattle, 1986). Children need to learn spatial concepts such as over/under, in/out, up/down, right/left, depth and directionality, and the limits of fingers, toes, and head. They also need to measure the risk of jumping, reaching, and falling. To learn these concepts, children need a variety of spatial experiences.

1)   High places such as knolls and towers from which to view activities.

2)   Differently sized spaces to crawl in, under, over, or through.

3)   Environmental cues such as textures and shadows.

4)   Opportunities to fall, jump, or drop safely (however, for children with brittle bones, a 6-inch drop may be too much).

16   *Play settings should provide a variety of spaces to facilitate social interaction and retreat.*

17 *Children need to learn spatial concepts such as in/out, up/down and right/left.*

18 *Play settings should offer nest-like spaces for quiet retreat and observation.*

19 *Children sometimes need to get away from the action.*

5) A variety of fixed reference points for orientation.

6) A variety of climbing experiences: up/down, in/out, over/under, etc.

s. **Retreats and Breakaway Points** (Moore, G.T. et al., 1979; Seattle, 1986; Schneekloth, 1985). Although children need to interact with their peers, they also need to be alone, to get away and dream, to escape from external pressure. They need secluded spaces to engage in quiet cognitive, social, and manipulative play, individually or in small groups. Nooks are required for solitary play and for watching others (Moore & Wong, in press).

At times, all children feel an acute need for privacy, to retreat from intense play or conflict, or from a new activity that is discovered to be too difficult or otherwise unpleasant. The design should allow a child to contemplate an activity before deciding to do it, and to leave before completing an activity without feeling failure, thus helping to maintain a positive self-concept.

An ideal retreat is neither too close nor too far from other children; it should provide privacy and the opportunity to observe the behavior of peers from a distance (Moore, 1979).

Escape opportunities prevent panic and provide encouragement for exploration by offering face-saving exits from unfavorable situations. Some groups can benefit by retreating from the larger population, thereby avoiding inappropriate comparison and conflict. There is some evidence that ethnic minorities play more easily when not outnumbered. The same may be true for children with disabilities. Children need places to test their own abilities without feeling that people are watching (the "fishbowl effect").

Provide more than one means of egress from challenging activities. For example, a ladder may have access to two platforms before reaching a top level or a platform may have both a slide and a ladder.

t. **Visible Completion Points** (Moore, G.T., et al., 1979; Seattle, 1986). For encouragement and to avoid frustration, children need evidence of their success and accomplishments—milestones which tell them they are improving their skills. Play settings should provide:

1) Clear stages of completion, such as climbing platforms at different heights, viewed by all.

20   *Play settings should include visible completion points.*

2) Positive signals at the point of completion or accomplishment, such as a bell to ring or something that can only be seen at or from the top.

3) Combinations of challenges and completion points scaled to children's capabilities.

u.   Spatial Orientation (Nordhaus et al., 1984). Settings must contain appropriate signage (see Chapter 7, Section 3, Program/Site Information). In addition, primary facilities such as restrooms, telephones, and program headquarters should be treated as landmarks and located so that they are visible from pathways. A direct view of a facility is the simplest and most effective means of orientation. (This does not apply to everything on the site. Less important facilities and opportunities need to be "discovered" by the users. Too much openness and visibility can destroy the pleasure of exploration.)

Spatial orientation also applies to inside-outside relationships. Siting and exposure to external landmarks can help users orient themselves to their surroundings.

v.   Landmarks/Visual Identity (Schneekloth, 1985; Seattle, 1986). Landmarks are key orienting devices used by all people to guide their movement through space. Because of their memorable form, or strategic location, landmarks tell us where we are in relationship to the whole.

Landmarks are elements that stand out strongly against their backgrounds because of their contrasting shape, silhouette, color, texture, or size. They help establish the identity of a place (Lynch, 1961).

Landmarks can be very effective in helping children orient themselves in space, establish a sense of inhabiting their "own place," and acquire clear memories of their environment. These are valuable means for children to develop psychological independence (Moore, 1966, 1978b).

Provide easily recognizable objects and experiences (acoustic, tactile, visual, olfactory) such as play structures, trees, hills, or ponds, which have known, permanent locations in the playground. Some should have a strong enough impact to provide an identifying image for the whole site.

Tall features from which children can view their surroundings and which can be seen from a distance are powerful landmarks (Moore, 1966).

Temporary landmarks such as flags and banners can be provided and, in some cases, made by children themselves.

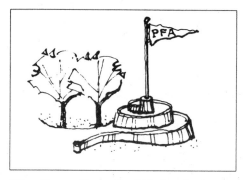

21   *Play settings should help orient children and provide a strong sense of identity.*

w. **Multisensory Cues** (AEC, 1980; Schneekloth, 1985; Flood Park case example, Chapter 22). A multisensory setting provides important cues for orientation and wayfinding for children with a variety of needs. The frequent repetition and reinforcement of cues can help capture attention and enable a child to cope with a strange environment. Sight, for example, can be reinforced by touch and sound.

Especially for children with sensory disabilities, play settings should emphasize all the senses: taste, touch, sight, smell, and hearing. Sites should be planned and settings designed to stimulate the development of all the senses.

The pairing or repetition of cues reinforces information for all children. Different levels on a play structure, for example, can have a different flooring to cue children about how high they are off the ground. At the same time, this tactile cue can reinforce the visual cues of safety rails, color coding, etc. This further aids learning since one child can use the cue most easily learned and teach others.

Sound. Sound can provide landmarks for children with visual and physical disabilities. Street lights, for example, can be coordinated with a pattern of sounds to allow the child to use an auditory cue for safe passage across the street.

Sounds are also important as a play phenomena. Children delight in producing sounds by striking things; it gives them a sense of interaction with the environment. Therefore, play settings should be designed to produce constant and patterned sounds (wind chimes, plants that make sounds like bamboo) to encourage children to rely on auditory sensations for orientation. Identify special areas with peculiar sounds. Giant musical instruments can be constructed (Sutton, 1985).

Children with visual, mental and physical disabilities can use echoes to determine their location in an enclosed space. There are many ways to design echoes. A tunnel is a classic example that children love. Use tunnels that have openings and closings at various places so that the experience of moving through an enclosed space becomes familiar. Paths with solids and voids along one edge can be used as sound cues to indicate the approaches to intersections.

Movement and orientation skills are dependent to some extent on locating oneself with respect to the mass/void continuum in the environment. Sound is used as a major cue in this respect. Children with visual disabilities also need practice to refine their "facial vision," i.e., the ability to sense physical barriers, and to stop before running into doors and walls. A combination of solids and voids on playgrounds can provide such experiences in a fun way.

22   Play settings should be places of multisensory stimulation.

23   Play settings should expose children to the acoustic environment.

24 *Tunnels can have sequences of solids and voids.*

25 *Tactile sensations can be exciting experiences.*

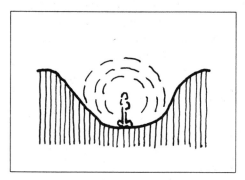

26 *Enclosed space.*

Touch. Everyone uses touch to gather information. It tells children about changes and continuations in their environment. Unclear cues are obviously confusing and can reduce the desire for exploration. Textures should be used to reinforce the kind of experience a child can expect: changes of texture where there is a change of activity or spatial relationship; different textures to designate different areas of the playground. Such treatments must be used consistently.

Sight. For the children with partial vision, "visual tracking" is an important learned skill for movement and orientation. To support visual tracking, settings should have bright reflective colors that stimulate vision and help children move through space. Use graphics that help children practice visual tracking. At the same time, take care not to visually overload the setting for users with full sight.

Smell. Fragrant plant materials can help orientate children with visual disabilities, especially if used to reinforce other sensory cues.

x. **Scale, Size, Shape, Enclosure, and Continuity.** These are the basic dimensions of spatial design which must be varied, juxtaposed, contrasted, and orchestrated to produce a range of spatial experiences suitable for different developmental and age requirements.

(**Scale** refers to the relative size of something; **size** refers to the actual dimensions; **shape** refers to the geometrical characteristics; **enclosure** is the sense of being contained by space; and **continuity** means the ability to move smoothly from point to point.)

y. **Play Above the Ground Plane** (Moore, 1974b; Seattle, 1986). Children need to play and travel above the ground plane in a challenging but safe manner, always with a choice of exits. Climbing is basic to development of gross motor skills, particularly body control, hand-feet coordination, and balancing on uneven, changing surfaces. Think of children's spatial experience in all three dimensions.

Children are particularly attracted to moving up, down, and through space. Think of free-flowing activities, such as swing ropes and safe trapeze-like experiences. Consider the "climb-ability" of all elements. Provide:

1) A variety of safe climbing experiences: both rigid surfaces (platforms, ladders, rocks, and trees); and flexible ones (cables, tires, nets).

2) Safe climbing and resting spots above the ground at many heights and levels.

3) Space for small groups to play together above ground.

27   *Open space.*

28   *Play settings should provide opportunities to play above the ground plane.*

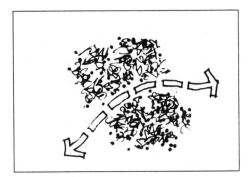

29   *Play areas should be structured as a system of differentiated (separate-yet-connected) settings.*

z.   **Differentiated Settings** (AEC, 1980; Moore & Wong, in press; Seattle, 1986). Different age groups use play spaces in different ways: some need private places within sight and hearing of their parents while others need places where different age groups mingle, learn from each other, and enjoy each other's company.

Children achieve different developmental goals at different times of their lives and at different rates. Developmental stages have varying skill levels which require settings to be used in different ways. Settings should therefore vary in space, size, and location, and be interconnected to give children choices between types of play.

Well-defined activity areas facilitate children's participation in all activities. The qualities of each space depend on the activities that go on there. Children who are easily distracted or have perceptual problems will benefit from clearly defined areas.

Children can recognize what activities are appropriate to certain spaces. Space dividers that separate areas with different functions can be as obvious as walls or as subtle as changed lighting. Carefully chosen signs, color cues, changes in level, and varying textures communicate the functions of particular areas.

For the most part, settings should be differentiated in terms of size and physical character, rather than by age or some other social division. Social divisions are unrealistic and usually create more problems than they solve, with the following exceptions:

1)   Areas should be set aside for the exclusive use of parents and caregivers with very young children.

2)   Raised areas with shade and adequate seating should be provided for adults and older children to oversee small children.

Further recommendations regarding the differentiation of settings include:

1)   Locate settings and equipment for large-muscle activity away from settings for small-muscle manipulative play.

2)   Locate high-density activity areas with care to avoid negative impacts on adjacent low-density settings.

30 *Well-defined activity areas may help children recognize appropriate activities for certain spaces.*

31 *Differentiation and linkage are critical considerations.*

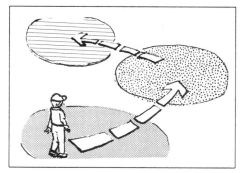

32 *Transition spaces allow children to move comfortably from one activity to another.*

3) Provide links between settings so that children can move easily from one to another and children of different abilities can see and interact with each other.

4) Differentiate between settings based on attributes such as:

- Types of play, either active or passive.
- Equipment size.
- Developmental task (quiet retreat, programmed, large muscle, etc.).
- Physical character (sand area, water play, moving equipment).
- Group size (single child, one to four children, six to ten and so on).

5) Identify settings by developmental goals rather than age groups (with the exception of separating toddlers and preschoolers). Provide links between developmental levels.

6) Within play areas, design the circulation in a looping form and use it to define activity settings. Looping circulation assures no dead-ends and allows children to progress steadily from one setting to the next.

7) Use circulation to encourage a developmental progression through graduated challenges. Links between settings of different levels of difficulty should be clear.

8) Avoid straight stretches of path that tempt children to run too fast, creating unsafe conditions.

9) Locate all settings to be at least partly visible from circulation areas so children can easily choose where they want to go.

10) Clearly separate main pathways from main activity settings and related circulation.

11) Design circulation routes to be wide and flat enough for wheelchairs and turnabouts and, where appropriate, for play activity and general milling-about. Circulation routes should not overlap with activity settings that can be easily disrupted by noise and movement.

12) Provide clearly defined transition spaces to allow children to move comfortably from one activity to the next. Children who have difficulty relating to new environments—young children, shy children, or children who are autistic—need clearly demarcated transitional spaces. Without them, they may have trouble joining in and focusing on new activities.

Children using wheelchairs and other special equipment may need extra space to transfer onto play features and to park or store their equipment.

13) Clearly define the play setting boundaries. This is important for supervision and to make sure children know what is acceptable behavior within each setting, especially when it is sharply different from adjacent settings. Locational awareness is important for children's psychological security and willingness to engage in new experiences (Schneekloth, 1985).

Edges are visually and tactually the most recognizable cue to differentiate settings. Even very small infants can see clearly defined edges as can many visually impaired children.

Accidents are more probable when objects, spaces, and activities are not clearly differentiated.

Define boundaries using objects and/or acoustic, tactile, visual, and olfactory cues so that the sequence of settings and their relationship to the whole can be clearly perceived. Articulate edges by contrasting field/ground relationships through color, materials, spatial relationships, and sun/shade patterns.

aa. **The "Edge" Effect.** To seek psychological and social comfort, children often prefer to gather around the edges of a space. The location of edges should be considered carefully in relation to other determinants, such as orientation, activity pattern, access points, etc. Where appropriate, build social/play elements into edges—design walls as places to sit, hide behind, climb on, walk along, etc.

Edges are also significant habitats where plants and animals (and people) can find shelter, especially internal corners (the meeting point of edges).

Edges can be readily created in the interior of a site along setting boundaries—many times multiplying the edge effect—to support a complex pattern of interactions, particularly between people and plants.

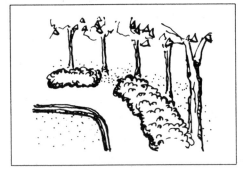

33 *Play settings should contain well-defined activity areas and edges.*

bb. **Undefined Places** (Chawla, 1990; Moore & Wong, in press; Schneekloth, 1985). Play settings can be used to stimulate creative and fantasy behavior. There is some evidence that undefined settings support dramatic play especially well (Hart, 1979; Moore, 1986c). In such settings, an undefined structure can become anything a child wishes, from a castle to a car.

34 *Open-ended, undefined spaces should be included in play settings.*

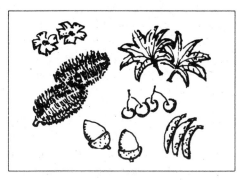

35 *People-plant interaction.*

36 *People-wildlife interaction.*

Avoid making play areas that are entirely made up of realistic play objects like trains. Some settings should be undefined in real world terms. If a platform is provided, be sure that it is not an explicit copy of a fort, so that the children can turn it into anything they want. A pile of rock, sand areas, and geometric structures all provide the opportunity for imaginative play. Settings which have more than one use will be used longer and by more diverse age groups, and will provide more learning potential.

Settings and objects which are not obviously representative of a specific thing (e.g., rocketship, castle, animal, etc.) allow the child to create his or her own fantasy play world. Undefined structures become whatever the child wants them to be, and the child will then create the story that goes with the imagined setting. "Let's pretend" games stimulate social interaction and help the child to experiment.

Military objects, such as tanks, cannons, and missiles, have no place on playgrounds. They should be excluded entirely (IPA, 1977).

cc.   **People-Plant Interaction.** A variety of settings are needed where users can make close contact with vegetation, including groundcovers, shrubs, and trees (Moore & Schneekloth, 1989; see Chapter 13, Trees/Vegetation).

dd.   **Wildlife Habitats.** Shelter and food for small-scale animal life—birds, small mammals, amphibians, reptiles, insects, and other small organisms—must be provided. This can be on a permanent or temporary basis.

If natural habitats and features already exist on an undeveloped site, make sure they are conserved and integrated into the site plan.

Vegetation, rocks, logs, marshes, and ponds can support the modest scale of wildlife that children find attractive, e.g., beetles, salamanders, snails, sowbugs, ants, fish, shrimp, worms, caterpillars, tadpoles, butterflies, spiders, and so on.

ee.   **Domestic Animals.** Domestic and farmyard animals are important resources for children, and are especially helpful for integration (*Children's Environments Quarterly*, 1(3), 1984; Handicapped Adventure Playground Association, hereafter HAPA, 1978; Shier, 1984). They require careful supervision and secure facilities for food and shelter. The City Farm concept is a viable idea here, as it stresses the needs of animals as well as children (Blue, 1986; Broadway, 1979; Schools Council, 1974a, b).

ff.   **Mix of People-made and Natural Elements.** Children need exposure to the full range of settings and objects that represent contemporary culture and our biological inheritance.

gg.   **Indoor-Outdoor Relationships.** A variety of transitions between buildings and the outdoors are recommended: terraces, decks, verandas, pagodas, etc. Adequate ramps are required (Allen, 1968; CMHC, 1980) (see Chapter 6, Section 17).

hh.   **Ease and Economy of Construction.** Playground budgets are always limited. Unnecessarily expensive features will mean cuts elsewhere. Playgrounds can be built in phases, as funds become available. The cost/play-value benefit ratio should be carefully evaluated for all settings.

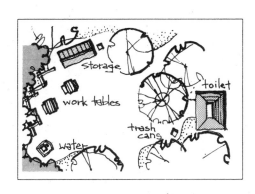

PART B:

Setting Design and Management

4. MANAGEMENT CRITERIA FOR PLAY SETTINGS

Eight criteria for managing play settings are emphasized throughout the guidelines.

4.1 Play Value

Play value is a measure of the developmental significance of a play setting, object, or material as a stimulus for children's play. Critical questions include:

a.   What are the play values and goals for integrated settings?

b.   How are they communicated to users, designers, managers, and manufacturers?

4.2 Programming Potential

Programming potential is a measure of the degree to which a given play setting, object, or material can be used as a resource for creative program development. Critical questions include:

a.   How can social and physical elements in a setting be extended to encourage a range of activity programming?

b.   What qualities should be included in physical settings to make them more flexible as potential programming environments?

c.   How can the program and environment be better designed to accommodate each other?

d.   Which environments and activities encourage integration of children with and without disabilities?

4.3 Play Leadership

Play leadership describes the role of those who enliven and inspire children to action, who support them, stimulate interest, encourage cooperation and integration, and who help adapt play environments to accommodate all abilities. Critical questions include:

a.   What are the roles and responsibilities of play leaders as facilitators and supervisors of children's activities?

b.   What are their roles in risk management, safety, and integration?

c.   What constitutes effective training for play leaders?

37   *Every type of child, no matter what level of ability, needs play opportunities.*

38   *Play settings should provide opportunities to learn about the physical world.*

4.4   Safety

Safety embraces the broad concept of caring for the health and well-being of all children under all circumstances, recognizing that they are a powerless group in society. Children are dependent on adults to provide safe, appropriate, high-quality settings for their development; specifically, this means ensuring that children are not exposed to hazardous situations and that known dangers are removed from their environment. Critical questions include:

a.   What are acceptable definitions of "safety," "risk," and "hazard" with respect to both physical and social aspects of play settings for children with and without disabilities?

b.   What do we actually know about these issues?

c.   How can we use the discussion of safety-related issues to increase awareness of the broader concepts of children's play, including play value, child development, and risk taking?

4.5   Risk Management

Risk management refers to management strategies and methods used to reduce the risk of accident, liability, and lawsuit with respect to children's play settings (Moreland et al., 1985b; see Chapter 25 for further details). The critical question is how we can implement a comprehensive set of risk management strategies, including:

a.   **Shared environmental control.** Control over the physical environment is essential to the safety and security of children. Entrances to every play program space should be able to be monitored. Where the space is shared with other organized groups, staff should get to know each other and their children so that the monitoring task can be shared.

b.   **Defensible settings** (Newman, 1972). Programmed activities can be dispensed into small group activity centers throughout the site. This decentralization of activity increases the possibility of informal surveillance of the whole site.

c.   **Shared site maintenance.** Effective site maintenance is essential to the health and safety of children. For most sites, this can be achieved most effectively as a shared responsibility of program staff, the parks and recreation department, or school district.

d. **High staffing/supervision ratios.** Clearly, the greater the ratio of trained staff to children the less likelihood of children getting into situations that could result in injury. The issue here is to ensure, through adequate training, that staff do not inadvertently block children from essential, nonhazardous risk-taking activity.

e. **Staff and leadership training.** Professional training is an essential requirement for adequate risk management (and all other aspects of effective play programming). How and where such training should be delivered is a matter of debate among professionals.

f. **Built-in risk-taking within programs.** This strategy is an excellent means of providing safe yet challenging experiences for children. It reduces the risk of children seeking challenges in more hazardous settings.

g. **Allowance for spontaneous play within programs.** To ensure play opportunities covering the full range of developmental needs, spontaneous play must be allowed. However, staff must take care that hazardous situations are avoided.

h. **Community involvement.** By encouraging the participation of children's families and neighborhood residents in play programs, they will become more knowledgeable and positive towards the program's goals and objectives. The chance of a negative (litigious) reaction in the case of a mishap will thereby be reduced. Community-based management means parents and community members must take leading roles, such as sitting on the board of directors.

i. **Documentation, record-keeping, and reporting.** As part of staff training, it is essential that everyone involved in a given play program follows standard record-keeping procedures and uses a pre-established documentation and reporting procedure in the case of an accident.

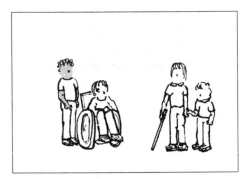

39   *Play settings must be accessible to children with all forms of disability.*

4.6   Accessibility

Accessibility is a measure of the degree to which users can experience all parts of an environment, recognizing that each will be more or less difficult for each individual. Critical questions include:

a.   What are the issues that hinder physical use, contact with, or sensory experience of particular elements or materials?

b.   Can all environments be physically designed for everyone? What role can managers play in facilitating access to settings and activity programs?

c.   What are the most effective management strategies for reducing psychological barriers to play settings (e.g., negative, uninformed attitudes towards children with disabilities, etc.)?

4.7   Integration

Integration is a measure of the degree to which children of different ages, sexes, ethnic and social groups, and ability or disability interact socially and play together. Critical questions include:

a.   What is a reasonable definition of "integration" for programs and settings?

b.   What are some common-sense criteria for evaluating integration?

c.   What are the major barriers at the local level to achieving properly integrated programs and play settings?

d.   What is the role of play leadership in integration?

4.8   Management

Management refers to the systematic and rational processes, procedures, and strategies used to allocate environmental resources to meet social goals. Included are policy, planning, participation, physical design, maintenance, and budgetary activities. Critical questions include:

a.   What are the most effective strategies for management and maintenance of integrated settings and programs?

b.   How can their success be measured?

4.9   Play Setting Concept

The concept of *play setting* is used throughout this book as a means of integrating behavioral needs and physical requirements in design. Play settings are functional entities that can be conveniently discussed and manipulated in the planning and design process to meet the developmental objectives normally proposed for most public play environments. The detailed requirements of seventeen types of play setting (reflecting the importance of choice and diversity in the child's environment) are discussed in the following chapters, ranging from entrance settings to storage settings.

5. ENTRANCES

Clearly defined entrances help orient, inform, and introduce users to the site. Entrances are a critical transition zone between transportation vehicle and program, especially for children with disabilities and parents with disabilities. It is therefore essential that all main entrances be fully accessible. Entrances are also places where people can meet and talk, and are locations for displaying community information.

Planning Criteria

Play Value. Entrances are an important social space, where children and parents can socialize and where neighborhood contacts are made.

Programming. Entrances are an important information node and provide an opportunity to advertise program details.

Play Leadership. Leaders need to recognize the program potential of entrance settings.

Safety. Moving cars, particularly when backing up, are a hazard. The chance of children running out in front of moving vehicles can be reduced by erecting barriers or by other means. A warning sign on its own is insufficient (in English law a child is assumed to be unable to read, or if they can, not to realize the full implications of the warning).

Risk Management. Entrances are good locations for signs about risk and liability.

Accessibility. Ramps are mandatory for entrances not at grade.

Integration. Entrances provide good potential for integration. Everyone arriving and leaving has to pass through, linger, and interact. Seating and shade must be adequate.

Management/Maintenance. Policies are required concerning public access and use of public space. Visibility of entrances and social support with benches, drinking fountains, etc., need careful consideration by site planners.

40 *Entrances should give a welcoming feeling to users and provide a multi-use zone for dropping off, information and gathering.*

5.1   Functional Requirements (Barrier Free Environments, Inc., hereafter BFE, 1980)

The principal public entrance of a play facility is of fundamental importance, legally and emotionally, to people with and without disabilities.

The principal entrance must be linked by accessible walks to public transportation stops, passenger loading zones, accessible parking spaces, and public streets and sidewalks. A person with a disability should be able to proceed independently from this entrance to all accessible spaces within the facility.

Entrances must be accessible and include drop-off and waiting zones.

5.1.1   Access (Kiewel, 1980)

a.   Provide grade-level or ramped walkways; stairs may be present but only in addition to the accessible walk.

b.   Use firm, continuous, nonslip walking surfaces.

c.   The walking surfaces should be kept free of leaves, ice, snow, and debris by regular maintenance, weather protection, or automatic snow-melting equipment.

5.1.2   Drop-off Zones (Robinette, 1985)

Entrances are where children often get dropped off and picked up, usually by vehicle. Wheelchairs, walkers, and other equipment must be accommodated in these areas. Requirements include:

41 *Drop-off zones should be provided close to play setting entrances.*

a.   Access aisles should be provided adjacent to vehicle pull-up spaces.

b.   The access aisle should be 12 feet wide and 50 feet long (Center for Accessible Housing, hereafter CAH, 1992). The cross-slope should be no greater than 1:50 and there must be a direct, accessible connection between the access aisle and the main entrance and circulation system of the play area.

c.   Where the zone is at the same grade as the adjacent walk, bollards or some other suitable device should be used to separate the two functions (bollards must be spaced at least 3 feet apart, 4 feet preferred). Where a curb exists and cannot be removed, one small ramp per car should be provided in accordance with the requirements listed for ramps in Chapter 6, Section 16.

d.   Walks adjacent to traffic lanes should be surfaced with a truncated dome pattern on the edge toward the traffic (at least 36 inches in width).

e.   In environments where children arrive and depart by bus, a protective canopy should be provided above the vehicle pull-up spaces. There must be a vertical clearance of at least 15 feet between the vehicular paving and the underside of the cover. The covered protection should be a minimum of 20 feet in length and extend a minimum of 6 feet over the stopped vehicle's drop-off lane or aisle (CAH, 1992).

f.   Signage should be provided to identify the drop-off zone and limit its defined use to a "pick-up/drop-off" function.

g.   Adequate lighting should be provided.

h.   Bollards:

1)   Bollards are useful as traffic control devices to allow pedestrian access while halting vehicular access. They should be spaced a minimum of 3 feet apart to allow a wheelchair to pass, though 4 feet is preferred.

2)   Bollards can provide useful seats if they are at least 12 inches wide and between 18 and 24 inches high.

3)   Bollards should be contrasting in color to the pavement around them. They should be well-illuminated at night to minimize the risk of a person inadvertently walking into them.

5.1.3   Waiting Zones

(See also Gathering, Meeting, and Working Places, Chapter 20)

Entrances are places of coming and going, where people have a chance for a few words with each other and to catch their breath, especially parents waiting to pick-up their children.

a.   Waiting areas should be large enough to comfortably accommodate the average number of people normally using them (Robinette, 1985).

b.   Seating should be provided for the average number of daily users, with space also allotted to park wheelchairs, strollers, and other wheeled vehicles (Robinette, 1985).

c.   Tables may also be provided to support social interaction and as a place to leave belongings.

d.   Bike racks must be provided.

42   *Bicycle stands should be installed at play setting entrances.*

e.   Litter receptacles are needed.

f.   An overhead shelter or canopy should be used to minimize the effects of the weather. Care should be taken to locate vertical support posts out of the paths of pedestrians using or passing near the shelter. If the shelter is enclosed, adequate space must be allotted for easy in and out movement (Robinette, 1985).

g.   Loading areas should be designed so that circulation from the waiting area is uncomplicated and over paved surfaces. The loading area itself should not have a curb that must be climbed (Robinette, 1985). If a curb cannot be avoided, it should conform with the standards presented in Chapter 6, Section 16.

5.1.4   Communications/Image

a.   Entrances should attract users and visitors, and give a positive first impression of the setting. They should present a welcoming, "please come again" feeling to people as they leave.

b.   Archways are a powerful welcoming element.

c.   Bulletin boards should be installed to advertise information about programs and related community events.

d.   Embellishments such as banners, flags, decorations, and posters can be produced as a program activity and displayed temporarily.

43   *Bulletin boards at play setting entrances should display program information.*

6. PATHWAYS

Pathways provide accessibility and help separate spaces that serve different functions; they enable users to move between and through elements and help to orient them in space. Pathways can also be a recreational and play facility in and of themselves.

Planning Criteria

Play Value. Different types of paths support different activities depending on their design. These activities include circulation, wheeled-toy play, chase games, and site exploration.

Programming Potential. Pathways provide potential for mobile activities.

Play Leadership. Leaders need to know how to use pathways for mobile games and interpretive activities.

Safety. Pathways designed for play must not be located near drop-offs. To ensure safety, adequate lighting and guardrails are sometimes needed.

Risk Management. Pathways must be well maintained; major paths must be clearly defined and well lit.

Accessibility. Pathways require good surfaces and correct gradients. Within the overall park, a hierarchy of path difficulties can be provided ("Accessible," "Usable," "Difficult," Nordhaus et al., 1984). Brochures, maps, and other materials should be provided to allow users to make decisions on access and difficulty before venturing out.

Integration. Pathways stimulate cooperation and interaction during circulation. They support both interpretive and mobile games. Pathways get children to destinations where they can interact with each other.

Management/Maintenance. Policies are needed to allow multimodal use (pedestrians, wheelchairs, tricycles, bicycles, skateboards, and other wheeled-toys) as well as different levels of use.

6.1   Accessible Routes (CAH, 1992; AEC, 1980)

a.   Park areas containing playgrounds should be linked to residential neighborhoods by accessible routes, otherwise getting to the park can be difficult.

b.   Routes can be classified by three levels of accessibility: Accessible, Usable and Difficult (Nordhaus et al., 1984). Be sure to provide a comprehensive, connected network of *accessible* routes to link accessible entrances and all main centers of activity on the site. This section lists the requirements for accessible routes in environments used by children.

In planning accessible routes, use site terrain to the best advantage. Secondary entrances that are nonprimary may be used if they are the best alternative and are made attractive. Appropriate placement of signs should indicate an alternate path or the location of a part of a facility. If the main route is inaccessible, a sign should guide people from there to the accessible route.

c.   Paths are the primary means for travel between activity areas and should be safe, accessible, and convenient (Bunin et al., 1980).

d.   **Dimensions** (CAH, 1992; AEC, 1980). Pathways must have a wide, continuous, even surface, and must be as level as possible. Overhead clearance must be at least 80 inches under tree limbs, signs, etc.; this is especially important for people with sight disabilities.

44   *Paths must be 44 inches wide minimum, though wider paths are preferred.*

To accommodate two children passing each other in wheelchairs, accessible routes should be at least 88 inches (CAH, 1992). This will also help accommodate baby strollers (Los Angeles, 1987). Wider pathway widths are also desirable to accommodate children using walkers and crutches, since children using walkers travel in a side-to-side motion and children on crutches tend to hold the crutches at a 50-degree angle from their bodies.

Minimum design specifications for accessible routes include:

1)   A minimum width of 44 inches (wider is preferred).

2)   No changes in level that exceed 1/4 inch (thresholds, doormats, heaved pavement, etc.). A 1/2-inch level change is allowable if it is beveled with a maximum slope of 1:2.

45   *Paths that are 88 inches wide allow two children in wheelchairs to pass.*

46   *Wheelchairs need 5 feet of turning space adjacent to benches.*

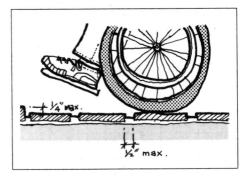

47   *Pathways should have no joints greater than 1/2 inch or changes in level greater than 1/4 inch.*

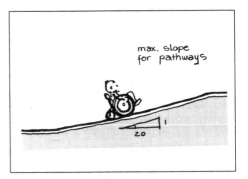

48   *Pathways should have a maximum slope of 5 percent.*

3)   A maximum slope of 5 percent (1:20), although less is desirable:

- 0—1% is level.
- 2—4% is moderate.
- 5—7% is steep.
- 7% is impossible.

4)   Surfacing must be of a nonslip material.

5)   No cross slope (from side-to-side of path) steeper than 2 percent is allowed; 1 percent is preferred (Zirpolo, 1987).

6)   Paths must have a "passing space" 74 inches wide provided at least every 100 feet (CAH, 1992).

7)   There must be headroom of at least 80 inches along the entire length and width of an accessible pathway.

e.   Children travel in straight lines in active play, and will do so unless diverted by substantial barriers or an especially desirable feature.

f.   If a pathway has a slope greater than 5 percent (1:20), it is considered a ramp and should be designed to meet the requirements that apply to ramps (see Section 16 of this chapter).

g.   **Third Dimension.** Some paths should lift users above grade to provide "overviews" of the setting. Bridges are an excellent solution (Robinette, 1985).

h.   **Bicycles.** Large or full-size bicycles present a hazard on main pathways (skateboards and rollerskates sometimes do, too). Without direct supervision, they are difficult to exclude, even with regulatory signs. The risk should be recognized by all caretakers in the play setting.

In a large setting, a separate bikeway path should be constructed along primary circulation routes. Bike racks should also be provided.

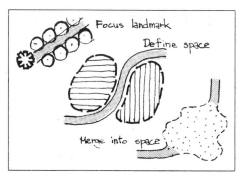

49   *Pathways should be used as a major structuring element in site design.*

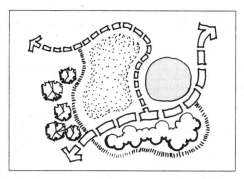

50   *A variety of pathway choices should be available.*

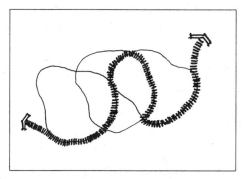

51   *Pathway layout should follow the principle of intersecting circles.*

6.2   **The Flow of Play Activity** (adapted from Seattle, 1986)

In diverse play settings, children's play activity takes on a complex, mobile form, especially when play props are freely available in the setting.

a.   Much mobile activity happens away from the main pathways. Play settings should allow for activities to ebb and flow continuously with multiple branching and decision points.

b.   Alternative choices of direction and activity should be visible.

c.   Because some children are easily distracted by too many choices, some subsettings should be visually separated.

d.   Branching should happen horizontally, vertically, and in a combination of directions.

6.3   **Choice of Route**

a.   **Variety.** Play areas should contain a variety of different types of paths, other than primary circulation routes, to accommodate hiking, triking, biking, interpretive activities, hide and chase games, and to meet the varied needs of children.

b.   **Indirect.** Some paths should be planned as indirect, informal routes, where children can explore the setting away from the main centers of activity. Other paths should be designed to reveal surprise, spatial contrast, sequential exposure to a wide variety of experiences, artifacts, views, etc.

c.   **"Intersecting Circles."** Minor paths should be laid out on the principle of "intersecting circles," to accommodate continuity of movement and provide complex settings for hide-and-chase games. Dead-ends and bottleneck situations where users might collide should be avoided.

6.4   **Wheeled-Toys**

a.   Major paths should accommodate appropriate wheeled-toys. They are an important means for children with disabilities to achieve independence and an important stimulus for integration between children.

52 *Special self-contained tricycle circuits should be provided.*

b. Special, circular, self-contained routes should be provided for tricycles and small bicycles to avoid potential hazards and conflicts with pedestrians.

6.5 Related Facilities

a. Sitting areas should be provided at regular intervals on main paths, in suitable locations.

b. **Rest Areas and Shelters** (Nordhaus et al., 1984).

1) Level 1: Accessible.

Provide 5 feet x 5 feet (minimum) level space for resting every 200 to 400 feet; provide seating and shelter every 1/8 mile.

2) Level 2: Usable.

Provide 5 feet x 5 feet (minimum) level space for resting every 400 to 800 feet; provide seating and shelter every 1/4 mile.

3) Level 3: Difficult.

Provide a level resting space at least every 1/4 mile; provide more frequent resting places for paths steeper than 1:20.

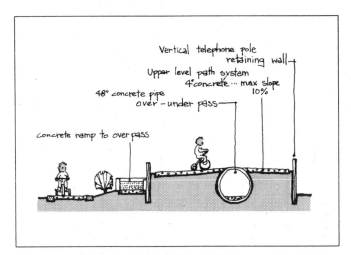

53 *Peach Playground gives tricycles their own domain.*

c. **Gates and Doorways** (Nordhaus et al., 1984). Gates and doorways must have a clear opening width of at least 32 inches. They also require a clear space adjacent to the approach that is large enough for a person in a wheelchair to maneuver and open the door or gate. The requirements for the clear space vary with the type of door and direction of approach. Be sure to consult the accessibility code for your area. In addition, in environments used by children, door hardware should be mounted no higher than 30 to 34 inches above the floor, and required opening force should not exceed 5 pounds (3 pounds if intended for use by pre-kindergarten age children) (CAH, 1992).

6.6 Surface Treatment Definitions

Pathway surfaces should be selected according to the following criteria: slip-resistance, accessibility, impact absorption, stability/rigidity, durability, maintainability, and aesthetics.

People with ambulatory disabilities need stable, firm, flat, nonslip, antiskid surfaces, as defined below (Kiewel, 1980).

a. **Stable:** Surfaces that do not shift unpredictably when subjected to pedestrian traffic. Examples of surfaces that are not stable are: loose gravel, sand, and carpet or sheet flooring that is not bonded to its backing or the floor and that may bubble, pucker, or ripple when stressed.

b. **Firm:** Surfaces that are highly resilient to deformation under concentrated loads. The bearing surface of a crutch or cane tip and the area of contact of wheelchair tires are considerably smaller than the net area of the average person's shoeprint. Therefore, surfaces need to be very resilient before they "feel" sound and can effectively support a person's mobility.

c. **Flat:** Surfaces without abrupt changes in level and without irregularities. Uneven surfaces pose problems for people with shuffling gaits and for some people who use crutches or canes. There are two principal concerns here:

1) Some tile or textured floor patterns can, when wet from maintenance or inclement weather, become a hazardous "sliding track" for crutch or cane tips and cause falls.

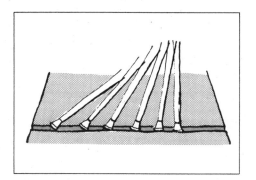

54   *Sliding track.*

2)   Surface jointing patterns can create a "washboard" ride for wheelchair users, which is uncomfortable and potentially harmful. Joints between pavers or materials must be tight, shallow (if not flush), and preferably short to minimize their potential for causing falls.

d.   **Nonslip, slip-resistant,** and **antiskid** describe the elusive opposite of "slippery." There has been considerable research on this topic, dating back to at least 1924, but it has focused on able-bodied people in "normal" straight-line walking.

6.7   Edges and Curbs (Seattle, 1986)

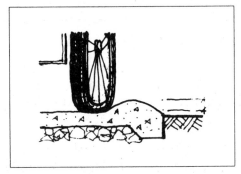

55   *Edge treatments stop wheelchairs from running off pathways.*

a.   Curbs may present a tripping hazard; therefore, provide a raised edge only where there is a hazard on the other side of the path. Better still, locate paths where edges are not required.

b.   Prevent abrupt, protruding edges or grade changes along paths and on informal paved areas where bikes, trikes, or wheelchairs might be used.

c.   Provide a minimum 3-foot radius for inside and outside corners on curved walks to minimize wear on plantings at corners.

d.   Where edging is omitted along asphalt surfaces, use a rolled edge having a taper of 30 to 45 degrees.

6.8   Warning Textures (Nordhaus et al., 1984)

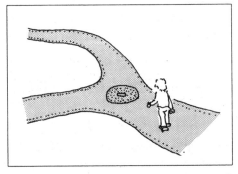

56   *Tactile treatments at path edges and intersections help people with visual disabilities*

a.   Changes in texture and material may be used as non-visual, tactile warnings for hazards and dangerous locations. However, this technique is not commonly used, and people may not recognize it. If warning textures are used at a site, they must be used consistently throughout. Partial or inconsistent use may be dangerous. Care must be taken not to create trip hazards for running children.

b.   Warning textures should begin at least 36 inches before a hazard is encountered.

c.   A texture that is easy to identify consists of truncated domes that are 0.9 inches in diameter, 0.2 inches high and 2.35 inches apart, as required by ADA on curb ramps (*Federal Register*, July 26, 1991).

d.   Materials with different noise and resiliency characteristics are more detectable than changes of texture alone. Warnings should be reinforced by contrasts in lighting value (light/dark).

e.   Changes in pathway texture may also be used to indicate a point of interest, seating area, sign location, etc. Textures used for communication must be used consistently throughout the site.

f.   Tactile warnings on the walking surface should be provided at locations potentially hazardous to people with severe visual impairments, such as crosswalks at roads, stairs, water areas, etc. Noise devices are required at busy street crossings. Such devices are educational for users with and without disabilities.

6.9   Levels of Accessibility (Nordhaus et al., 1984)

Accessibility requirements must accommodate mixed-ability groups, such as an able-bodied child and a parent with a disability.

As previously mentioned, three levels of accessibility have been defined which present a more realistic prediction of degree of difficulty for people with ambulatory disabilities. Note, however, that levels will vary according to standards of maintenance.

a.   **Level 1: Accessible.**

Hard surface with light texture. Vertical joints less than 1/4 inch. Horizontal joints less than 1/2 inch. Gratings only when necessary, with openings less than 1/2 inch perpendicular to the direction of travel.

b.   **Level 2: Usable.**

Firm surface with moderate texture. Vertical joints and texture less than 3/8 inch. Horizontal joints and grating openings less than 1.2 inches.

c.   **Level 3: Difficult.**

Passable in a wheelchair.

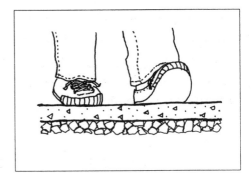

57   Concrete.

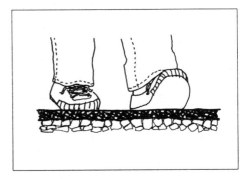

58   Asphalt.

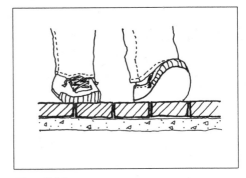

59   Brick.

6.10   Pathway Surfaces (Bunin, et al., 1980)

In large part, the surface of a path determines its accessibility. Balancing topography with the need to provide a wide range of pathway accessibility, one can choose from a variety of pathway surfaces. In order of decreasing accessibility, possible choices include: concrete; asphalt; pavers on concrete; crushed stone or decomposed granite; wood decking; pavers on sand; grass; "turfstone"; untreated soil; gravel; woodchips; and sand. By using surfaces (adapted to regional climatic variations) in combination with other features such as slope, pathway width, and rest areas, a large and extremely varied constituency of users can be satisfied.

a.   **Concrete** (Nordhaus et al., 1984). Concrete must be poured on a well-prepared base that is clean and free of debris. Finishes should have a light texture, such as a broom finish, so that the surface will not be slippery when wet. The texture should drain water off the pathway so that it does not stand or freeze.

b.   **Asphalt** (Nordhaus et al., 1984). Asphalt pathways may be used if they are carefully constructed and maintained. Typical construction should include:

1)   Subgrade cleaned and cleared to a depth of 6 inches below finished grade, compacted to 95%. A soil sterilizer may be utilized to control weed growth.

2)   Four-inch base of course aggregate, compacted to 95%.

3)   Primer coat.

4)   Two-inch surface course of hot mix bituminous concrete, compacted to 95% density. An epoxy finish, coated with sand, may be used to give a natural appearance and reduce softening problems in hot climates.

5)   Slope to drain.

    Asphalt surfaces should not be used in very hot, sunny locations because it may become soft and cause difficulty for people using wheelchairs. Also, maintenance is important for asphalt pathways to keep them from becoming degraded by weeds, cracks, and erosion.

c.   **Pavers on Concrete** (Nordhaus et al., 1984). Brick, tile, or concrete pavers set on a properly constructed concrete base can provide a Level 1 pathway surface. Joints between pavers must meet the requirements of the designated Level of Accessibility.

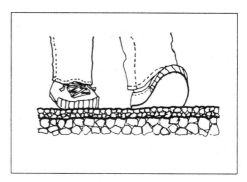

60 *Crushed stone.*

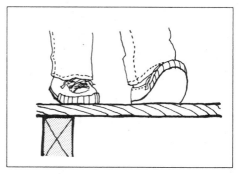

61 *Wood decking.*

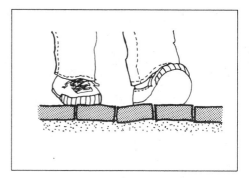

62 *Pavers on sand.*

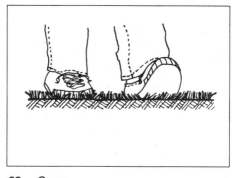

63 *Grass.*

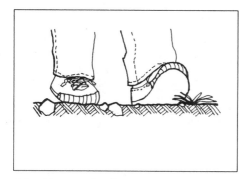

64 *Untreated soil.*

d. **Crushed Stone and Decomposed Granite** (Nordhaus et al., 1984). Crushed stone can form an accessible surface if it is correctly designed and constructed, and adapted to regional climatic conditions.

1) Subgrade cleaned and cleared to a depth of 6 inches below finished grade, compacted to 95% density. The use of a soil sterilizer is recommended.

2) Four-inch base course, 3/4-inch crushed stone, compacted to 95% density. A binder of 2 to 3% Portland cement with water and gravel may be used.

3) Two-inch surfacing course of crusher fines, rolled and compacted to 95% density. Cement binder recommended.

4) Maintenance is essential to ensure a consistent surface.

e. **Wood Decking** (Nordhaus et al., 1984). Wood decking may be used as a pathway and flooring surface for all levels of accessibility, providing joints meet the requirements of the Level. Warpage and movement of the material must also be controlled.

f. **Pavers on Sand** (Nordhaus et al., 1984). Brick, tile, concrete, or other paving materials set in sand are not recommended for Level 1. Winter heaving and movement of the material over time may cause unacceptable irregularities. They may be suitable for Level 2 or 3 if properly installed.

g. **Grass (Turf)** (Nordhaus, et al., 1984). A grass surface can be passable as a Level 2 or 3 surface if it is level and well-maintained.

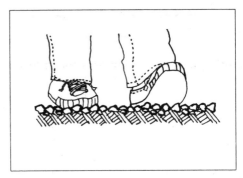

65   Gravel.

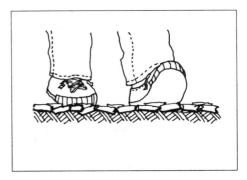

66   Wood chips.

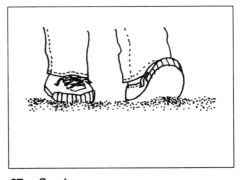

67   Sand.

h.   **Turfstone.** This surfacing material consists of honeycomb concrete blocks filled with topsoil and seeded with grass. The result is a wear-resistant, well-drained, soft, grassy surface that is accessible to some, but not to all. While wheelchairs can roll over it, the honeycomb pattern can make it difficult to walk with crutches, a cane, or a walker.

i.   **Untreated Soil** (Nordhaus et al., 1984). Untreated soil is highly variable. Some situations may be acceptable for Level 2 or 3 if level and maintained. Soil is likely to change significantly due to precipitation, erosion, wear, etc.

j.   **Gravel** (Nordhaus et al., 1984). Loose gravel is not recommended. It can be very difficult for a person using a wheelchair or walking aides. Packed gravel may be suitable for Level 3.

k.   **Wood chips.** Small gauge chips make an attractive surfacing material. They have a pleasant smell. When well-compacted on a level subsurface, the surface is accessible at Level 2, otherwise Level 3 is more likely. On the negative side, wood chips are splintery (especially when freshly ground) and have a high bacteria count.

l.   **Sand.** Sand is not recommended for pathway surfacing.

6.13   Treatment Definitions (Kiewel, 1980)

a.   **Abrupt changes in level:** This is a change in the height of a walking surface greater than 1/4 inch. A change of 1/2 inch is acceptable if it is beveled with a 1:2 slope. Changes in level greater than 1/2 inch must be avoided in pathways.

b.   **Change in elevation:** This is a change in the height of a walking surface greater than 1/2 inch, regardless of the angle at the edge of the change. Changes in elevation must be avoided in pathway design, or ramps must be provided to ensure accessibility.

c.   **Crutch stop:** This is a low curb or rail along the edge of a ramp or wall, designed to stop crutch or cane tips from sliding off the surface.

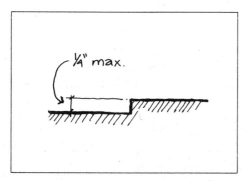

68 *Level changes up to 1/4 inch are acceptable on the pathway surface.*

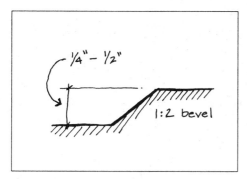

69 *A change in level is allowable up to 1/2 inch if it is beveled at a 1:2 slope. Changes greater than 1/2 inch are not allowed.*

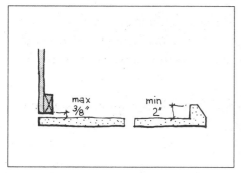

70 *Crutch stops.*

6.14   Components (Nordhaus et al., 1984)

a.   Curbs and Railings

Curbs and railings should be provided according to the requirements for different levels of accessibility:

Accessible	Usable	Difficult
Provide a 2-inch high curb at the edge of paths that slope at the side. Provide a 34- to 38-inch high railing at hazardous pathway edges. In children's environments, provide an additional handrail surface at a height of 16 to 26 inches.	Provide a 2-inch high curb and 34- to 38-inch high railing at difficult and dangerous locations. In children's environments, provide an additional handrail surface at a height of 16 to 26 inches.	Provide curbing at difficult and dangerous locations.

Be aware that children can use curb and railing structures as play features.

b.   Pathway Edge

Accessible	Usable	Difficult
Provide a distinctive edge on at least one side of the pathway as a "shoreline" for visually impaired people who use canes. A 2-inch high curb is preferred unless it is in an active play area where it could create a trip hazard.	Provide a distinct change of material at the edge of the pathway that is detectable by a person with limited vision.	Edge treatments on these paths may be more natural, though some definition that is perceptible to people with limited vision should be provided (e.g., plantings or a change in surfacing material).

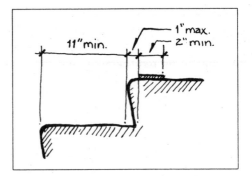

71 *Stair treads with indicator stripes.*

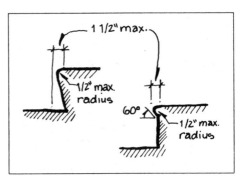

72 *Accessible stair nosings.*

73 *Stairs should provide handrails on both sides.*

6.15   Steps and Stairways (Kiewel, 1980)

One of the most frequent misconceptions regarding accessible design is that stair design has nothing to do with accessibility. There are, however, people with disabilities who actually prefer to use stairs. Therefore, step or stair design is critical to the safe and efficient use of the built environment.

There are four components of accessible outdoor stair design:

a.   **Risers.** The physical existence of risers is important for two groups of people. People wearing prosthetic or orthotic devices on their legs often use the riser face to guide their leg(s) up the step. Other people with impaired coordination, who use crutches or canes, place their crutches against the riser of a step above them for balance as they maneuver up the stairway.

b.   **Nosings.** Open riser stairs represent the worst kind of nosing design, that is, the stair with the greatest tripping hazard. Poured sloped-riser stairs provide the best nosing design, that is, the stair with the least tripping hazard.

Accessible stairs must have risers that slope out to meet the leading edge of the tread. The nosing should be shallow (preferably less than 1 inch) and either be beveled at 60 degrees or more from the horizontal, or rounded to minimize its potential to trip. Every nosing of every tread must have a 2-inch wide stripe of color that contrasts with the tread color. The stripe must be flush with the tread surface and no further than 1 inch from the tread edge (Goltsman et al., 1992).

c.   **Handrails.** It is critical that stairways have handrails on both sides. People who have had strokes, amputations of a hand or arm, or who have hemiparisis from disease or accident will have only one hand to use the handrail. Handrails must be available on both sides so that no matter which direction the person is going, he or she will always have a handrail on the "good" side.

Handrail projections are also important. Handrails on stairs must extend at the same angle of descent for the distance of one tread length before leveling off and extending an additional 12 inches parallel to the ground surface. This is to provide the person using the handrail with consistent support all the way to the stair landing. The handrail at the upper landing need not continue at the angle of ascent, but must project horizontally to the upper landing at least 12 inches to provide continuous support (Goltsman et al., 1992).

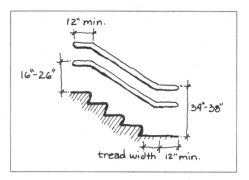

74   *Stair handrail projections*

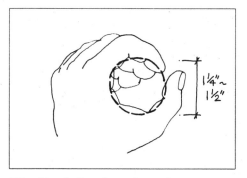

75   *Handrail surface dimensions.*

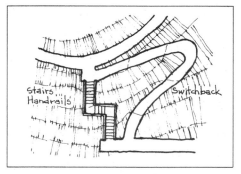

76   *A ramp that switches back.*

Handrails must be designed to fit the human hand. The preferred shape is round with a diameter between 1-1/4 and 1-1/2 inches, which enables the hand to almost close. Handrails must also be 1-1/2 inches from any adjacent vertical surface or farther than 18 inches. If they are closer, there is not enough space to get a good grip. If they are between these two distances, they may trap a person's arm if they lose their grip.

Finally, handrails must be mounted between 34 and 38 inches above the stair nosings. This is the required height range as stated in the ADA (*Federal Register*, July 26, 1991). However, the Uniform Federal Accessibility Standards (UFAS) requires a handrail height of 30 to 34 inches. This standard may also be applied, although it is likely to be changed to reflect the height range used in the ADA. In environments for children, an additional gripping surface should be mounted between 16 and 26 inches, depending on the age of the primary user group (CAH, 1992).

Detectable Warnings. In environments used by children, a combination of two or more warning cues should be provided, extending a minimum of 36 inches from the top nosing. Detectable warnings must contrast from the adjacent walkway surface through the use of sound, resilience, texture, or inclined surfaces as warning cues. Physical barriers such as gates, doors, or bollards should also be used on exterior stairs to prevent wheelchair access (CAH, 1992).

6.16   Ramps

Depending on the topography and design of the site, ramps may play an important role in the pathway system and in ensuring access to all parts of the site. Actually, any time a pathway's slope exceeds 5 percent (1:20), it is technically a ramp and must be designed to meet all of the standards that apply to ramps.

It is important that ramps be fully integrated with the site's conventional or central circulation system. People with mobility impairments expend a great deal of energy moving around a site. Ramps, in particular, can be very tiring and it can be exhausting to travel extra distance to gain access to a ramp. When possible, ramps should be designed as the most direct route of travel with stairs provided as an alternate route.

The most important factor in ramp design is the slope. In a study completed by Syracuse University for the revision of the American National Standards Institute (hereafter ANSI) A117.1 specifications showed that 44 percent of the wheelchair users tested

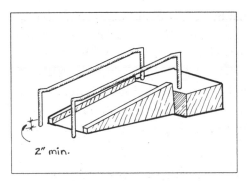

77   Ramp with 2-inch curbs at the edges.

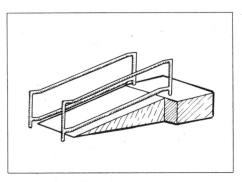

78   Ramp with a continuous railing at the ramp surface.

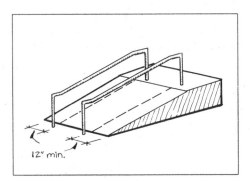

79   Ramp with a surface that extends beyond the handrails on each side.

could not traverse a 30-inch rise in elevation at the slope of 1:12, while all persons tested could negotiate at least a 24-inch change in elevation at a slope of 1:20. (Note: The test ramp was not long enough to test rises in excess of 24 inches at the 1:20 slope.)

The following guidelines apply to accessible ramps in environments used by children:

a.   **Slope.** The maximum slope of a ramp should be 1:20. Where 1:20 is not feasible, the minimum feasible slope must be built to insure access and usability by children. When 1:20 is not feasible, a maximum slope of 1:16 is permitted. In alterations, when a 1:16 ramp is technically unfeasible, a maximum slope of 1:12 is permitted if the level change does not exceed 6 inches (CAH, 1992).

b.   **Length.** The maximum horizontal run of any ramp should be 20 feet (CAH, 1992).

c.   **Width.** The minimum clear width of ramps should be 44 inches. The minimum clear width for two wheelchairs to pass should be 88 inches (CAH, 1992).

d.   **Surfacing.** The surface of the ramp should be brushed concrete or a similar surface to prevent slipping. If the ramp is in an area where children will be playing, particularly if it is near play equipment, the ramp itself will likely become a play element. In such cases, a shock-absorbing, resilient surfacing should be used.

e.   **Cross Slope.** If the ramp is not level side-to-side, it will be difficult to navigate for a person in a wheelchair, particularly a child. Cross slope should not exceed 1:50 (Goltsman et al., 1992).

f.   **Ramp Edges.** Ramps must include protection from drop-offs at the edges. This can be accomplished with walls, 2-inch minimum curbs, or railings that provide a suitable barrier at the ramp surface (e.g., a continuous rail immediately above the ramp surface or vertical posts). Alternately, the ramp surface may be widened to extend at least 1 foot past the handrails on each side (Goltsman et al., 1992).

g.   **Landings.** Landings must be provided at the top and bottom of each segment of a ramp as well as between segments if there is more than one run. The top landing must be at least 5-feet square while the bottom landing needs to be 6-feet long and as wide as the ramp. Intermediate landings must be 5-feet long and as wide as the ramp. When a turn into vehicular traffic is required at the bottom of a ramp, the turn must be located beyond the 5-foot clear landing (CAH, 1992).

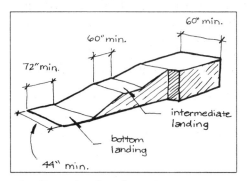

80   *Ramp landing dimensions.*

h.   **Handrails.** Handrails on access ramps must be designed and installed in accordance with the requirements for your area. However, special consideration should be given to the age of the intended user groups when deciding on the appropriate handrail height. While ADA requires mounting heights between 34 inches and 38 inches (*Federal Register*, July 26, 1991), this is too high for children. Additional handrail gripping surfaces should be mounted between 16 inches and 26 inches above the ramp surface, depending on the ages of the children being served.

i.   **Vertical Clearance.** There should be 80 inches of clear space above the ramp.

6.17   Pathway Development (Bunin et al., 1980)

Following are additional standards that should be applied in pathway design:

a.   If ramps or switchbacks are needed, provide stairs for a more direct alternate route.

b.   Expansion joints should be 1/2 inch or less.

c.   Storm drain gratings should be placed off of pathways. If they are in the path, openings should be less than 1/2 inch and perpendicular to the path of travel.

d.   Prune overhanging tree branches to a height of 80 inches. If pruning will damage or detract from a tree, consider rerouting the path around it.

e.   Use separate texture and color cues to indicate areas of high risk, such as a steep embankments, steps or intersections; and functional changes, such as seating areas, fountains or plazas.

f.   Avoid bold patterns or colors that may be disorienting over a continuous surface.

7. SIGNAGE

Signs that can communicate to people of all abilities are vital. They ensure good orientation, direct traffic flow, satisfy requirements of effective risk management, and provide information about site and programs.

The need for signs depends on the size of the play setting. Play settings should not be over-signed. Signs should be designed in the spirit of play.

A realistic assumption is that children (and people whose native tongue is not English) cannot read written signs or, if they can, the implications of the message are not fully understood. Hence the need to emphasize graphic signs, especially those that are child-oriented and child-designed. International characters and standards should be used as much as possible.

Planning Criteria

Play Value. Signs can be designed as play objects or sometimes become unintended play objects.

Programming. Signs provide permanent interpretive information about the site. Temporary signs can advertise special events and add to the site's aesthetic appeal.

Play Leadership. Responsibility for using and managing temporary signs should be shared by play leaders and park maintenance staff.

Safety. Signs alert users to the special features of equipment, improve users' sense of security, and reduce the risk of getting lost or feeling lost.

Accessibility. Appropriate heights, depths, colors, pictographs, and tactile qualities can be used to communicate information to all types of users.

Risk Management. Signs provide information about appropriate use of equipment and facilities.

Integration. Signs must communicate an image of "ALL users welcome."

Management/Maintenance. A clean, readable, up-to-date, secure sign system is essential. Signs should be designed as part of the total design concept, not as an afterthought. Signs should be attractive and consistent with the overall aesthetic style.

81　*Informational signs.*

82　*Directional signs.*

83　*Identification signs.*

7.1　**Types of Signs**

a.　**Informational Signs** present general information in words and graphics (for those who cannot read) about the organization of a site, the programs available at the site, and the circulation system, including accessible pathways, that leads to those facilities and programs.

Informational signs placed at the entry to a site should identify and locate accessible facilities, describe the site's level of accessibility and indicate where additional assistance may be obtained (Nordhaus et al., 1984).

Entry signs should convey a welcoming attitude to the user, and emphasize support rather than restriction of activity. However, it may also be important to communicate safety rules as a risk management strategy.

b.　**Directional Signs** present information that indicates direction to a space or facility, change in route, or confirmation of correct direction. They usually include an arrow. They are located at the site entry and all decision points (Robinette, 1985).

"You are here" signs help people find their way around. They should be oriented in the same direction as the visitor and show prominent landmarks within view.

Directional signs must be provided to direct people arriving at the site to the accessible site and facility entries. Directional signs should also be systematically placed on the site to direct visitors, including:

1)　Signs at site entry, indicating the direction to parking and facilities.

2)　Signs at parking areas to identify access to pathways and facilities.

3)　Signs at all decision points along a pathway.

Signs should be visible from pathways and within reach for touch reading. Indications of direction must be clear.

c.　**Identification Signs** present information in both words and pictograms to identify specific features or facilities. Identification signs for accessible entries must display the International Symbol of Accessibility. They should also:

1)　Visibly and unambiguously identify the facility from the approaching pathway.

2)　Indicate the level of accessibility of the facility ("accessible," "usable," "difficult").

84   *Regulatory sign.*

85   *Signs must be readable by children and adults with senses other than vision.*

86   *Raised letters are better than Braille signs.*

d.   **Regulatory Signs** present notification of rules, requirements, warnings, and restrictions and are used for traffic delineation and control.

7.2   General Guidelines for Readability (Bunin et al., 1980)

Signs should be "readable" by touch and hearing as well as by sight. Raised lettering and symbols convey information to people reading with either hands or eyes. Raised letters are actually preferable to Braille since many people with sight disabilities, especially the partially sighted, do not read Braille. When possible, the most effective method of communication for people with limited sight is a sighted guide or audio tape device, such as those often found at zoos, nature centers, museums, and other recreation areas. In general, however, more research and development is required on types of signs that will accommodate people with sight disabilities.

Signs can have a strong positive (or negative) educational value for both parents and children. That is why it is important to consider what the sign is trying to "teach" when considering how best to design it. Once you have identified this, simply follow the marketing advice of "making the media match the message." Whatever you do, don't limit yourself to words only when designing a "readable" sign.

That said, following are some general considerations for designing readable signs:

a.   Place signs logically, within easy range of vision and reach, at main intersections and nodal points. People should be able to approach to within 3 inches of signs.

b.   Place signs so that they are unobstructed by vegetation and buildings.

c.   Place signs so that they cannot be inadvertently walked into.

d.   Place signs at a comfortable height for children and seated or standing adults. The appropriate height for standing adults is 60 inches above the ground surface. This is the mounting height required for permanent identification signs in buildings. However, if signs are intended for use by children the appropriate mounting height is 48 inches or lower (depending on the age of the children being served). Decide which height or heights are most appropriate for your users and mount signs consistently throughout the site.

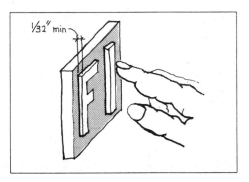

87 *Raised letters should contrast with the background.*

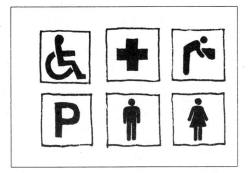

88 *Pictograms should be used in addition to written information.*

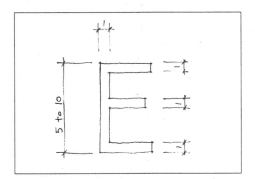

89 *The ratio of stroke width to letter height must be between 1:5 and 1:10.*

e. Use light-colored letters or symbols on a dark background for maximum readability. Use bright, noticeable colors with a matte, non-glare finish.

Letters on permanent identification signs must be raised 1/32 inches; they must also be 5/8 inches to 2 inches in height. For overhead informational or directional signs, letters must be 3 inches or more in height with a ratio of letter width to letter height of 3:5 and 1:1. Line weight of letters on these signs should have a ratio of line width to letter width of between 1:5 and 1:10 (*TAC*, 1992). These dimensions, when used with a matte finish and a high contrast between the color of the character and its background, can increase readability.

When determining letter height for signs that must be read from a distance, increase the letter size to ensure that it can be easily read. This is particularly important if the sign must be read from a moving vehicle while entering the parking area.

f. Use Arabic numerals and standard sanserif letter typefaces.

g. If there are predominant foreign language groups in the population being served, include these languages on multilingual signs. Be sure to use a professional translator to ensure precise, clear instructions and direct, concise language.

h. Pictograms should be used in addition to written information, using simple, high contrast, bold, clear graphics. Symbols must be understandable as well as visible and must be presented with borders that are at least 6 x 6 inches. They must also be accompanied by a written description. Rely on standard symbols such as those used by the U.S. Department of Transportation for ease of recognition.

Regular street signs can be used for "Stop," "Yield," etc., which also have an educational advantage.

i. Where possible, consider using signs which engage children in cause-effect learning (e.g., pressing a button gives a verbal response). Allow children to make their own signs in supervised play areas as part of play programs.

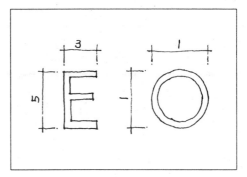

90   *Character width-to-height ratio 3:5 and 1:1.*

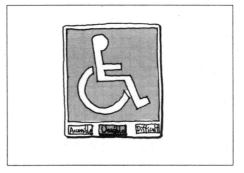

91   *International Symbol of Accessibility with "level of accessibility" indicated.*

j.   **The International Symbol of Accessibility** is a standard symbol which indicates that a facility or route is fully accessible. The symbol should not be modified, nor should extraneous elements be added. Supplemental signs and symbols which indicate level of accessibility, provide direction, or identify a facility may be used in combination with the symbol of accessibility.

The International Symbol of Accessibility must be displayed as a white figure on a blue background or as a blue figure on a white background.

The wheelchair figure should always face right unless it is used as a directional sign pointing to the left.

The width of the border should be equal to the stroke width of the figure.

Good quality, vandal-resistant, weather-resistant materials should be used.

The International Symbol of Accessibility should be used to:

1)   **Identify accessible parking spaces.** Each space should be marked with a vertical signpost as well as pavement markings. Signs must be at least 70 inches square and display the symbol of accessibility. Spaces must also be marked with a painted symbol of accessibility on the pavement.

2)   **Indicate beginnings of pathways.** Use the symbol with level of accessibility signs.

3)   **Indicate accessible facility entrances.** The symbol must be used to identify which facility entrances are fully accessible. For entrances that are not accessible, there must be signs directing users to the nearest accessible entrance.

3)   **Indicate accessible facilities.** Use sensibly and with discretion to convey areas and facilities that are not obviously accessible to the user, or situations where the level of accessibility is unclear. In heavily vegetated areas, for example, users may need details of accessibility before venturing forward.

7.3   Program/Site Information

a.   Provide interpretive signs for parents and teachers at the entry of all playgrounds to indicate special features or opportunities offered by the area; for example, a water play area.

Parents need to know whether a site is fully or only partially accessible.

b.   Provide signs on individual items of play equipment that inform parents and caregivers about special features or opportunities. Signs can show how spaces and facilities can be used for creative play, for example, making a "house" by draping a sheet over a play structure or branch of a tree.

92   *Signage should be designed as an information system directing and explaining to users the opportunities of the site.*

8. FENCES/ENCLOSURES

Fences are a primary means of defining, protecting, separating, and creating activity settings. They perform a crucial function in vegetation management of protecting resources from severe impact. If used inappropriately, they can also restrict play opportunities unnecessarily and cut children off from the environment (in a park, for example), or create play "ghettos."

Planning Criteria

Play Value. If used correctly, fences provide a sense of security, enclosure, and support for activities.

Programming. Fences provide physical support and places to hang or attach objects, strings, etc. They are useful for defining play areas.

Play Leadership. Fences can help improve supervision and create defensible space (Newman, 1972).

Safety. Fences are important safety devices; they can define zones of legal responsibility, but can become hazardous if used unintentionally as climbing structures.

Risk Management. Attention must be paid to climbing risks inherent in fences. Gateways must be clearly observable by staff.

Accessibility. Entrances must be clearly visible and wide enough for wheelchair passage (at least 3 feet 6 inches).

Integration. Fences should not be used to separate children in such a way that unintentional segregation results, especially between children with disabilities and children without disabilities.

Management/Maintenance. Policies for the location and modification of fences with respect to vegetation management should be developed. Fences should be kept in good repair.

8.1   Design Considerations

Fences have a primary function of directing pedestrian movement, enclosing or defining activity areas, and protecting vegetation.

Locking sites at night is often ineffective or causes more problems than it solves. Children still climb over fences, and liability is still an issue because the playground can be legally considered an "attractive nuisance." Only very high fences will keep able-bodied children out of an area. Fences will get climbed and can present a hazard unless an easier means of access is provided.

Play experiences should be incorporated into fencing design where appropriate; for example, with peek-a-boo holes, chalking surfaces, child-created mosaic walls and murals. Think of fences as positive design elements integrated with other elements like play equipment, or as a play element in their own right (walls to walk along, for instance).

Fencing and barrier systems should reflect the physical structure of the site and the pattern of movement and activity within it. In the case of vegetated areas, the barrier system should reinforce the spatial structure of the maturing landscape. When designing fences, the following criteria should be considered:

a.   **Height** should be sufficient to stop direct forward movement. Children's mid-chest height is about right. For young children, this means that a single rail is often sufficient, but it is not a good solution for someone with a cane (the single rail cannot be detected and a person with a visual disability may fall over the rail; a textured surfacing should be used in such situations as a tactile warning). For higher fences, a double rail is necessary—otherwise, small children will scoot under. A second rail also increases climbability. Some fences should be set low or have multiple rails so they can be sat upon. The top rail should be set at a good "leaning height" (this varies according to age).

b.   **Visual Privacy/ Visual Access.** The transparency of a fence should relate to what is on the other side. If it is planting, then the fence should be as unobtrusive as possible so visual contact is unimpaired. If privacy is important, the fence should be more solid.

It is often a good idea to let planting grow through the fencing which increases the strength of both the fencing and the plants.

93   Barriers can be designed as play elements in their own right.

94   Fences make good hangouts.

95   *Barriers can define different degrees of privacy.*

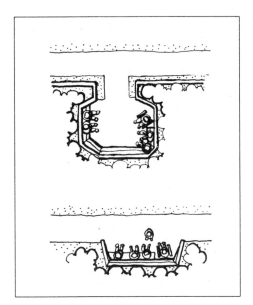

96   *Fences can be used to define gathering places.*

c.   **Spatial Definition/Visual Interest.** Barriers are used to differentiate and modulate interrelationships between people and vegetation, and to define main pathways and social spaces within vegetated areas.

The definition of potential social space should always be kept in mind when designing fencing. Straight-line fencing is boring and antisocial. All manner of nooks, perches, and hangouts can be formed by modifying fence lines.

d.   **Degree of Protection/Permanence.** Longevity requirements of barriers used for different purposes vary considerably. Temporary protection of plantings may be needed only for a few months; at the other extreme, permanent definition of vegetation and activity zones is usually required. Construction of all permanent fences must be robust. Chain link fencing is an effective, low-maintenance fencing medium. Welded mesh is even better. Both require aesthetic enhancement with plantings or other applied materials or surfaces.

1)   Use vinyl-coated mesh for chain link fencing around children's play areas (Seattle, 1986).

2)   Wood fencing should be used in approved locations only, taking into consideration visibility and design details which prevent decomposition (Seattle, 1986).

e.   **Multiprotection Techniques.** To protect vegetation, barriers of differing degrees of permanence can often be used as successive "lines of defense." The objective is *not* to keep children out of planted areas, but to reduce impact so that planted areas have a better chance of survival. Main planting areas can be enclosed by a permanent barrier, behind which shorter-term, less obtrusive protection can be provided according to the growth, protection, and aesthetic needs of specific plants. Individual plant stakes provide a further degree of protection.

f.   **Aesthetic Appearance.** In public play areas, fences and barriers must be attractive. Shrub plantings, ground covers, and vines can be used to camouflage unsightly fences.

97 *Fences can define intimate social corners.*

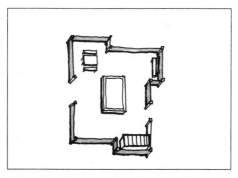

98 *Fencing should enclose specific settings.*

99 *Sturdy, temporary fencing protects new plants.*

100 *Fences protect plants from "running through" behavior.*

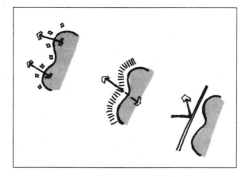

101 *Fences can provide varied degrees of protection and penetration of planted areas.*

102 *Fences can support vines and shrubs to hide unattractive elements.*

103 *Peepholes, color, varied textures, and patterns of solids and voids make fences attractive play settings.*

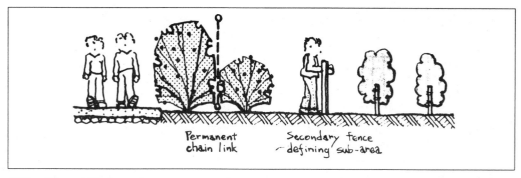

104 *"Lines of Defense."*

9.   MANUFACTURED PLAY EQUIPMENT SETTINGS

Most equipment settings stimulate large muscle activity and kinesthetic experience, but they can also support non-physical aspects of child development. Equipment can provide opportunities to experience height and can serve as landmarks to assist orientation and wayfinding. They may also become rendezvous spots, stimulate social interaction, and provide hideaways in hiding and chasing games. Small, semi-enclosed spaces support dramatic play. Seating encourages social play. Properly selected equipment can support the development of creativity and cooperation, especially structures that incorporate sand and water play. Equipment settings must be designed as part of a comprehensive multipurpose play environment. Isolated pieces of equipment are ineffective on their own.

Planning Criteria

Play Value. Equipment can support large muscle, psychomotor coordination as well as social interaction and dramatic play.

Programming Potential. Play structures can be converted to other temporary uses like stage settings; loose parts can be strung from and attached to the equipment such as backdrops or banners for special events and dramatic play activities.

Safety. There are a number of well-documented safety issues related to manufactured play equipment (Root, 1983; Simm, 1985; U.S. Consumer Products Safety Commission, hereafter CPSC, 1991): falls, entrapments, protrusions, collisions, splinters. Loose clothing, scarves, and cords on clothes present a potential of strangulation when caught on equipment. All of these issues must be addressed in the design, maintenance, and supervision of play equipment.

Play Leadership. Trained supervision is necessary; leaders must know how to adapt equipment to other program purposes.

Risk Management. Equipment should be properly sited, selected, and installed over appropriate shock-absorbing surfaces. Procedures and standards for equipment purchase, installation, and maintenance must be developed. A systematic safety inspection program must be implemented. Site and program supervision standards must also be developed and accident and incident records must be kept. Parents and caregivers must be warned about the dangers of loose clothing and about the effect of extreme weather on equipment and surfacing safety.

Accessibility. Equipment should be accessible, but must be designed for children, not wheelchairs. Transfer points should always be marked both visually and tactually. The most significant aspect of making a piece of equipment accessible is to understand that children with disabilities need many of the same challenges as children without disabilities.

Integration. Play equipment provides opportunities for integration, especially when programmed with other activities. Play settings should be exciting and attractive for parents as well as children—adults accompany children to the park or playground more often today than in the past. It is equally important to design for parents using wheelchairs who accompany their able-bodied children.

Management Issues. Strict policies and standards are needed. A safety inspection schedule is mandatory. The CPSC guidelines (1991) provide an important base, but they are limited. Play settings should be re-evaluated and renovated periodically, about every five years. This should be allowed for in the budget. Manufacturers' catalogs should be used as part of a community education process to broaden and deepen the understanding of play by decisionmakers.

9.1   Design Criteria for Manufactured Equipment

9.1.1   Safety

a.   **Hazard versus Challenge.** Children will use equipment in all possible ways, regardless of the original design intent. Since the idea of play is to explore the potential of any play setting, children will test its use beyond the limits of their own ability—that is how they discover their limits (Bruner & Sherwood, 1976; Collard, 1979). Unfortunately, such "testing" can sometimes put children in situations that compromise their safety. As a result, a fundamental aspect of play—children being able to challenge the limits of their abilities—is being eroded by adult concerns (sometimes unfounded) about liability and risk of suit (Bruya & Beckwith, 1985).

When children test their limits, they learn new skills. Good play setting design allows for such tests and anticipates the consequences of this normal behavior. Children will run up slides, and they will jump out of swings. Play setting designers must understand this and adjust the environment so that misjudgments by children do not become injurious (Beckwith, 1982).

A hazard is the unforeseen consequence of a child's inability to handle a given challenge. It can result from a poorly designed feature which children see without comprehending the behavioral implications, such as insufficiently high guard rails and nonlevel surfaces at slide entries. A hazard can also result from poor maintenance (rather than design) as something children cannot see, like broken glass in sand (CPSC, 1991).

A challenge is something the child can see and chooses to attempt. The playground designer's responsibility is to maximize challenge and minimize hazard (Beckwith, 1985a; Herron & Sutton-Smith, 1971; Redl, 1959).

b.   **Separation of Play Areas for Different Age Groups**

The CPSC (1991) recommends that separate play areas be designed for different age groups. Accident reports and claim records show that very young children have been gravely injured while playing on equipment intended for older children, sometimes while the parents are actually facilitating their play (Mount, 1985). Similarly, accidents can occur when older children use equipment designed for toddlers.

105   *Children will use equipment in novel ways regardless of original design intent.*

106 *Separate play areas should be designed for each age group.*

107 *Every reasonable effort must be taken to keep toxic substances out of play settings.*

Separation of activities should be based on developmental needs, activity characteristics (separation of noisy or large muscle activity, for example), safety considerations, and environmental requirements (separation of water play areas, for example). However, physical separation of different age groups should be designed to allow mixed-age groups of siblings and friends to play in the same general vicinity and to allow parents to observe children of different age groups from one supervising position.

c. **A Range of Play Opportunities.** Equipment should be designed to provide a wide range of behavioral options for children of varying abilities.

d. **Chemical Pollutants.** Environmental contaminants are a special problem around children and people with environmental illnesses. Diagnosis and treatment are difficult because individual responses vary. Symptoms for the same exposure often range from flu-like, to allergy-like, to behavioral reactions.

Unfortunately, a surprising number of playgrounds are located on former industrial sites or landfills. Many are adjacent to major highways with high levels of windborne asbestos, lead and rubber (Freedberg, 1983). Likewise, park management practices sometimes include weed abatement and insect control measures which introduce significant levels of contamination. Occasionally entire playgrounds are heavily sprayed with no effort made to restrict access while the chemicals are active. This is not true everywhere, however; some communities (e.g., Berkeley, CA) have laws and integrated pest management programs that severely limit the use of herbicides and pesticides in public areas.

The chemicals of greatest concern are those recognized as toxins and carcinogens. Most petroleum products, asbestos, reactive metals, and some agricultural/industrial by-products fall into this group. Lead in paint and wood treatments is also a concern (CPSC, 1991). The wisest policy is to remove all materials from children's environments which have not been proven safe.

1) Every effort must be made to reduce chemical contamination of play areas (see National Playing Fields Association, hereafter NPFA, 1983, for a discussion of the working definition of "reasonably foreseen," as developed in the English courts).

2) The public must be notified and access restricted when there are detectable levels of chemicals, whether permanently or temporarily present, in a play area.

9.1.2   Play Value

a.   **Options.** Research has shown that a diversity of settings stimulates a wide range of play activity and supports the needs of children at all levels of development (Moore, 1966, 1974a,b, 1978b, 1980; Rothenburg et al., 1974; Frost & Klein, 1979; Bruya, Robbins & Fowler, 1983; Frost & Campbell, 1985; and others).

Playgrounds that are insufficiently diverse are often underutilized (Gold, 1972). Although traditional equipment settings are appealing to many children (Moore, 1978b), a broad diversity of settings is necessary to maintain interest and to provide developmental challenges for all children (Herron & Sutton-Smith, 1971; Redl, 1959). Successful playgrounds usually have a high manipulative factor (Moore, 1989a,b). Even a well-designed composite structure with many options still provides only one type of play setting and is not equivalent to a multi-setting playground (Frost & Klein, 1979; Frost & Strickland, 1985).

b.   **Sensory Variety.** Play structure settings present a good opportunity to provide sensory stimulation and discrimination. Children can be exposed to the qualities of processed materials in a structured sensory experience over which the designer has considerable control. These materials can be intentionally manipulated to increase access (Playing and Learning in Adaptable Environments, Inc., hereafter PLAE, 1981–87). Primary dimensions are:

- hot—cool—cold
- light—shade—dark
- color

- rough—smooth
- hard—soft
- noisy—quiet

Sensorially diverse environments stimulate more complex patterns of activity for a greater number of children.

c.   **Spatial Complexity.** Developmental potential is increased by emphasizing three-dimensional, connected paths of movement (Page, 1976; Bruya, Carter & Fowler, 1985). In this way, children can learn spatial concepts such as over-under, in-out, up-down, right-left, spatial depth, and directionality. They thereby begin to realize the limits of their own fingers, toes, head, and body, and are able to measure the risks of jumping, reaching, and falling (Seattle, 1986).

Play equipment should be designed to support the maximum potential for creative physical action by all children (Beckwith, 1982).

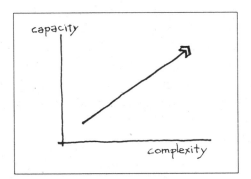

108   *Capacity of equipment increases with complexity.*

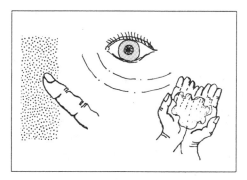

109 *Play structures need to stimulate all of children's senses.*

110 *Play structures should support crawling.*

111 *Play structures should support jumping.*

d. **Large Muscle Activity.** The primary purpose of some play structures is to accommodate large muscle activities (Bower, 1977, 1979) from which complex patterns of activity are built up (Moore, 1974b). Individually and in combination, activities vary according to the physical characteristics of the structure and the psychosocial characteristics of the users. The following are desirable large muscle activities:

- climbing
- swinging
- bouncing
- balancing
- jumping
- crawling
- hopping
- skipping
- creeping

- sliding
- rolling
- lifting
- pushing
- pulling
- knee walking
- hand-over-hand
- hanging by arms
- twirling/spinning

e. **Movement.** Children love movement and they derive great pleasure from the stimulation of their kinesthetic senses. In response, designers should:

1) Build a variety of movement, as an end in itself, into manufactured equipment settings.

2) Provide interactive play equipment which responds to children's input (Frost & Klein, 1979).

"Up-down" activity stimulates a special sense of movement through space and encourages dramatic play (Parten, 1971). "Up-down" movement is a basic dimension in spatial perception ("I am higher than you," "I can see you, you can't see me").

Children with physical disabilities have few opportunities to get "above the action." Equipment should be designed to allow a child with a physical disability the opportunity to slide, crawl, tumble, or pull themselves up to an "overview" position (Shaw, 1980). Design considerations for providing equipment access are discussed in Section 9.1.6 of this chapter. In addition, safe, accessible "overviews" should be built into play settings where feasible.

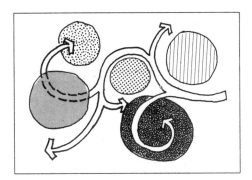

112   *An effective play structure emphasizes sensory variety and many psychomotor opportunities.*

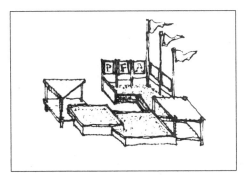

113   *Play settings should emphasize linkage and flow.*

f.   **Linkage and Flow.** Psychomotor activity involves children in mastering the flow of their own bodies through space, in a continuous sequence of movement. Continuity of physical support is very important; it enables the child to make a variety of "play circuits" through the play environment (Moore, G.T. et al., 1979).

Early playground designs provided many separate play events to avoid competition and crowding. But this idea failed to recognize that children play in small groups (Scholtz & Ellis, 1975; Wade & Ellis, 1971; Ellis & Scholtz, 1978). More recent concepts of linkage and concern for traffic flow have resulted in use of decks and linking devices, such as balance beams, to create flexible traffic flow patterns (Bruya, 1985b).

Where the emphasis is on movement and large muscle activities, linked equipment settings are normally preferable to isolated pieces (Moore, 1974b; Shaw, 1976; Bruya, 1985a; Beckwith, 1985b). However, where a manufactured equipment setting is provided to support quiet social activity, it should be separated from the main cluster of equipment.

- Each main "play circuit" should provide a choice of "subcircuits" to maintain interest and avoid the potential boredom of "one-way-to-go" systems.

g.   **Motor Challenge.** Children will always suffer bumps, bruises, and grazes when they play. However, the risk of serious injury must be minimized by the design of equipment settings. The most important design parameters for managing risk are the distance of potential falls and the shock-absorbing properties of the surfacing materials. While attention to these parameters will not stop accidents, they can help reduce the severity of injuries. Further aspects of height in relation to shock-absorbing surfacing materials are discussed in Chapter 11:   Ground Covers/Surfacing, Section 11.3.1, Surfacing Depth and Critical Height.

Where possible, equipment should be designed with only a few feet of sheer drop to ground level (Bowers, 1977).

Since falls from unsafe elevations have been established as a major playground hazard, characteristics other than height must be found to provide appropriate challenges to children.

1)   New and traditional equipment settings should provide physical challenges that are not based on height, including upper body movement and balance (Beckwith, 1985a).

114 *Multilevel, pyramidal structures provide a graduated challenge and reduce fall distance.*

2)   Challenges should be "graduated" (Moore, G.T. et al., 1979). Upper body development activities, for example, would include turning bars, chinning bars, parallel bars, ring treks, and track rides, in addition to traditional elements such as horizontal ladders.

3)   Graduated challenges should be provided at varying heights to facilitate accessibility (PLAE, 1981–87).

4)   Fall distances should be reduced in multi-level structures by using a pyramidal form with intermediate decks or other components such as nets and ramps (Bruya, Sullivan & Fowler, 1979).

h.   **Differentiation.** Refuges away from the main currents of activity are needed by some children. Small tributary spaces should be designed into equipment settings to increase the variety of activity options.

•   Differentiate equipment settings to provide tributary and refuge spaces to accommodate activities for all children.

9.1.3   U.S. Consumer Products Safety Commission (CPSC)

The CPSC *Handbook for Public Playground Safety*, first issued in 1978, was the result of an extensive investigation with the active participation of both the public and equipment manufacturers. The most recent edition, published in 1991, represents the current "standard of care" for play area safety from a legal perspective.

The CPSC mandate does not fully address the problems of accessibility and integration, neither is it concerned necessarily with maximizing developmental benefits for all children. The *Play For All Guidelines* expands on the CPSC *Handbook* to address these issues and to promote better play environments for all children.

The following safety guidelines meet or exceed CPSC:

a.   **Entrapment.** Entrapment occurs when any part of a child's body (head, hand, finger, etc.) becomes lodged within a space and cannot be withdrawn. The result can be strangulation, loss of a finger or limb, or emotional injury. Openings on play equipment must be carefully designed so that there are no opportunities for entrapment. CPSC (1991) recommends specific test procedures and testing tools for evaluating entrapment hazards. Entrapment criteria include:

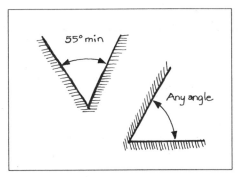

115   *To prevent head entrapment, angles must exceed 55 degrees or be oriented so that one of the edges is horizontal to the ground or down-sloping.*

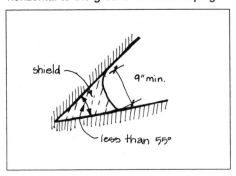

116   *Where angles are less than 55 degrees, shields must be installed to prevent head entrapment.*

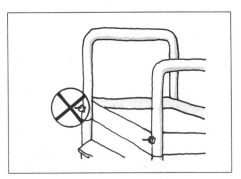

117   *All nuts and bolts should be recessed, fitted with tamper-proof locks, and the holes plugged.*

1)   **Head entrapment—opening size.** In general, any opening between 3-1/2 inches and 9 inches which is closed on all sides may present a head entrapment. This includes both vertical and horizontal openings. The only exception is when the ground surface serves as the opening's lower edge.

2)   **Head entrapment—opening shape.** No vertical angles less than 55 degrees are permitted unless one leg of the angle is horizontal or slopes downward. The angle can be exempt if filled with a rigid shield to prevent entrapment.

3)   **Head entrapment—flexible openings.** Head entrapments can be created by openings that appear to be safe but that change size during equipment use or when pressure is applied. An example of this type of opening is the spaces in a climbing net.

4)   **Head entrapment—depth of opening.** The depth of an opening is limited when there is a barrier behind it. When determining entrapment potential, opening depth must be considered along with opening size in accordance with CPSC test procedures.

5)   **Finger entrapment.** Do not allow openings between 5/16 inch and 1 inch on play equipment.

b.   **Protrusions.** Protrusions are components which extend in any direction from play equipment, site elements, or site furnishings and which might entrap a child's clothing, cause a child to loose his balance or pose a potential impact hazard. Any protrusions must meet CPSC requirements as determined through standard test procedures (CPSC, 1991). It is preferable that *all* nuts and bolts be recessed, fitted with tamper-proof locks, and the holes plugged.

c.   **Sharp Edges or Corners.** A sharp corner is any wooden or metal edge which is not rounded to prevent injuries if struck during a fall. Sharp edges are any surfaces which may cut or puncture a child's skin. Neither sharp edges nor sharp corners are allowed in a play area.

d.   **Crush, Pinch, and Shearing Points.** Crush, pinch, and shearing points are junctures which could cause contusion, laceration, abrasion, amputation, or fracture during use. These points are created when components move in relationship to each other or to a fixed component. There must be no accessible crush, pinch, or shearing points in the play area that could injure children or catch their clothing.

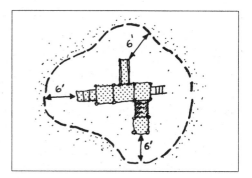

118 *Fall zones must extend a minimum of six feet in all directions from play equipment over 20 inches high (preschool) and 24 inches high (school-age).*

e. **Use Zone.** The *use zone* is defined by the CPSC as the area around each piece of equipment or composite structure. It consists of two parts: the *fall zone* and the *no-encroachment zone*.

1) **Fall Zone.** The fall zone is "an area under and around the equipment where protective surfacing is required . . ." (CPSC, 1991). In other words, it is the clear area under and around play equipment where a child could be expected to land when falling or jumping from the equipment. For school-age play areas, all play equipment over 24 inches high must have an unobstructed fall zone with shock-absorbing surfacing. For preschool and toddler play areas, this fall zone requirement should be applied to all play equipment over 20 inches high (CPSC, 1991; U.S. Army, 1992). The CPSC guidelines state that fall zones should extend a minimum of 6 feet in all directions from the perimeter of the equipment. Ratté et al., 1990 (based on Beckwith, 1988) recommend that the fall zone be extended one foot for every additional foot of height above six feet. Thus, an eight-foot high piece of equipment (or section of a composite structure) would require an eight-foot fall zone.

Fall zones for swings and slides must meet additional CPSC requirements (see Sections 11.2 and 11.3 of this chapter). With the exception of spring rocking equipment and equipment under 24 inches in height, the fall zones of adjacent pieces of equipment should not overlap. However, adjacent pieces of equipment may share a single no-encroachment zone.

2) **No-Encroachment Zone.** A no-encroachment zone is an additional area beyond the fall zone where children using the equipment can be expected to move about, engaged in activity related to the piece of equipment. These areas should be free of obstacles. The CPSC *Handbook* (1991) states that:

> No specific dimensions can be recommended for the no-encroachment zone around individual pieces of playground equipment. These dimensions will vary according to the types of adjacent pieces of equipment and their orientation with respect to one another.

> For example, the recommended fall zone at the side of both a slide and a swing is 6 feet. Since fall zones should not overlap (with the exception of certain adjacent spring rockers), a slide could be placed with its side no closer than 12 feet to the side of a swing. Therefore, there may be no need to add an additional no-encroachment zone. Conversely, it

would not be desirable to have a slide exit facing the front or rear of a single axis swing.

No-encroachment zones extending beyond the fall zones are recommended for moving equipment or equipment from which the child is in motion as he or she exits. This allows more space for children to regain their balance upon exiting the equipment and also provides added protection against other children running into a moving part.

f.   **Shock-Absorbing Surfacing.** Shock-absorbing surfacing material is required to reduce the likelihood of severe head and upper limb injuries that often result from falls from play equipment. To meet the CPSC criteria, the surfacing material must attenuate the impact of a head-first fall from the highest point of the equipment onto the shock-absorbing surface such that the impact will not exceed 200 g's peak deceleration and a Head Injury Criteria (HIC) of 1,000. (See also Chapter 11: Ground Covers/Surfacing, Section 4, On-Site Testing.)

The HIC values are derived from a mathematical formula that combines both the deceleration of the head during impact as well as the time duration over which the head decelerates to a halt.

The most widely used test method for evaluating the shock-absorbing properties of a shock-absorbing surfacing material is to drop an instrumented metal head-form onto a sample of the material from a specified height and record the deceleration/time-pulse during impact. (For further details, see ASTM F1292, *Standard Specification for Impact-Attenuation of Surface Systems Under and Around Playground Equipment.*)

g.   **Multiple Exits.** All play equipment, including composite structures and playhouses, must have a minimum of two exits. If the equipment is intended for preschoolers, then climbers, such as rung ladders, climbing nets, and arch climbers cannot be the sole means of access. In playhouses, a window can qualify as an exit if it is large enough to be climbed through by a child.

h.   **Guardrails and Protective Barriers.** Guardrails and protective barriers create nonclimbable enclosures that help keep children from falling off elevated decks. While they are essential for safety (e.g., in a multi-deck structure where a high deck is adjacent to a low deck), they also support the many "chase" and "hide-and-seek" games that children always adapt to play structures.

119   *For safety, play equipment should have multiple exits.*

The recommendations for guardrails and protective barriers vary with the age group of the intended user:

- For toddlers, only full protective barriers should be used. Protective barriers should be provided for all decks 20 inches high or higher. The protective barriers on these decks should be 20 inches high minimum as measured from the deck surface (U.S. Army, 1992). CPSC does not address the design of protective barriers for toddlers.

- For preschool age, full protective barriers are preferable and should be provided for all elevated decks over 20 inches in height (CPSC, 1991). Protective barriers must be 29 inches high. CPSC also allows guardrails for this age group for platforms between 20 inches and 30 inches high. However, full protective barriers should be used unless a guardrail is needed for the functioning of a specific play event (e.g., a clatter bridge). If guardrails are used, the height of the top rail from the deck surface should be 29 inches. The height of the lower edge of the guard rail to the deck surface should be 23 inches maximum.

- For school-age children, full protective barriers continue to provide the greatest protection against falls and should be provided for all elevated decks over 30 inches in height (CPSC, 1991). Protective barriers must be 38 inches high. CPSC also allows guardrails for this age group for platforms between 30 inches and 48 inches high. However, the use of full protective barriers is encouraged, unless a guardrail is needed for the functioning of a specific play event. If guardrails are used, the height of the top rail from the deck surface should be 38 inches. The height of the lower edge of the guardrail to the deck surface should be 26 inches maximum.

All protective barriers and guardrails should be nonclimbable and free from entrapments. In addition, protective barriers should not have any openings which would allow a child's torso to pass through (3.5 inches by 6.2 inches, or larger).

The recommendations for protective barriers have created confusion as various manufacturers try to determine what is "nonclimbable." For the most part, the industry agrees that horizontal rungs constitute a "climbable" barrier since these are generally constructed in the same manner as ladders. Vertical rungs are preferable, provided they meet entrapment specifications. Some companies simply wall in the opening completely. Such a barrier may indeed be nonclimbable, but it also greatly inhibits supervision.

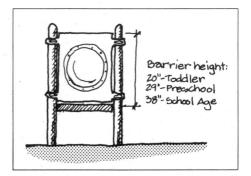

120 *Protective barriers must be nonclimbable and at the appropriate height for each age group.*

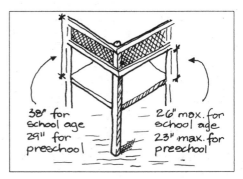

121 *Guardrails must also be nonclimbable and at an appropriate height.*

Three designs which seem to meet the CPSC guidelines and supervision requirements without creating entrapments are: vertical wooden slats or metal rails with 3-inch spaces, panels with cutouts covered with clear plastic, and wire mesh panels.

Be certain that platform enclosures are provided at appropriate heights for the age group that will be using the equipment and that there are no entrapments or footholds for climbing.

Children with Motor Disabilities may require additional railing details to support their movement through the play environment. However, care must be taken to ensure that additional handrail support does not create opportunities for children to climb over a barrier. For example, providing two parallel banisters is not an acceptable solution because it creates a ladder for able-bodied children. Additional support for children with motor disabilities should be provided at transition points where there are changes in surface, activity, or elevation. This support can be in the form of vertical grips or handholds that provide the needed security while complying with the CPSC guidelines.

i. **Signs.** The CPSC looked at the issue of warning signs and found the issue too complex for a guideline. They do, however, suggest color-coding equipment to indicate degree of difficulty. Substantial research is required on this issue before any guidance can be offered (Quality, 1987). For instance, "red for danger" may encourage rather than inhibit hazardous activity if children interpret such signs as a challenge.

In the years since the first publication of the CPSC guidelines, several liability cases have established the requirement for warning signs on the basis of the public's right to be informed of hazards (Bruya & Beckwith, 1985). Currently there is no generally accepted language for such signs. Compounding the problem, many users may not read English or may not read at all. Therefore:

- If provided, play equipment should have both word and graphic playground safety signs (see Chapter 7: Signage).

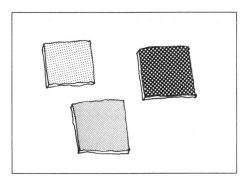

122 *It is often assumed that children respond to primary colors. This assumption may have no basis in fact.*

123 *Most "thematic" elements have a pronounced effect.*

124 *Equipment settings should allow children and play leaders the opportunity to program them for dramatic purposes.*

9.1.4 Appearance Considerations

a.　**Color.** It is generally believed that children respond best to primary colors, although little research exists to support this assertion.

b.　**Theme.** Making slides look like rocket ships and climbers look like castles is based on the assumption that thematic play structures will better support and stimulate dramatic play activities. But these are adult ideas that have little grounding in research.

Do figurative expressions have developmental value? Certainly they attract young children, especially if the expression is taken from nature. But over time, children will tire of such expressions, especially if they are exposed to them day after day. Non-thematic equipment is more adaptable for informal as well as programmed activity (PLAE, 1981–87).

The effect of thematic equipment is different for different ages and closely matches developmental stages. For most ages, the more abstract the thematic representation the more supportive the setting is for the imagination. Modest "thematic" elements can have a pronounced imaginative effect. A simple "steering wheel" fixed on a piece of equipment will be enough to turn it into a "fire truck," "locomotive," "space ship," "wagon train," etc. (Moore & Wong, in press).

Thematic elements provide strong visual identity and clear landmarks in play settings (see subsection **c.** below).

1)　Equipment should be designed to allow for a variety of dramatic play opportunities.

2)　Equipment settings should allow the child and/or play leader the opportunity to program the setting for a variety of dramatic play experiences.

3)　Since the impact diminishes rapidly, thematic equipment is best suited for large "magnet" playgrounds in community parks which are not frequently visited by the same children.

4)　In school and neighborhood parks which are used daily by the same children, thematic equipment has a lower priority. However, it can still provide strong identity.

125   *Play structures should have strong identity and expression.*

c.   **Visual Identity.** Because play structures are usually centrally sited, it is important that they have a strong visual identity. This identity can be expressed in abstract or figurative terms.

An advantage of figurative expression is that it gives visual identity to a setting and is therefore an aid in orientation and recognition. It provides a sense of belonging (Moore, 1978b; Moore, G.T. et al., 1979). Child interviews suggest that a visit to a playground with significant visual impact creates a lasting impression (Moore, 1986c).

The meaning and psychological impact of visual expression will be increased if the community, especially the children, participates in designing and executing the work.

1)   Strong visual identity should be designed into equipment settings, using both figurative and nonfigurative means.

2)   The local community should participate in deciding on the visual expression and identity of play settings.

9.1.5   Scale

Few items of manufactured equipment are scaled to meet the needs of very small children. However, for other age groups and to the extent necessary, equipment should be based on anthropometric data and conform to the physical size of children.

9.1.6   Specific Population Requirements

a.   **Visual Disabilities.** Children with vision impairments must be able to "read" the environment to be able to use it. To assist them, provide the following (Schneekloth & Day, 1980; Schneekloth, 1979):

1)   Use two- or three-dimensional representations of the equipment as part of a mapping system to communicate the equipment's appearance and location.

2)   When practical and necessary for safety, equipment should have guiderails.

3)   All means of entering or leaving a piece of equipment should be indicated by a change in texture and/or material on the rail and/or floor. Care should be taken that this does not create a trip hazard for running children.

126   *Use two- or three-dimensional representations of the equipment as part of a mapping system.*

4) Areas of entry and exit should occur only after some distinct physical movement has been initiated (e.g., turning a corner, stepping up or down).

5) Swings should be oriented away from main circulation and separated from the rest of the play area. Swings should never be attached to a composite structure (CPSC, 1991).

6) Surfacing materials should change at the junction of safety zones and circulation pathways. The change should be distinct and standardized.

7) All edges of equipment settings must be well-defined.

b. **Motor Disabilities.** In addition to grip enhancements and the concept of graduated challenge, children with motor impairments benefit especially from soft settings. Play events such as nets, hammocks, and resilient surfaces are particularly appealing and beneficial.

c. **Nonambulatory.** Children using wheelchairs, canes, walkers, or crutches like to play in equipment settings as much as other children. Manufacturers should be urged to make equipment accessible so that children using mobility aids can come adjacent to it and transfer onto it. An important part of providing equipment access is ensuring that accessible routes lead to the equipment (see Chapter 6: Pathways, Section 1). Within fall zone areas, that surfacing must also be shock absorbing (see Chapter 11: Ground Covers/Surfacing, Section 3). Accessibility for nonambulatory users can be facilitated by providing the following facilities:

1) **Transfer Points.** A transfer point should be provided to allow a child to transfer between a wheelchair and the play structure. This transfer point must be located on an accessible route (CAH, 1992) and should meet the following design criteria (Golstman et al., 1992):

- **Clear space.** A 5-foot by 5-foot clear, level area must be provided on one side of the transfer platform.
- **Parking space.** For each transfer point, a 30-inch by 48-inch space should be provided adjacent to an accessible route and out of the equipment's required fall zone, where a child's wheelchair can be left while he or she is on the play structure.
- **Size of platform.** The transfer platform must be at least 2 feet by 2 feet.
- **Height of platform.** The height of the transfer platform should be between 15 inches and 17 inches (CAH, 1992).

127 A transfer point should be provided to allow a child to transfer between a wheelchair and a play structure.

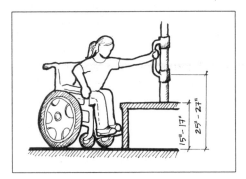

128 *Handholds help children transfer onto the play equipment.*

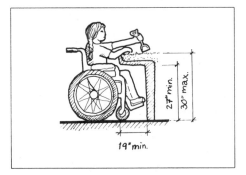

129 *Accessible sand and water trays can be a valuable play element for children with disabilities.*

- **Handholds.** At least one handhold, positioned 25 inches to 27 inches above the ground, should be provided at the rear of the transfer platform or the transfer platform should have an edge which can be gripped to help a child slide from a wheelchair onto the platform.
- **Surface of platform.** The platform surfacing material must be smooth enough to slide on and off without cutting, scraping or burning.
- **Adjacent platform heights.** There must be no more than 6 inches between the transfer platform height and the height of the deck surfaces which lead to the main structure. To avoid head and finger entrapments, there should be no openings between different platforms.
- **Grab bars.** Grab bars or handholds should be provided at each level change on the play structure.

2) **Vertical Play Walls.** Any type of play equipment that can be used while sitting in a wheelchair should be located adjacent to an accessible route and mounted between 20 inches and 36 inches above the deck or ground surface (Goltsman et al., 1992).

3) **Sand and Water Tables.** Accessible sand and water tables or trays can provide valuable play experiences for children using wheelchairs or other assistive devices. To ensure accessibility, the play surface of the table or tray should be no more than 30 inches above the ground. In addition, adequate wheelchair clearance should be provided (27 inches high and 17 inches deep) and there should be a clear, level area 48 inches long and 30 inches wide in front of the table or tray area for forward approach. Additional sand and water features should be positioned at ground level for use by children using prone boards. See Chapters 16 and 17, respectively, for more details about water and sand play settings, and further comment about the difficult design issue of reconciling the dimensions required for access with the dimesions needed for adequate depth of sand or water.

4) **Bicycle Control.** Playgrounds with good access for wheelchairs also support access for bikes (and skateboards and roller skates). Simple "No Bikes" signs are unlikely to fully discourage bike riding and its hazards.

- Install bike racks and "no bike" signs at playground entrances, with "thank you" signs next to bike racks. This would make the "no bikes" rule abundantly clear and encourage adults within the play area to exercise supervision.
- Provide attractive bike riding facilities elsewhere in the playground.

130 *Supervision of children with hearing disabilities is improved when clear sight lines are provided.*

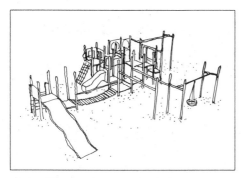

131 *Play equipment should have many ways on and off.*

d. **Hearing Disabilities.** Children with hearing disabilities comprise one of the largest child disability groups. The major issue with hearing disabilities is communication with playmates and supervising adults.

Supervision of all children, including those with hearing loss, is improved when sight lines within the playground are clear, especially for settings such as benches, entrances, and gathering areas.

1) Children with hearing disabilities are more dependent on visual cues; therefore, make sure that important information is clearly visible. Provide warning signs and other visual cues to alert children to potential hazards.

2) Each element of the equipment setting should be easily visible from multiple points. However, a balance must be struck so that possibilities for exploration and discovery are retained.

3) Play equipment must be configured so that children with hearing loss can see potential hazards, including other children playing on the equipment.

4) Vibrations, or materials which cause vibrations, can be used to warn of others on the equipment. However, it can also cause metal fatigue, especially at weld points.

e. **Cognitive Delays.** Orientation is a major issue when equipment settings are designed for children with cognitive delays. Equipment elements must be visually understandable, not confusing. There are a number of ways to help orientation through use of color, shape, and texture. Throughout the play area, these orientation cues should remain consistent.

Children with developmental disabilities sometimes find it easy to climb to some portion of a piece of equipment, but then become fearful and unable to proceed. They discover that backing down is also too frightening and are stranded. This situation is more likely to be avoided by using the linkage concept in equipment setting design. In addition, the potential injury from an equipment fall will be minimized if the equipment and the surfacing meets the CPSC guidelines and the recommendations set forth in this document.

f. **Behavioral Disability.** Children with psychological, emotional and behavioral disabilities need an environment that is well-structured and focused. Interaction with other children is sometimes difficult.

Children with behavior disabilities and their caregivers benefit from carefully designed, enclosed settings which help to safely retain children.

Diverse, linked settings reduce the need for turn-taking and competition, thereby contributing to a more successful play experience for these children.

g.   **Allergies and other Environmental Disabilities.** Some children have extreme sensitivity to certain plants, synthetic and environmental pollutants, noise, etc. Known aggravations of these disabilities must be avoided in play settings.

h.   **Multiple Disabilities.** Special consideration must be given to the needs of children with more than one disability. For children with severe multiple disabilities, watching or "vicarious play" may become a major form of interaction. For these children, places to sit and observe in the middle of the action may be especially important.

9.2   Inspection and Maintenance Program

The need for carefully planned and professionally administered maintenance programs has become a critical aspect of public play provision (Root, 1983; Simm, 1985; Beckwith, 1983b; McIntyre et al., 1989), especially for risk management (Bruya & Beckwith, 1985). A maintenance program must be implemented as part of regular safety inspections. Trained maintenance personnel must be available to address equipment and site problems as they arise. A missing bolt, a piece of glass, or a broken plank can result in serious injuries if left unaddressed. Proper maintenance will add to the longevity of play settings, and ensures that a play area that is designed for safety remains safe.

132 *Daily and monthly inspection is a critical aspect of maintenance.*

A safety and maintenance inspection program, complete with baseline, routine and annual inspection forms, will be available from MIG Communications by January of 1993.

a.   **Play Area Inspections.** There is considerable variance in the frequency of playground inspections across the nation (Frost & Klein, 1979). Not only do similar municipalities with similar conditions have quite dissimilar standards, but equipment manufacturers also differ greatly in their recommendations.

A basic inspection program should include the following components:

• Daily to weekly (depending on site usage) visual review of the play environment, checking for hazards as specified in an approved checklist. For example, some cities have instituted daily inspections of equipment.

133   *Rotten structural wooden members can be very hazardous.*

- Monthly to three times monthly (depending on site usage) recorded inspection by a trained operative using an approved checklist (FPC/NPFA, n.d.; Root, 1983).

- Bi-annual to annual (depending on site usage) "tear down" inspection to examine features such as bearings and footings for deterioration as detailed in manufacturer's specifications and on approved checklists.

- A comprehensive maintenance program (NPFA, 1983) including staff training, provision of inspection checklists, prompt repair of discovered problems, follow-up quality assurance, and detailed documentation (Bruya & Beckwith, 1985).

9.3   Installation

a.   **Footings.** The tops of playground equipment footings must be covered by shock-absorbing surfacing to the same specifications as the rest of the play area. The top edges of the footing must be smoothed with a two-inch radius. Frame members should rest on a well-drained bottom of gravel to prevent encasement of posts and subsequent deterioration (Friedberg, 1975).

b.   **Installation Instructions.** Most manufacturers supply detailed installation instructions with their equipment. Problems arise when installers do not (or cannot) read these documents, or do not receive them. Companies which rely heavily on export trade have begun to use purely graphic instructions. Not only does such an approach resolve translation problems but it also provides appropriate guidance for the nonreading installer.

1)   Check the quality and quantity of material supplied before installation. The supplier should include a parts list against which quantities are checked.

2)   Check that suppliers provide appropriate installation instructions and that these are followed precisely. Retain these documents in the project file.

c.   **Factory Support.** Ideally, factory representatives should inspect final installations of play equipment for compliance with manufacturers' standards.

- Request that the factory inspect the installation and document its compliance with factory specifications. Because these specifications may be different from those of the CPSC, ask the manufacturer to identify (in writing) what those discrepancies are, if any.

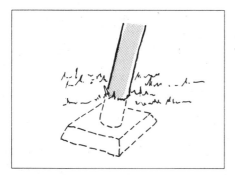

134   *The tops of playground equipment footings must be covered by shock-absorbing surfacing.*

- Get a letter from the manufacturer stating the equipment has been installed to factory specifications.

9.4 Surfacing

Surfacing is a critical factor in play area safety and accessibility. Section 1.3f of this chapter describes the CPSC requirements for surfacing in play equipment use zones. Surfacing is also covered in detail in Chapter 11, Ground Covers/Surfacing.

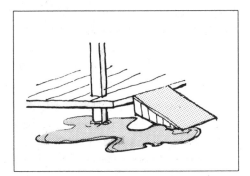

135 *Good drainage around structural supports is essential.*

9.5 Drainage

Drainage is one of the most frequently overlooked aspects of playground installation. In most sites, few investments have better cost/benefit ratios than improved drainage. Even locations with infrequent rain can have mud problems due to irrigation.

At the same time, wet sand and mud are important play materials, so opportunities for wet sand and mud play should be encouraged in appropriate locations (Heseltine & Holborn, 1987; Hogan, 1982; Hewes, 1974). Such play opportunities should be deliberately designed into the playground rather than left to chance. Careful design of the drainage system is one way of providing temporary water and mud play opportunities (Moore, 1987).

1)   Install positive drainage, utilizing French drains or similar systems for best results.

2)   Ensure that areas where sand is to remain in place are kept fairly level (unless there are effective retaining features). Locations under swings and at the end of slides (because they tend to become the lowest points) need the most active drainage.

9.6 Retainers and Edge Detailing

(See also Chapter 6: Pathways, Section 6.7, Edges and Curbs)

Edging, curbing or other containment is required around play areas that are filled with loose surface materials (Beckwith, 1983a, 1983b; Bruya, 1985). These retainers have a significant visual impact on the play area. Care in their design and installation will enhance the play area's appearance and help minimize the need for maintenance over time.

136   *Edges can be designed for sitting.*

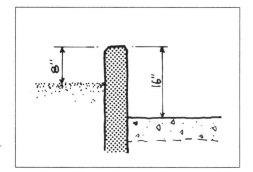

137   *Such a detail presents little trip hazard since it must be intentionally climbed.*

a.   **Surfacing Material.**   Wood retainers must be treated for ground contact, although a nontreated wood cap may be advisable.

Berms covered with grass or other appropriate vegetative cover can retain loose material just as effectively as a concrete wall. However, the berm must be carefully designed to ensure proper drainage and easy maintenance.

b.   **Use Zones.**   As discussed earlier in this chapter, different types of play equipment require different sizes of use zones—the area that should be kept clear of obstructions and be properly surfaced to prevent serious injury to children who may fall from the equipment. It is important that retaining walls and other elements that define the edge of the play equipment area be located outside the use zone. In general, the requirements for use zones range between 6 feet and 8 feet, with swings being a notable exception (see part 2e in Section 11 of this chapter).

c.   **Height Differential and Trip Hazards.**   The height of retaining walls and other surface material barriers should be determined by two considerations: retaining loose material and ensuring that the border does not create a trip hazard. Logically, the higher the barrier, the better the retention of loose material. An eight-inch difference between the top level of the loose material and the top level of the retaining wall is usually adequate to retain material; however, it is not high enough to stop material from being thrown out of the retained area.

Trip hazards exist in both directions: in and out of play areas. If the ground cover is added over an existing grade, which greatly simplifies drainage requirements, then the approach height should be a minimum of 16 inches: 8 inches for loose material and 8 inches for retaining. Such a detail reduces the trip hazard since it must be intentionally climbed. A minor problem exists on exit, however, since the child may be unaware of the additional 8-inch differential. Alternately, an 8-inch pit with an additional 8-inch barrier presents the same obstacle entering and exiting, while a 16-inch pit with 8 inches of material presents an obstacle in the exit direction. If the pit is surrounded by concrete, exiting a 16-inch pit may present a minor trip hazard, with the possibility that children will fall onto the concrete. When surrounded by grass, any of the above combinations are acceptable. Note, however, that there has been no research on this issue.

Note also that the issue of accessibility must be addressed in areas with retaining walls and fall zones where the shock-absorbing surfacing is sand or a similar loose material. Such provisions might include ramps for access and/or accessible routes surfaced with a firm, resilient, shock-absorbing surface. For details, refer to Chapter 6, Pathways, and Chapter 11, Ground Covers/Surfacing.

d.   **Transition Zones Outside Equipment Areas.** The area around the surface material retainer, extending out about five feet, is an area where significant future maintenance will occur. Material thrown out of the retainer will be deposited here and should be anticipated. A popular solution is a five-foot pathway of decomposed compacted granite around the edges of the play area. When a hard surface like concrete is used for such a path, the ejected material can act as roller bearings and create a significant slip hazard.

9.7   Structural Considerations

a.   **Testing.** The CPSC recommends thorough testing of play equipment using a number of testing procedures. However, manufacturers are not required by law to perform these tests. In addition, it is not required that consumers be informed about whether a product has been tested or the results of any tests that might have been performed. Therefore, consumers must request documentation from manufacturers on the test performance of play equipment considered for purchase. If test results are unavailable, it may be wise to keep looking.

b.   **Modularity.** Composite systems use a few simple parts which combine to make complex structures. Such structures can be added to and modified as new products or safety trends emerge. Currently, many products in a wide variety of materials use modular parts. Such systems offer designers more flexibility and more possibilities for adapting play structures for all children. Additional railings, deck height adjustments, and other modifications are easy to accomplish.

9.8   Materials

a.   **Wood.** Wood has been used longer than any other material in the manufacture of play equipment, and has enjoyed repeated periods of fashionability over the years. However, because it is subject to rotting and insect invasion, it has also been periodically replaced with more durable materials. At the turn of the century, most wood equipment was replaced by equipment constructed from steel. After a brief comeback in the 1960s, wood equipment was again replaced in the late 1970s, this time by composite systems that combined use of wood with a variety of materials, including metal alloys and molded high-density plastics.

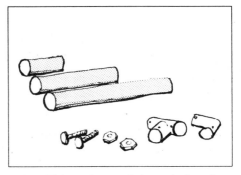

138   *Play equipment is best designed with modular parts.*

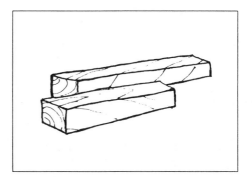

139 *Wood must be naturally rot-resistant or be properly treated to make it durable and safe.*

The following considerations should be kept in mind when considering a purchase of wood play equipment (CPSC, 1991):

1) Wood used in play structures should be naturally rot- and insect-resistant or should be treated to avoid such deterioration. The most common wood treatments used for playground equipment are the inorganic arsenicals. These should be applied by the manufacturer or wood preserver in accordance with the specifications of the American Wood Preservers Association C17 standard (American Wood Preservers Institute, n.d.). This standard states that the treated wood should be visibly free of residues which may contain high levels of arsenic. Chromated copper arsenate (CCA), which causes a greenish coloration, is acceptable if the dislodgeable arsenic on the surface of the wood is minimized. Lee (1990) found that technology exists to treat playground equipment wood with CCA so that dislodgeable arsenic is below detectable levels.

2) Preservatives that have low toxicity may be suitable for playground equipment wood. These include copper or zinc naphthenates, and borates. Creosote, pentachlorophenol and tributyl tin oxide are too toxic or irritating and should not be used as preservatives for playground equipment wood. Finishes that contain pesticides should also be avoided.

3) All paints and other similar finishes must meet the current CPSC regulation for lead in paint: 0.06% maximum lead by dry weight.

4) Insist on complete documentation of wood treatment chemicals and procedures. Manufacturers must ensure that the users of playground equipment cannot ingest, inhale, or absorb potentially hazardous amounts of substances as a result of contact with equipment. Purchasers and installers of playground equipment should obtain documentation from the manufacturer that the preservatives or other treatments applied to the equipment do not present a hazard to the consumer.

5) A consumer information sheet on playground equipment should be available at the point of sale. This sheet contains important health precautions and disposal information that should be read by installers, builders and consumers before performing any wood-working operations such as sanding, sawing, or sawdust disposal.

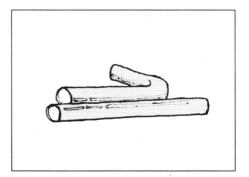

140   *Metal must be treated to prevent it from rusting.*

b.   **Metal.** Steel predominates as the basic material for play equipment frames due to its high strength and ease of fabrication. Unfortunately, steel is also prone to rust which can diminish its strength over time and ultimately result in structural failure.

1)   To prevent rust, most steel is galvanized and painted. However, since steel on play equipment is usually in the form of structural tubing, and since tubing is not galvanized on the inside, interior rust can continue to be a problem. Interior rust can be minimized by ensuring proper footings that will reduce water accumulation in pipes. Some manufacturers have tried to address the problem of interior rust by using water pipes instead of structural tubes. But since these pipes are not fabricated for structural use, they require heavy gauges to approximate the strength of structural tubing.

To overcome the rust problems associated with steel, some manufacturers now use aluminum frames. While the cost for aluminum is slightly higher and its strength is less than that of steel, its superior resistance to rust makes it an attractive choice.

2)   To determine the best metal choice for a site, consider the site conditions and the life expectancy for the play area. In locations that do not have significant problems with standing water, steel can be used effectively, provided that the manufacturer's footing details are followed precisely. In coastal locations and areas that are often wet, aluminum frames should be considered.

3)   All paints and other similar finishes must meet the current CPSC regulation for lead in paint: 0.06% maximum lead by dry weight.

c.   **Plastics.** Hundreds of different types of plastic are now available; nearly every piece of play equipment available today uses some form of plastic. Plastics are typically used to increase the visual appeal of environments by offering a great range of color and form and to increase the safety of play equipment. Plastics are used to round corners and add a soft coating to otherwise hard surfaces. They are also valuable as a coating on metals that would otherwise become too hot in direct sunlight and cause contact burns.

Among the plastics used on play equipment, the most common is high density polyethylene. It is used for rotational molded slides, panels, and spring-mounted animals. It can also be used in injection molds as a "structural foam" and has

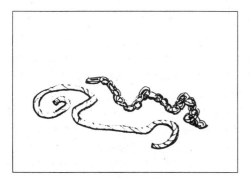

141   *Ropes and chains provide flexibility and durability. Chains should be covered in vinyl to avoid pinch points.*

142   *Play equipment must be vandal-resistant.*

been employed for spiral slides and deck planks. Polyvinyl chloride (PVC) is also popular as a soft coating on chains and decks.

Fiberglass should be avoided in unsupervised play settings because it has low impact resistance (Bruya, 1985a).

d.   **Rope and Chain.** Flexible elements like cargo nets are appealing to children, but require frequent inspection and replacement when used on public playgrounds because of their low durability (Bruya, Sullivan & Fowler, 1979). To improve durability, chain is sometimes substituted for rope. However, chain is harsh and can produce pinch points. Chain should only be used if it is covered in a vinyl coating. However, under conditions of high use, the vinyl coating can start to disintegrate within an unacceptably short time. Alternately, wire cable woven within polypropylene rope can provide a higher degree of flexibility and durability.

9.9   Hardware

a.   **Vandal-Resistant Hardware.** Play area equipment can be made unsafe by vandalism and theft of equipment parts.

While manufacturers of playground equipment have long sought to make their equipment resistant to vandalism, their efforts must be supplemented by a routine maintenance program that checks equipment daily to ensure that it is properly functioning and safe. In addition, play area designers and managers must make sure that efforts to deter vandals do not also diminish the safety of the play area for its users.

If special fastening devices are used to discourage the removal of equipment, they should be properly installed and free of protrusions which could cause injury. Old-fashioned hex head bolts which were once common on play equipment should not be used because they are unsafe and easily vandalized. It was once common practice to spot-weld these bolts on-site and paint them with "cold galvanize" to achieve acceptable levels of durability. Most modern equipment is powder-coated and will be damaged by welding.

Nails should never used to hold together play equipment.

- Make sure that the fasteners used on play equipment are vandal-resistant and that protrusions meet CPSC guidelines.

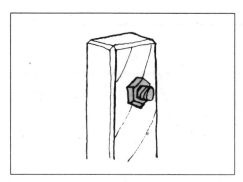

143 *Eliminate dangerous protrusions.*

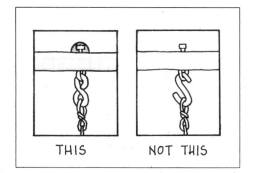

THIS   NOT THIS

144 *Moving joints should use bearings, not simple metal-to-metal "S" hooks.*

b.   **Protrusions.** Most new play equipment is built in accordance with the CPSC guidelines regarding protrusions. Older pieces of equipment should be inspected to ensure that fasteners and other hardware conform with the CPSC guidelines for protrusions (see Section 1.3 of this chapter).

c.   **Moving Joints.** Moving joints are one of the most troublesome maintenance features on playgrounds. Although modern nylon bearings perform significantly better than traditional roller bearings or bronze bushings, any bearing will eventually fail. For this reason all moving joints must be disassembled periodically to inspect for wear. As sealed joints cannot be disassembled, replacement records must be kept. There are many moving joints on play equipment which are not immediately obvious, such as the connection of rings to support beams and chain events to fixed structures.

When purchasing new play equipment, consider the following:

1)   The manufacturer should supply all moving joints with bearings. Simple metal-to-metal "S" hooks are not acceptable.

2)   Bearings used in all moving joints and chain connections to fixed structures should be high quality and durable. Make sure they are designed to facilitate ease of inspection and maintenance.

9.10   Finishes

While rust-resistant galvanized finishes are still commonplace, "powder coating" has replaced nearly all other paints. Powder coating is an electrostatic process which applies epoxy, nylon or polyester plastic as a very fine dry powder which is then oven-cured and bonded to the surface of steel or aluminum. Powder coating is the most durable choice of finishes where many color options are important to the consumer. When using steel, the powder coat can be put over the galvanizing to provide extra protection from harsh environmental conditions. However, this additional protection should be weighed against the increased costs.

9.11 Play Events

9.11.1 Slides

Slides are a popular play area item, especially when integrated into varied play settings. They need to conform to the developmental needs of children. Slides for preschoolers should have different dimensions to those for older children. Safety features also need careful consideration.

a.   **Slide Heights.** Falls are the most frequent playground hazard and can be reduced considerably by installing high quality shock-absorbing surfacing materials and by reducing equipment height. The suggested maximum slide heights by age of the user are: 36 inches for toddlers; 48 inches for preschoolers; 70 inches for school-age children. Slides may be higher if installed on slopes. Access decks must be properly enclosed.

   1)   Slides which are attached to composite playground equipment are preferred over freestanding slides because of reduced risk of falls from the entry deck.

   2)   Restrict slide height to limits defined by the age of the intended user group and test results of the fall zone's shock-absorbing surfacing material, whichever is smaller.

   3)   To guide slide height decisions, charts should be developed to describe the relationships between distance of fall, resiliency of surfacing, and severity of potential injury. See Chapter 11: Ground Covers/Surfacing, Section 11.3.1, Surfacing Depth and Critical Height.

b.   **Slide Gradient.** While standards in other countries may differ, the current CPSC guideline states that "the average incline of the sliding surface should not exceed 30 degrees."

   Wave slides may have portions which are steeper so long as the total slope requirement is not exceeded. However, changes in slope on a wave slide should not allow a child to lose contact with the sliding surface.

c.   **Slide Chute Side Rails.** The CPSC guideline for slide rail height is 4 inches minimum, but in other countries it is even greater. England requires 6 inches but also allows a steeper angle of descent.

d.   **Slide Chute Width.** A disadvantage of standard slides is that they prevent adults from sliding down with a child between their legs. Wide slides solve this

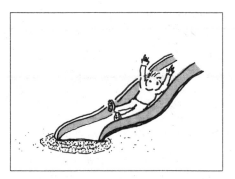

145   *Design of the slide exit needs careful consideration.*

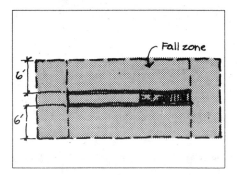

146   *Slide fall zones are generally 6 feet in all directions.*

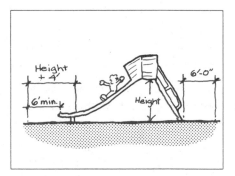

147   *The fall zone at the slide exit is determined by the height of the entry platform plus 4 feet.*

problem and offer the advantage of group play experience (Beckwith, 1985b); however, they are sometimes threatening to young or children with disabilities.

e.   **Slide Entry Platforms.** Slide platforms should have a minimum length of 22 inches. The platform should be at least as wide as the slide. The platform should be surrounded by appropriate protective barriers and there should be no gaps between the slide platform and the slide surface. There should also be no protrusions which can snare body parts or clothing. (CPSC, 1991)

f.   **Slide Exit Zones.** The CPSC requires that slide exit zones be a minimum of 11 inches long. For slides that are no more than 4 feet in height, the exit region should also be no more than 11 inches in height above the protective surface. For slides that are over 4 feet in height, the exit region should be at least 7 inches but not more than 15 inches in height above the protective surface. In addition, slide exit edges should be rounded or curved to prevent lacerations or injuries which could result from children falling back onto the slide when exiting.

Prior to CPSC, some slides were available with shorter exit regions placed directly at surface level with the advantages that, a) children were prevented from falling back on the exit lip of the slide, b) children tended to move out of the path of following players more quickly, and c) better exit transitions were provided for nonambulatory children. While the new CPSC guidelines allow for exit zones to be at surface level for slides that are less than 4 feet in height, more research is needed on the preferred height of slide exits, particularly for accommodating children with disabilities.

Note: Many children with disabilities and those 18 months and younger frequently lack sufficient trunk strength and control to remain upright while sliding. In motion they fall supine and could injure their head and/or neck on exiting a slide which is raised above the surface.

g.   **Slide Fall Zones.** The fall zone in front of the access to the slide should extend a minimum of 6 feet from the perimeter of the equipment (excluding slides installed on an embankment). The fall zone in front of the exit of the slide should extend a minimum distance of 6 feet from the end of the slide chute *or* for a distance of 4 feet plus the distance between the ground and the underside of the entry platform, extended from the point on the slide where the incline gradient has been reduced to 5 degrees from the horizontal, as illustrated at left (CPSC, 1991).

h.   **Freestanding Slides.** Decades of slide use by millions of children have demonstrated both the popularity of slides and their hazards. The vast majority of the slide accidents occur in three areas:

1)   Slide stairs are the source of numerous accidents (Mount, 1985). Very young children find themselves fearful of progressing and unable to climb down while older children often use stairs for horseplay.

2)   The slide entrance area is often used for king-of-the-mountain games.

3)   The top section of the slide chute, where sliding children collide with children running up the slide, is also a problem.

The risk of injury from these ancillary behaviors is reduced significantly when slides are attached to composite play structures, when decks replace stairs, or when slides are installed on mounds or berms.

The CPSC guidelines allow slide access via a ladder with rungs or steps, a stairway with steps, or by other means as part of a composite play structure. For ladders with rungs or steps with open risers, it is important that the open space between steps be less than 3-1/2 inches or greater than 9 inches to prevent head entrapment. For toddlers and preschoolers, fully enclosed steps should be provided with a maximum vertical rise of less than 9 inches.

To support accessibility, open risers should be avoided. However, while closed treads are preferable, they can fill with sand and create a slip hazard. Therefore, the tread surface should have small holes to let grains of sand pass through without clogging (but smaller than 5/16 inch to prevent finger entrapment).

1)   Freestanding slides should be avoided, unless steps are fully enclosed.

2)   When stairs are fully enclosed, be sure that they are designed so that they do not become sand traps (and therefore slip hazards).

i.   **Slide Entry Areas.** When standard narrow slides are attached to play structure decks, railings or loops are used to facilitate entrance and reduce the possibility of falling. For many years a single rail has been the standard solution. However, this design encourages children to use the safety bar as a play element in and of itself, creating an even more dangerous situation. Solutions to this problem include use of a double rail or a hood across the entryway. Whatever solution is adopted, the child's transition from deck to slide must occur without significant exposure to falling.

148   *Access for nonambulatory children can be facilitated if there are steps alongside the slide.*

Access for nonambulatory children with transfer skills can be facilitated if there is a large, smooth platform at the end of the slide, 16 inches above an accessible, shock-absorbing surface. The platform should connect directly with a cleated ramp or accessible stairs parallel to the slide to provide access to the deck. Such a configuration provides a fully accessible (for the intended population) slide experience and does not introduce significant new hazards.

j.   **Slide Materials.** Traditionally, stainless steel has been the material of choice for slide surfaces. However, because of problems that stainless steel can pose, it is increasingly being replaced by high density polyethylene.

Stainless steel, while very durable, becomes extremely hot in direct sunlight and can cause second degree burns. To minimize this problem, slides should be installed pointing in a northerly direction (for play areas in the Northern Hemisphere). While this technique is somewhat effective in reducing burns, it greatly reduces design and configuration options. Alternatively, slides must be provided with adequate shading.

A second problem with low-grade stainless steel is that when it fails, it tends to expose razor sharp edges. Routine inspections and proper maintenance are the best insurance against this hazard.

Plastic slides solve the problems of heat and sharp edges. When first introduced, plastic slides were made of fiberglass. While these slides accomplished the goal of adding color and reducing burns, they proved to be flammable and subject to impact fracture.

Currently, high density polyethylene slides solve the durability problem and add an element of permanent color. They are not combustible themselves, but will melt if a fire is built around them. Unless well-made, they can also be light sensitive and can be damaged by sand and heavy objects being thrown against them.

- Evaluate carefully the possible replacement of stainless steel slides with polyethylene slides.

149   *Slides should be varied and challenging*

k.   **Variety and Challenge of Slides.** Modern equipment settings have many innovative slide designs (wave, spiral, wide, tunnel, banister, even slides with rollers) in addition to standard narrow slides. All of these designs must allow children using the slide to see the slide exit region from the entry area. This helps reduce dangerous collisions between children.

Roller slides should be purchased with caution. While extremely interesting to children, they have a number of unique characteristics. Although normally not a pinch hazard, roller slides tend to induce "surf riding" play. Thus, roller slides from decks not higher than 4 feet are preferred. Frequent maintenance is also required. Roller slides are not recommended for public playgrounds unless frequent maintenance can be guaranteed (CPSC, 1991).

Roller slides should not use ball bearings and cannot be installed over pea gravel. The best resilient material under roller slides is rubber matting.

Tube slides should be installed with care, making sure that barriers are provided or surfaces treated to prevent children from sliding on the top of the tube. The minimum internal diameter of the tube should be no less than 23 inches. Tube slides also raise questions of supervision.

- Creating play settings with several different types of slides makes the playground more interesting, developmentally more challenging, and safer, since children can select the types of slides best suited for their own skill levels.

1. **Slide Joints and Seams.** The seams which result from the construction and assembly of slides must be carefully inspected. Butt seams (i.e., those which do not overlap) offer a significantly greater chance for foreign objects to become lodged in the cracks and protrude into the sliding regions.

    - CPSC (1991) recommends that the slide bed and rails be composed of one piece. If this is not possible, select slides with lap joints rather than butt joints to avoid foreign objects being inserted into the chute area.

150 *Select slides with lap joints rather than butt joints.*

9.11.2 Swings

Swings can take a variety of forms, depending on the method of suspension, type of seat, length of arc, character of takeoff and landing, etc. The traditional single-axis, double-hung swing (with a reinforced vinyl seat) is still probably the most popular piece of play equipment ever invented (Moore, 1986c, 1987b; Bruya, Robbins & Fowler, 1983a).

Several types of swings are possible; "triple-hung," multi-axis auto tires are a well-tried idea. The suspension hardware is a crucial detail and should be a high-quality, manufactured item.

a. **Swing Height.** Swings should be suspended from a variety of heights to cater to different age groups and to provide a range of movement. Don't assume that small swings will always be used by small kids. Big kids often enjoy the quicker rhythm of small swings; they should be made just as robust as big swings.

While high swings appeal to children, the danger involved both from falls and collisions makes high swings unacceptable in public facilities. The maximum recommended height for swing crossbeams is 8 feet for school-age children and 7 feet for toddlers and preschoolers.

b. **Swing Seats.** Most swing injuries result from swinging children hitting other children in their path (Page, 1976). Even empty swing seats with significant mass and/or sharp edges can cause injury when thrown. To minimize the likelihood of children being struck by a moving swing, it is recommended that no more than two single-axis swings be hung in each bay of a supporting structure. Single-axis swings should not be attached to a composite structure.

Swing seats made of wood or metal should be removed, including animal figure swings, because their rigid frameworks present a high risk of impact injury. For school-age children, only rubber-belt seats and triple-hung auto tire swings are recommended. If swing seats are reinforced, they should not allow sharp edges to be exposed.

"Tot swings" are single-axis swings designed for use by very young children with adult assistance. The seats and suspension systems of these swings, including the related hardware, should follow all of the criteria for conventional single-axis swings. Additionally, tot swing seats should provide support on all sides of a child. It is important that such supports do not present a strangulation hazard. Openings in tot swing seats should conform to the entrapment criteria in Section 1.3 of this chapter.

Swing seats for special applications are allowed so long as they conform to the CPSC guidelines. Accessible swings must have a back and side support or a hole/indentation (as in a tire swing with a cloth or webbed bottom) for the child's backside.

c. **Swing Clearances.** To minimize collisions between swings or between a swing and the supporting structure, adequate swing clearances must be provided. There should be a minimum of 30 inches between a swing and the nearest structural element, and at least 24 inches between swings. In addition, to reduce side-to-side motion, swing hangers should be spaced wider than the width of the swing seat (CPSC, 1991).

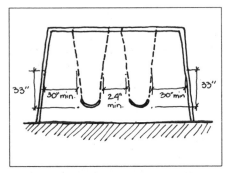

151 Adequate swing clearances must be provided.

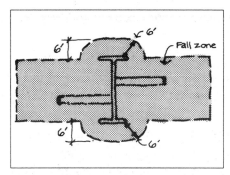

152   *Swings require an ample fall zone to protect children who may fall or jump from a moving swing.*

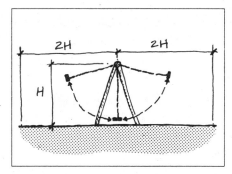

153   *Swing fall zones in front of and behind the swings must be two times the height of the swing crossbeam.*

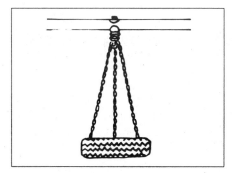

154   *Tire swing universal joint.*

d.   **Isolation and Traffic Flow Barriers.**   Because swings can act as battering rams and small children commonly walk into the swing-use zone, swings should be isolated from other play equipment.   They should not be added to composite structures.   Also, do not provide more than two swings in each section of a swing support structure (CPSC, 1991).

The CPSC suggests that additional protection be provided by designing a traffic flow barrier around the swing area.   However, care must be taken to ensure that such a barrier does not become a play event itself (e.g., a turning bar).   Separation is the best way to handle conflicts of use.   Also, entrances to the swing zone should be located to maximize visibility between the swing area and the rest of the play environment.   For example, if there is a logical "front," such as a view of the playground itself, this should be the location of the entrance.

- Locate swings in their own enclosure separate from the rest of the playground or on the edge of the play equipment area.

e.   **Swing Fall Zones.**   Swings require an ample fall zone to protect children who may fall or jump from a moving swing.   For swings, the fall zone is equal to two times the height of the swing crossbeam.   This fall zone must be provided both in front of and behind the equipment.   A 6-foot circulation zone must also be provided on both sides of the swing.   When two swings are located adjacent to each other, the swings may share the 6-foot circulation zone at the side.

1)   The minimum setback requirement for swings is two times the height of the swing cross-beam.

2)   Swing areas should be defined by distinct differences in ground texture.

f.   **Tire Swings.**   Tire swing hangers are one of the most critical hardware items used on playground equipment.   This is due to the stress that is applied when a number of children climb on the swing at the same time (Bruya, Robbins & Fowler, 1983a).   The amount of weight and centrifugal force which can be applied during normal use warrant extensive testing by manufacturers.   Failure of these hangers is potentially catastrophic.

Two types of hanger design are available: ball joint and universal joint.   Each has their advantages and disadvantages.

Ball joints are a clean design and present no pinch points.   A shortcoming of these joints has been their limited degree of motion which can cause wear and

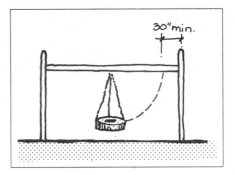

155   Tire swing dimensions.

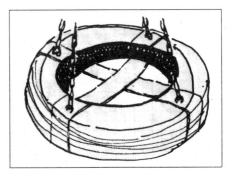

156   Accessible tire swing.

157   "Tarzan" ropes are popular, but are not recommended for public playgrounds.

eventual failure. Tire swings require about 170 degrees of freedom and most ball joints provide only 145 degrees.

Universal joints are not prone to such limitations. However, they do present pinch points. Commonly, these are covered with a protective boot and, if well designed and maintained, provide satisfactory protection from pinching.

The other common failure of tire swings results from movement of the mounting hardware. Permanent positive attachment of the bearing to the beam is essential. Routine inspection and maintenance is also required.

Tire swings, since they move in all directions, require a beam support span which is two times the swing length plus 5 feet. A swing with support chains that are 4 feet long would require a 13-foot cross-beam.

Tire swings are easily made accessible by strapping webbing to the bottom or inserting plasticized canvas in the hole and bolting it in, thus creating a "nest." If children are to be able to transfer onto the swing, the seat height must be at 15 to 17 inches above the ground surface and an accessible, shock-absorbing surface must be provided.

Heavy truck tires should be avoided on tire swings. If steel-belted radials are used, they must be routinely inspected to ensure that no steel belts are exposed that could cause injury. Holes should be provided in tires for drainage (CPSC, 1991).

g.   **"Tarzan" ropes.** Although popular, Tarzan-type, freestanding swing ropes are not recommended in public playgrounds unless installed under the strictest conditions of maintenance and supervision. Ropes should be removed when supervision is not available.

h.   **Swing Accessibility.** Unless a means of holding swings in a stationary position is provided, swings are hard to get into at transfer points. A challenge for manufacturers is to design a swing into which a child in a wheelchair can transfer effectively, paying particular attention to: positioning, visibility, and security.

Currently, no adequate solution has been developed for independent nonambulatory access to swings. Seats need to be 15 to 17 inches off the ground rather than the customary 12 to 24 inches, but more research is needed on this issue. Exerglide is a make of swing that can be operated without lower body movement; however, upper body strength must be robust. Wheelchair swings are not recommended for public play settings.

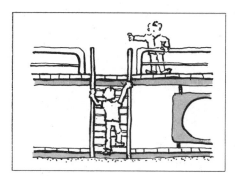

158 *Play structures should support climbing.*

9.11.3 Climbers

a. **Climber Heights.** As noted in several other guideline categories, height limitation is one of the best means of reducing injuries from falls.

In the case of slides, height is required for the equipment to perform its function. Climbers, on the other hand, do not require heights above 56 inches to be fully challenging. The height of a climber should be based on four factors:

1) Type and quality of the shock-absorbing surface.

2) Location.

3) User group.

4) Ability to maintain the equipment and surfacing.

Climbers, including ladders, are attached to play structures to achieve proper traffic flow patterns. But even in these applications the child never needs to be exposed to a fall greater than 56 inches. Critical Height is an esential criterion; it is defined by the shock-absorbing properties of the surfacing material in the use zone (see Chapter 11: Ground Covers/Surfacing, 11.3.1 Surfacing Depth and Critical Height, for a complete discussion. Tunnel climbers and net climbers are designed to reduce the total drop to which a child is exposed.

b. **Climber Rung Size.** Consensus among manufacturers favors a climber rung diameter between 1 and 1.67 inches. The actual diameter selected should correspond to the age of the intended user group. If the equipment is intended for use by many age groups, then one rail size should be selected.

- Rails and grips on climbers should be between 1 inch and 1.67 inches in diameter (CPSC, 1991).
- For rungs used to support the user's entire body weight by their hands, the rung diameter should be between 1 inch and 1.55 inches in diameter (CPSC, 1991).

c. **Climber Fall Zones.** In addition to the standard fall zone requirements (see Section 1.3e of this chapter), climbers should not have climbing bars or other stuctural components in the interior of the structure onto which a child could fall from a height of greater than 18 inches. Therefore, arch climbers are preferred over cube climbers because they do not have interior bars.

In addition, the configuration and spacing of climber rungs and structural elements must not create any entrapments (see Section 9.1.3a of this chapter).

d.   **Climber Variety and Flexibility.** As with other play events, climbers will provide more benefits with greater safety if they are presented in several types to provide for graduated challenge. Of particular importance is the provision of flexible climbers, such as nets, which require dynamic balance instead of simple static balance.

- Ensure that a variety of climbers is included in each play environment. Flexible climbers have additional developmental benefits.
- Arch climbers and flexible climbers should not be used as the sole means of equipment access for preschoolers (CPSC, 1991).

9.11.4 Balance Events

a.   **Static Versus Dynamic Balance.** Child development specialists point out that, except for children under four, dynamic balance (i.e., balance on surfaces which move) has more developmental value than static balances, such as beams.

Such activities can be incorporated into playgrounds through the use of cable, clatter, chain/log bridges, rolling barrels, or spring platforms.

However, suspended balance events like cable walks and nets place very large loads on play structures which must be carefully engineered to accommodate these stresses.

- Include dynamic balance activities in equipment settings.

b.   **Balance Height.** The most effective balance activities are at ground level or slightly elevated above grade. In most cases, 12 inches is sufficient.

- Balance activities should not be greater than 12 inches in height (CPSC, 1991).
- For preschoolers, locate balance events directly on the shock-absorbing surface.

159   *Play equipment should support balancing, both static and dynamic.*

160   *The most effective balance activities are slightly elevated above grade.*

c.   **Balance Linkage.** Balance activities are more frequently used when they link parts of the playground. Because of their low height and minimum potential for injuries from falls, they may be used to link play structures with surrounding walkways (Hewes, 1975; Beckwith, 1979a; Moore, 1974b; Moore & Wong, in press).

1)   Balance activities should be used as linkages.

2)   To make balance activities accessible to children with visual disabilities, provide at least some events with guiderails (PLAE, 1981–87).

9.11.5 Upper Body Events

a.   **Graduated Challenge.** Examples of upper body events include turning bars, chinning bars, horizontal ladders, ring treks, and track rides. Safety in the use of upper body development equipment is promoted by the use of many different events with differing levels of skill.

- Include upper body development events with graduated skill levels in each equipment setting.
- Horizontal ladders and ring treks are not intended for children under 4 years old.
- Track rides are for use by school-age children.

161   *Play equipment should provide for differing levels of skill.*

b.   **Linkage and Size of Upper Body Events.** Upper body events such as ladders and treks stimulate more use when they are used to link parts of the play environment because they become part of the flow of children's games. Grouping these events also encourages children to demonstrate their abilities to each other.

Horizontal ladders are used with less conflict if they are wide enough for more than one child. For children from three to five, a ladder with a 5 degree incline and six-foot length aids learning. For older children, spans of 12 feet are appropriate. Ladder rungs should be spaced greater than 9 inches apart to avoid entrapment, but not further than 15 inches apart. Overhead rings may be spaced further apart.

- Upper body events should be used to link sections of the play environment and should be sized to challenge children of various abilities.

c.   **Mount-Dismount on Upper Body Events.** The mount and dismount of upper body development devices such as ladders and treks is important. Children often approach the dismount in a fatigued state and must be able to dismount with ease and security.

To prevent children from falling onto the rail or deck and facilitate safe mounting and dismounting, the first and last handholds should not be placed directly above the dismount rail or deck, but should be inset by 8 or more inches.

- Upper body development equipment must have appropriate, easily used mount/dismount features.

162   Child going hand-over-hand along a climber.

d.   **Grip Size for Upper Body Events**

(see Section 9.11.3b for discussion of this topic)

e.   **Height of Upper Body Events.** The following guidelines should be followed in determining the appropriate height for upper body events on play equipment:

1)   The height of horizontal ladders should be limited to 96 inches for school-age children and 60 inches for preschoolers.

2)   Horizontal ladders can be lowered to make them accessible for children using wheelchairs who have upper body strength. An appropriate ground surface for both fall-cushioning and wheelchair access will need to be installed (PLAE, 1981–87).

3)   The height of ring treks should be limited to 96 inches for school-age children and 72 inches for preschoolers.

9.11.6 Spinning Equipment

Children are attracted by the circular movement of merry-go-rounds and other forms of spinning equipment. The safety issues, however, are substantial.

163   Children are attracted by spinning play equipment.

a.   **Size and Speed of Spinning Equipment.** Injuries on spinning equipment (merry-go-rounds or whirls) consist largely of falls against or under the moving equipment and are made more serious by its size and mass. One of the most common accidents occurs when young children attempt to dismount while older children (or even adults) are spinning the whirls. The most obvious means of reducing these injuries is to limit the size of whirls. A four-foot diameter whirl will hold four children and is much less likely to cause serious injury. In addition, the rotating platform should not have any sharp edges or parts that protrude beyond the rotating base.

The CPSC requires that the peripheral speed of platforms be limited to a maximum of 13 feet per second (CPSC, 1991). Several manufacturers now supply speed limiters on larger whirls. While not as effective as limiting size, such measures should reduce accidents.

b. **Surfacing for Spinning Equipment.** The use of whirls causes loose material to be pushed away around their base. This exposes the underside for possible entrapment. Some installers attempt to solve this problem by mounting the units over rubber matting. If the matting is sufficiently resilient and properly maintained, this may be an acceptable practice. However, it is imperative that there be no access to the underside of the equipment.

- Be certain that rotating equipment is installed in such a manner that children do not have access underneath it such that they can become entrapped.

c. **Design Requirements of Spinning Equipment.** Finger loss is a frequent injury on whirls due to gaps between the central support post and the whirl that create finger entrapments. Such gaps are usually the result of poor maintenance. Newer designs shroud this connection so that even with negligent maintenance no finger entrapment occurs.

For many years whirls where fabricated from pipe and had open centers. Such designs have proven extremely hazardous as children become easily entrapped.

- Remove whirls with open frameworks. Ensure that the equipment is properly maintained and that the bearings do not present possible finger entrapments. There should not be any openings on the equipment that are 5/16 inch in diameter or larger.

9.11.7 Rocking/Spring-Mounted Equipment

Children respond dramatically to opportunities for bouncing and rocking.

a. **Appropriate Age Group.** Spring-mounted animals are especially appealing to children five and under. They should therefore be included in areas designed for preschool play. Because this equipment is intended for young children, it is important for them to be able to hold on without falling. Grips of 3/4-inch diameter and footrests are recommended.

Designs which contain and correctly position and support the child are preferred so long as they are not too heavy for small children to activate (which is the case

164 *Play equipment should support bouncing activities.*

165   Young children love to ride "springing" animals.

with some vehicle theme designs). Designs should minimize the likelihood of the rocker being used by more than the intended number of users.

Conventional seesaws, while providing support for cooperative play and remaining popular with children, present a significant chance for back injury and crush points. They are not recommended, except for spring-loaded seesaws which have solved some of these problems. More research is required on this issue.

b.   **Spring Performance on Rocking Equipment.** Springs designed for use on playgrounds must meet difficult criteria: they must be soft enough for small children to move yet strong enough to avoid damage when used inappropriately by large children. In addition, they must be designed to minimize the possibility of children pinching either their hands or their feet between the coils or between the spring and a part of the rocker.

9.11.8 Manufactured Inflatables.

Inflatables have a great potential for use by children with and without disabilities. They can be used by people of all ages and abilities either in integrated settings or in specific programs for children with physical, mental, or emotional disabilities. Inflatables are mobile and can be used as the basis for a mobile play environment in parks, playgrounds, recreation centers, and during summer programs.

Select units with welded construction as opposed to stitching so that they are strong enough to be used by adults as well as children. Welded construction eliminates the need for protective covers when the structures are exposed to water or other liquids.

More research and development needs to be conducted in this area of equipment.

9.11.9   Interpretive Play Equipment

Conventional play equipment can be greatly enhanced by the addition of equipment settings that act like interpretive stations, stressing environmental education and hands-on experience rather than physical education. They are especially appropriate in settings with trained play leadership and have a broader potential for the integration of children with disabilities. The concept also extends the developmental potential of public playgrounds.

Pipes of different lengths for different tones

166   Equipment settings that resemble interpretive stations enhance the play environment.

9.12   Documentation

Play equipment manufacturers' promotional materials, catalogs and installation documents accompanying specific pieces of equipment should be improved as sources of information for prospective users. Many catalogs could be more informative in relation to the criteria used in the CPSC guidelines and the *Play For All Guidelines*. Safety could also be more visibly promoted, with inspection schedules included with new equipment. If properly designed and used, manufacturers' catalogs can become significant vehicles for public education.

9.13   Documentation Checklist

The following list itemizes most of the documentation required for a comprehensive playground risk management program (Bruya & Beckwith, 1985). While every attempt has been made to be as complete as possible, the program for a specific site may require additional information. Not every site needs documentation as this list indicates. Final determination of the proper files to keep, the information they should contain, and the length of time they should be retained must be made by each agency and organization in light of its unique needs.

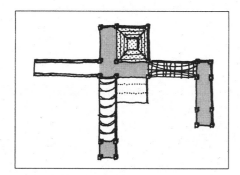

167   *Site layout and installation details.*

a.   **Assessment**

1)   An inspection of the site's compliance with the CPSC guidelines.

2)   An environmental inventory identifying unusual features, such as open bodies of water.

3)   Written descriptions of the site's activities and programs.

4)   Profiles of the key user groups.

5)   An assessment of community recreation and play needs.

b.   **Design**

168   *Site inspection.*

1)   Project's goals.

2)   Names and roles of individuals and organizations involved in developing the project.

3)   Design team qualifications.

4)   Equipment specification requirements.

5)   Manufacturers' catalogs.

6)   Site layout (conforming to master plan) and installation details.

7)   A summary of public (playground task force) and administrative review processes, including written approvals.

c.   **Purchase**

1)   Purchasing agent's procedures and qualifications.

2)   Manufacturer's guarantee.

3)   Permitted and actual deviation from specification.

4)   Purchase orders.

5)   Verification of correct shipment.

d.   **Installation**

1)   Installer qualifications and insurance.

2)   Provisions for on-site safety of workers and public during construction.

3)   Manufacturer's installation manual.

4)   Manufacturer's verification of proper installation.

e.   **Supervision**

1)   Staff/child ratio guidelines.

2)   Manufacturer's use guidelines.

3)   Student and/or community safety awareness program.

4)   Warning signs.

5)   Accident monitoring and systematic review.

f.   **Maintenance**

1)   Post-installation design review.

2)   Daily inspections.

3)   In-depth inspections.

4)   Equipment amortization schedule.

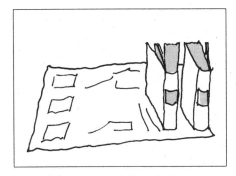

169   *Manufacturer's installation manual.*

9.14 Prototypical Language For Purchase Documents And Criteria For Purchasing

To be considered for purchase, all vendors of play equipment shall provide the following:

a. **Certificate of Insurance** for both products and general liability of not less than $1,000,000. The issuing underwriter shall be AA rated. Self-insurance requires the posting of a bond.

b. **Manufacturer's Certificate of Compliance** with the Consumer Products Safety Commission's Playground Equipment Guidelines.

c. **Structural and Materials Specifications** with complete details and performance specifications on all connection hardware, materials and structural components.

d. **Site Inspection.** Purchaser shall be provided with a clearly detailed checklist by the manufacturer for on-site verification that the equipment has been installed according to manufacturer's specifications. This checklist should be filled out by the vendor or a qualified equal.

    After receiving this completed document, the manufacturer will issue a Warranty Validation Certificate to the owner. Special care should be taken to ensure adequate shock-absorbing surfacing throughout the fall zone and appropriate minimum setbacks from adjacent equipment.

e. **Warranty.** The minimum required warranty is one year on materials and workmanship. In addition, a special ten-year **Post and Deck Integrity Warranty** is also required.

f. **Maintenance Schedule,** provided by the manufacturer, shall estimate the frequency with which inspection and maintenance should be performed in relation to time and use.

g. **Use and Safety Information,** including a manual listing appropriate activities for each play feature. For school site installations, lesson plans for increasing student and staff safety awareness and encouraging proper use shall also be provided. Specific hazards and consequent potential injury, if any, shall be identified.

h. **Equipment.** Where applicable, all integrated play structures shall be modular in nature; that is, their framework shall be composed of similar elements which can be configured in a variety of ways so that expansion and modification can be easily accomplished.

i.   **Materials.** Considerations include:

1) **Attachment Hardware.** There should be a minimum number of types of attaching hardware. All hardware shall be vandal-resistant. Hex-head bolts are not acceptable. Bolts and nuts must have vandal-resistant fastening methods. Nails should never be used to secure play equipment.

2) **Posts.** Posts shall be steel, aluminum, wood, or plastic. All posts should be warranted for ten years.

3) **Decks.** Decks shall be retained without exposed hardware. Nails are not permitted. Metal decks are permissible if vinyl-clad.

4) **Plastics.** All plastics shall be high-grade polyethylene, polyvinyl chloride, or polycarbonate. They shall be stabilized against ultraviolet light degradation and shall be self-extinguishing.

5) **Chain and Cable.** All chain or cable on climbing structures shall be covered with a durable plastic coating which is cut-resistant. Joints shall be smooth and free of burrs.

6) **Wood Treatment.** All wood shall be treated, free of residual chemicals, and certified for compliance with the C-17 standard of the American Wood Preservers Institute. Coating or sealer may also need to be applied.

Checks may not exceed 18 inches in length or 1/8 inch in width when received. Wood may not check after installation for a period of one year to a check dimension of 24 inches in length and 3/16 inch in width.

7) **Metal Treatment.** Touch-up scratches in posts. Paint shall be supplied by the manufacturer. (Be aware that dents can affect the integrity of posts.)

j.   **Population Capacity.** The maximum number of users for each play activity and for the overall environment should be specified. This population estimate shall be adjusted to consider developmental characteristics and use by both same-age and mixed-age groups.

k.   **An Inventory of Educational Benefits** shall detail the specific learning experiences provided by the apparatus.

l.   **Fall Zones and Setbacks.** The minimum fall zone shall be illustrated in a plan view drawing of the play equipment. Specific detail shall be provided as to the manufacturer's recommendation for type and depth of shock-absorbing surfacing in accordance with the standards set forth by the Consumer Products Safety Commission and ASTM Standard F08.52.

m.   **Installation Manual.** The installation instructions shall be complete in all details and provided prior to purchase. The minimum required information shall include the site layout process, order of assembly, footing requirements, and list of parts by subsection or component. Estimated construction hours and number of people required shall also be provided.

10. MULTIPURPOSE GAME SETTINGS

Flat open spaces support team sports, large group games, traditional games, and ball play (NPFA, 1985). For wheelchair use, these spaces need to be hard-surfaced; otherwise, turf is the best surface.

Planning Criteria

Play Value. Game areas support activities which promote cooperation, team spirit, and large muscle development.

Programming. A high level of expertise is required to program game areas appropriately for all children.

Play Leadership. Ensure that leaders balance sports and team games with other program opportunities. Encourage training in cooperative games.

Safety. Do not locate hard surfaces near fixed equipment from which children could fall. Recognize that pedestrian falls onto hard surfaces are one of the most common forms of minor injury. Hurts from falls and collisions are common and difficult to avoid.

Risk Management. Safe, well-maintained ancillary equipment is required. Ensure that children and parents have a knowledge of the rules. Prepare settings so that accidents can be dealt with expeditiously: telephone, transport, emergency procedures, first aid supplies, and staff training.

Accessibility. Partial shade is required for adequate comfort. Viewing areas for parents, children, and other spectators should be fully accessible.

Integration. Cooperative games (Orlick, 1978 & 1982; Orlick and Botterill, 1975) have more potential for integration than traditional sports, although modifications of mainstream sports can also be tried. Besides the inherent pleasure for children with disabilities generated by sports like bowling, swimming, basketball, and football, major enjoyment is derived from their recognition that the nonhandicapped world also enjoys these activities. The children feel part of the larger whole and not "different." However, some design modifications are necessary (HUD, 1978).

Management/Maintenance. Policies are needed to specify who is allowed to play on teams. An important issue is that ball game areas are underused compared to the space they occupy, and are not often used by girls (Moore, 1978b).

10.1   Places to Run (Schneekloth, 1985)

Children need to run. For children with visual or physical disabilities, opportunities are often limited to certain areas and times when adult supervision is available. They need safe places to run without supervision. Running lanes, rope guides, or other devices can be provided to make running possible for specific disabilities. Runs for children using wheelchairs can also be installed. Appropriate running surfaces need to be provided (see Chapter 6, Pathways, and Chapter 11, Ground Covers/Surfacing).

10.2   Court Games

Supervised play areas can provide more challenging games (volleyball, basketball, racquetball, tetherball, and badminton). They require hard-surfaced areas, special equipment stored at the site and, perhaps, leadership and supervision for some age groups.

10.3   Hard-Surfaced Play Areas

There may be some hard-surfaced areas for less-structured activities: bike rodeos, skateboarding, and roller skating In Glasgow, Scotland, a BMX/roller skate/skateboard facility was developed as a shallow hard-surfaced bowl about 45 feet wide, with a side-to-center fall of about 12 inches and a central drainage vent. It is surrounded on three sides by seating and shrub planting (P. Heseltine, correspondence).

10.4   Ball Play Areas

Ball play is a universally popular play activity, ranging from simple informal games that can be played alone or with one or two others (Moore & Wong, in press), to organized team sports. Important considerations when designing ball play areas include:

a.   **Time-Sharing.** Ball games go through "seasons," climatically and culturally. Informal games are different from organized team games. This means that various ball play areas can be superimposed on each other to create a "time-shared" space, particularly basketball, handball, and kickball areas.

b.   **Irregular Boundary.** Beyond the actual pitch size, there is no reason to make ball play settings rectangular in shape. An irregular boundary adds to the visual interest of the space and makes it look less monofunctional. If the boundary has "depth" (e.g., vegetation rather than a chain link fence), other uses are more likely to be encouraged.

170 *Ball walls are an important addition to ball play areas.*

171 *Multipurpose asphalt game areas can include formal ball courts, places for spectators, and areas for community activity. Shade is especially important for children with disabilities.*

172 *Lowered basketball hoops allow use by children using wheelchairs.*

c.   Half-Size Courts. Most basketball games use only about one-third of a regular court. Demand for full-size courts is much less than for half-courts, which are also easier to incorporate into an irregular layout.

d.   Adjacent Ball Walls. In addition to an asphalt ground surface, the most important ball playing accoutrements are walls; and in contrast to asphalt, there never seem to be enough. The best way to get ball play to happen in some places rather than others is via the strategic location of "strike-out" walls and other dividing walls. Ideally, several walls should be provided, with one or two curved ones to add interest. They should be high enough to stop fly balls (10 to 12 feet high). They also make terrific surfaces for artwork such as murals.

e.   Multipurpose. Ball playing areas can also accommodate other functions requiring large spaces, such as community events and festivals. Design considerations like microclimate, visual appearance, shady sitting places, trash cans, etc., should be carefully considered.

Multipurpose game areas should contain rectangular ball playing pitches, but may also have an irregular outer boundary of "ball walls" and places to sit and watch the game, read a book, and meet friends. Trees for shade and climatic control and additional vegetation for reducing visual impact should also be provided. They should be designed as places where people can hangout, rest, or converse (See "Kickabout Areas," NPFA, 1977).

10.5   Game Ideas (CMHC, 1977)

a.   Basketball Hoops. Basketball hoops lower than the standard 10 feet height allow young children and those using wheelchairs to enjoy the game. Some designs allow hoop heights to be adjusted.

b.   Ping-Pong. Outdoor ping-pong tables need protection from the wind; sometimes solid fencing is used if the area is too exposed. Paddles and balls must be provided at the site. Ping-pong is a school-age, teen, and **adult** game that takes up little space and develops skills and team play.

c.   Badminton and Volleyball. Badminton and volleyball do not need fancy court surfaces or even regulation dimensions, only a relatively flat surface. These games are enjoyed by all ages.

173 *Box hockey.*

d.   **Box Hockey** (CMHC, 1977). This simple game is very popular in Sweden and is perfect for school-age children; it is also a space saver. It can be played with four as well as two. The hockey stick needs to have a shorter foot for maneuverability. Swedes use a round stick more like a cane with a curve at the striking end. The object is to get the puck out of the opponent's end through one of the holes in the middle board and the goal hole.

e.   **Tetherball.** This is a game for school-age children that does not take up too much space. Children can develop their own rules or use standard ones.

11. GROUND COVERS/SURFACING

Both soft and hard play surfaces are needed to support different types of play activity. Shock-absorbing surfacing materials are mandatory throughout the fall zones of all manufactured equipment. These materials should also be firm and resilient along accessible routes leading to transfer points onto equipment (see Chapter 9, Section 1.6c). A range of natural ground covers can provide contact with nature and a habitat for small animals. The surfacing addressed in this chapter includes: turf and natural ground covers, hard surfaces, and shock-absorbing surfacing materials.

The surfacing in each part of the play environment must respond to the needs of the intended activities and user groups. Considerations include: durability, toxicity, allergenicity, slip-resistance, all-weather use, climatic zone, maintenance, aesthetics, accessibility, and required shock absorbancy. By providing a diversity of materials that meet the needs of different areas, users and activities, surface materials can ensure a wide variety of play opportunities for the widest number of users.

Play Value. Soft surfaces help promote and extend social interaction. Hard surfaces or accessible shock-absorbing surfaces are necessary for ease of access and activities such as ball play.

Programming. Soft surfaces and natural ground covers are a source of play props and sensory stimulation. Hard surfaces are necessary for particular games.

Play Leadership. Leaders need knowledge of how to use various surfaces.

Safety. Surfacing in play equipment fall zones must meet the CPSC guidelines for shock-absorption. Allergenic, toxic, hurtful, and spikey varieties of plants must be avoided.

Risk Management. Shock-absorbing surfacing materials must be installed in all equipment settings. Careful maintenance is required for all surfaces.

Accessibility. Accessible shock-absorbing surfaces must be provided in play equipment settings. Long grass is difficult to wheel through and walk through. Hard-surface pathways are needed.

Integration. The potential to support integration varies from surface to surface.

Management/Maintenance. Provide shock-absorbing surfaces for play equipment settings. All surfaces require frequent maintenance to provide for safety, accessibility, and play value.

11.1 Turf and Natural Ground Covers

Turf and other natural ground covers create ecosystems at a smaller scale than trees and shrubs. They are more manipulable for children but also more vulnerable and prone to wear. Attention to circulation design can help avoid unnecessary erosion and the need for replanting.

Some ground cover species change according to the season, which enhances the sense of the passage of time. Some species attract small insects, which are a source of learning and excitement for children. Flowering and scented species add sensory diversity. Scented species are attractive to children with low vision; however, poisonous species and species with thorns must be avoided.

Pest and weed management practices must be carefully evaluated to avoid exposing children to toxins. All weeds should be removed manually. Small animals should be managed by trapping. Other pest problems should be evaluated by certified pest management personnel. Should chemical treatment be necessary, the least toxic alternative should be chosen. After treatment, the play area should be closed until safe for use.

a. **Turf/Grasses** (Mason, 1982). Turf is found in play environments throughout the world. It is a living thing, however, and can take only so much wear and tear before it dies.

Turf is used in one of three situations:

- Sport playing surfaces.
- Unstructured recreation areas.
- Surfaces on mounds and slopes.

Turf is **not** suitable as a shock-absorbing surface under equipment.

Turf normally contains a mixture of plants (not always grasses—clover is also common). There are two types of plants: tussock-forming and creeping. Creeping plants have a far greater power to rejuvenate, and thus are always an advantage in heavily used areas (see "Grass Seed Mixtures for Children's Play Areas," NPFA, 1986).

Another important consideration is the width of leaf and stem. Plants with wide leaves and stems make a less smooth surface than plants with very fine leaves. However, wide-leaved plants are more durable than fine-leaved plants.

The best playing surfaces are constructed with turf on a bed of sand, irrigated and fertilized from below.

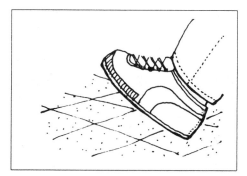

174 Appropriate surfacing materials should be chosen according to use patterns.

175 Surfacing materials need careful consideration.

Consider the following when determining which species of ground cover to use in a play environment:

1)   Different species have different abilities to withstand wear.

2)   Different species have different abilities to regrow after being damaged.

3)   Some species have a dormant period during which they turn brown.

4)   Turf and other natural ground covers require more work to maintain than non-living surfaces.

5)   Turf turns to mud in wet weather if an unsuitable variety of grass is used or site furnishings are not moved regularly.

6)   Turf can be soft and cool to look at and is relatively soft (but still firm) to play on.

7)   Turf is difficult for wheelchairs to move through over a long distance (10 to 15 feet). It is not suitable for an accessible playing field.

11.2   Hard Surfaces

Hard surfaces include: dirt, concrete, asphalt, artificial grass, and decomposed granite. These surfaces should never be used in play equipment fall zones.

a.   **Dirt.** Dirt varies in hardness, but never meets the requirements for shock absorption under equipment.

b.   **Concrete and Asphalt.** These are very hard surfaces to fall on and, therefore, cannot be used under equipment. However, they are necessary for activities where turf surfaces are impractical, such as for ball play. They are very accessible to people using wheelchairs and are easy to maintain and to keep free of broken glass.

Asphalt must be laid to a fixed, solid timber or concrete edge or it will crack and become broken around the edges.

c.   **Artificial Grass.** Artificial grass is an expensive material that is suitable for general play and games areas. It must be laid on a hard, smooth, flat surface. It should not be used under play equipment, and it can be damaged easily by fire.

d.   **Decomposed Granite.** This material is a good all-weather surface for picnic areas, pathways, or around trees. It should not be used under play equipment.

176   *Turf provides a soft, but not resilient, play surface.*

11.3 Shock-Absorbing Surfacing Materials (see also Chapter 6: Pathways, Section 10, Pathway Surfaces)

From all corners of the country, park and recreation personnel and school administrators have recognized the fact quoted by CPSC (1981) that approximately 70% of all playground injuries are due to falls from equipment onto unsafe surfaces. Adequate surfacing throughout play equipment fall zones is an essential safety requirement. The principal standard of adequacy (CPSC, 1991) is that the surface must yield both a peak deceleration of no more than 200 g's and an HIC value of no more than 1,000 for a head-first fall from the highest accessible point of the play equipment when tested in accordance with ASTM F1292, *Standard Specification for Impact Attenuation Under and Around Playground Equipment* (see Chapter 9, Section 1.3f). Consumers should require that manufacturers supply the results of such tests, conducted by an independant laboratory, before specifying a given safety surface.

Surfacing is a critical aspect of manufactured equipment settings. A number of alternative treatments are available. Each has positive and negative points. Most surfaces are costly. All require regular maintenance, some more frequently than others.

11.3.1 Surfacing Depth and Critical Height (CPSC, 1991)

The CPSC has conducted tests to determine the relative shock-absorbing properties of some loose-fill materials commonly used under and around playground equipment. The table on the following page summarizes the Critical Heights of playground equipment at each depth of material. The Critical Height is the maximum height at which a headfirst fall from equipment onto the playground surface meets CPSC shock-absorbancy requirements. Each material was tested at three "uncompressed" depths and one "compressed" depth. Notice that the ability to absorb impacts reduces when the material is compressed. This table may be used as a guide in selecting the type and depth of loose-fill materials that will provide the necessary safety for equipment of various heights. Keep in mind that materials must meet the specifications listed in Appendix D of the CPSC *Handbook* (1991) if they are to accurately reflect the performance data listed in the table.

Critical Height (in feet) of Tested Materials			
	Uncompressed Depth		Compressed Depth
Material*	6 inch	9 inch	12 inch	9 inch
Wood Mulch	7	10	11	10
Double-Shredded Bark Mulch	6	10	11	7
Uniform Wood Chips	6	7	>12	6
Fine Sand	5	5	9	5
Coarse Sand	5	5	6	4
Fine Gravel	6	7	10	6
Medium Gravel	5	5	6	5

Source: CPSC, 1991
* Materials must correspond with the specifications listed in Appendix D of the CPSC Handbook.

11.3.2 Organic Materials

Organic materials, such as pine bark mini-nuggets, pine bark mulch, shredded hard-wood bark, and cocoa shell mulch share the following characteristics (CPSC, 1991; PLAE, 1987):

1)   Cushioning properties depend on the air trapped within and between individual particles. In rainy weather, or during periods of high humidity, these materials absorb moisture and tend to compact. Under these conditions, they may lose some of the trapped air necessary for protective cushioning.

2)   They should never be installed over existing hard surfaces.

3)   With the passage of time, these materials may decompose and become pulverized, thereby losing their cushioning effect and needing to be replaced.

4)   When wet and exposed to freezing temperatures, they freeze and lose their cushioning protection.

5)   Good drainage is required underneath the material. When wet, they are subject to microbial growth.

6)   Strong winds can blow these materials, reducing the thickness necessary for adequate cushioning. A method of containment must be provided.

7)   They are gradually displaced by the playing action of children, thereby reducing the thickness of protective layers in vital fall areas. A method of containment will help reduce displacement.

8)   They harbor and conceal various insects which are usually harmless, and provide learning opportunities for children.

9)   They also can conceal animal excrement and other trash such as broken glass, nails, pencils, and other sharp objects that puncture and cut.

10)   With use, they may combine with dirt and other foreign materials resulting in a loss of shock-absorbing properties.

11)   They may be deliberately removed (stolen) for use as mulch by residents.

12)   They can be flammable.

13)   Generally, these materials require replacement and frequent maintenance such as leveling, grading, and sifting to remove foreign matter.

14)   A major benefit of wood-based shock-absorbing surfacing materials, when compared to inorganic materials such as sand, is that they are less abrasive when tracked into buildings.

15)   When used as a surfacing for informal play (circulation and social areas not under equipment), several of the above reservations that relate to reduction in shock absorbency no longer apply. Under these conditions, organic materials provide a viable, wear-resistant alternative to grass. They also provide children with useful "props" to support dramatic play.

Common Organic Surfacing Materials:

a.   **Bark Nuggets.** The principal wood product used for surfacing under play equipment is bark nuggets from 1/2-inch to 1-inch screen size. Its shock-absorbing characteristic is due primarily to its compressibility.

However, bark nuggets tend to retain water and decompose over time. Their softness allows them to abrade and become pulverized, which accelerates this process. Thus, in time, the nuggets are reduced to a dusty, soil-like composition. Some children are allergic to bark dust. When dry, it blows in their eyes.

Bark nuggets can get thrown around. This makes the play setting look untidy and can be hazardous for pedestrians and ball players on adjacent hard surfaces. Bark nuggets are inaccessible to people with ambulatory disabilities.

The initial cost of bark and its maintenance requirements make it an expensive alternative. Sawdust is occasionally used as a less expensive substitute, but it decomposes very rapidly and is not recommended.

b.   **Wood Chips.** Wood chips are in many ways preferable to bark nuggets as a surfacing material. Once matted down, wood chips provide a wheelchair accessible surface. However, it is not accessible to people using other ambulatory aids. Wood chips are produced by "chippers" used in tree-pruning operations and are readily available from Parks Departments or tree servicing companies. Chips come in different sizes. The smallest chips work best.

Suitability depends on the source. Coniferous chips are the best because the chips are not as splintery as hardwood when first spread. Pine scent is an added attraction and the pine needles help to make a soft "mat." Softer hardwoods such as sycamore do almost as well.

When wood chips are first put down they are spikey and splintery, but these characteristics disappear with wear and weathering, and the chips soon "mat" into a comfortable play surface. They have good drainage, and provide an excellent habitat for insects. Children like to explore this microcosmic world for living organisms and other "finds" like coins, bottle tops, and small plastic toys. Wood chips are much easier than bark nuggets or sand to police for broken glass, and do not attract cats and dogs. There are also manufactured wood chip products.

1)   Maintain a minimum depth of 4 inches in nonequipment areas.

2)   Use chips rather than bark nuggets except where the initial abrasiveness of chips will be a problem.

11.3.3 Inorganic Materials

Sand and pea gravel are common inorganic shock-absorbing surfaces. They have the following characteristics (CPSC, 1991):

1)   Sand can be blown, and either material can be thrown into children's eyes.

2)   They can be displaced by the playing action of children, thereby reducing the thickness of protective layers in fall zones. A method of containment is required.

3)   They can harbor and conceal various insects, animal excrement, and other trash such as broken glass, nails, pencils, and other sharp objects that can cause puncture and cutting wounds. Sand is particularly attractive to cats.

4)   With use, these materials may be combined with dirt and other foreign materials, resulting in a loss of cushioning properties.

5)   With increasing amounts of moisture, sand becomes cohesive and less cushioning. When thoroughly wet, sand reacts as a rigid material when impacted from any direction. Good drainage is required underneath the material.

6)   When wet and exposed to freezing temperatures, these materials will freeze and lose their cushioning protection.

7)   They are difficult to walk on and inaccessible to wheelchair users.

8)   Generally, these materials require replacement and frequent maintenance such as leveling, grading, and sifting to remove foreign matter.

9)   These materials must never be installed over existing hard surfaces.

Synthetic inorganic materials include rubber matting and chopped tire. They have the following characteristics:

1)   They often require near-level, uniform surfaces and are therefore difficult to lay.

2)   They may be subject to vandalism (defaced, ignited, cut, etc.).

Common Inorganic Surfacing Materials:

a.   **Sand and pea gravel.** These materials are most frequently chosen for shock absorbing surfacing under play equipment. Since they have no compressibility, their shock-absorbing characteristics are due to their ability to deform to the shape of the falling child. They spread the area of impact while increasing its duration (a slow, large area impact is less injurious than a narrow quick impact).

Sand is more popular than gravel as a shock-absorbing surface, and has been used throughout North America and Europe for many years (Los Angeles, 1987). Pea gravel offers some advantages as a surfacing solution for very cold and very hot climates. Sand particles must be round in shape and as uniform in size as possible. Particles 1/32 inch or less will be significantly affected by the surface tension of water and tend to bind together when wet. Fine sand is most effective as a shock-absorbing surfacing material (CPSC, 1991).

177   *Sand is a good fall surface.*

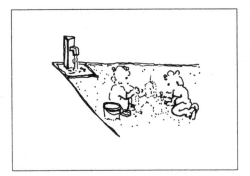

178 *Sand is the most responsive, malleable ground surface, but accessibility is problematic.*

Particles larger than 3/8 inch have sufficient mass to cause serious eye injury when thrown. Sand of the type required is produced by interaction with water and exists in river and ocean deposits. It is sometimes known as washed river bed sand, grain, or bird's eye sand.

The species of original stone affects the longevity of sand. Hard sand will last longer than sand composed of soft stone particles. Because of the weight of sand, the major cost is transportation.

If sand is used as a surface under play equipment, additional sand areas must be provided for sand play. Sand under and around equipment cannot serve both purposes. If additional sand areas are not provided, children will play in traffic areas, a potentially hazardous situation, and the products of their sand play will get stomped on, causing much frustration and unnecessary social conflict.

If sand is used as the primary shock-absorbing surface, then it should be used in combination with manufactured resilient surfaces to provide access to the equipment for people with mobility problems.

b.   **Synthetic Shock-Absorbing Surfacing.** Synthetic surfaces have been used on playgrounds for decades. They include synthetic tiles, poured resilient surfacing, and chopped tires. The traditional form was a one-inch thick interlocking mat with a waffle pattern on the underside. CPSC tests showed that it performed satisfactorily for falls less than four feet in height. More recently, new surfaces have come onto the market that meet CPSC guidelines for greater heights.

Chopped tire is also an effective shock-absorbing surfacing. Like sand and bark nuggets, it will spread outside its containment barrier. To prevent this, some suppliers add a flexible plastic binder. The material retains most of its shock-absorbing characteristics, but the surface tends to deteriorate with wear and is subject to vandalism. To counteract this, a skin of the binder material or artificial grass is added. Such composite materials are available up to 3 inches thick.

Synthetic tiles and poured surfacing provide access for wheelchair users and the ambulatory disabled. They should be used on pathways which come within the fall zone of an equipment setting and to provide access to equipment.

A major drawback of chopped tire and similar composite materials, with and without binders, is that some materials may be flammable. Some also may have a highly unattractive rubbery odor.

When purchasing these materials, there are a number of factors to consid:

1)   Does a drop onto this surface from the height of the highest accessible point on your play structure result in a g-force rating of less than 200 g's and an HIC of no more than 1,000? (see Chapter 9, Section 1.3f)

2)   Does the surface allow for water drainage?

3)   Is it slip-resistant?

4)   What are the installation requirements?

5)   What are the maintenance requirements?

6)   Can it be easily cleaned?

7)   Will it look attractive and complement the appearance of your playground equipment?

8)   Does it smell okay?

9)   Is the surface durable and capable of withstanding extremes of temperature, frost, vandalism, etc?

10) Is it easily repaired?

11) What is the warranty and estimated life of the surfacing material?

c.   **Other Proprietary Surfacings.** New or improved manufactured surfacings are continually appearing on the market. They vary greatly in suitability for different play settings and climatic conditions.

11.4   On-Site Testing

The protection of children from major fall-related injuries is directly related to the fall distance and the shock-absorbing surfacing. The only way to truly know if the surface meets CPSC criteria is to test on site. Until recently, this has been unrealistic due to cost.

Paul Hogan has developed a head-form that can be dropped from any height onto a surface to determine the g-force and HIC value of a fall. It is called a Surface Resiliency Tester. The head-form will provide managers of children's playgrounds immediate feedback about shock-absorbing surfaces and the necessary maintenance action which should be taken. For more information, contact Paul Hogan, Playground Clearinghouse, Inc., 26 Buckwalter Road, Phoenixville, PA 91460.

SUMMARY OF SHOCK-ABSORBING SURFACING MATERIALS FOR USE IN PLAY EQUIPMENT FALL ZONES

MATERIAL	SHOCK ABSORBING CHARACTERISTICS	ADVANTAGES	ISSUES TO CONSIDER
I. ORGANIC LOOSE MATERIAL (pine bark, bark nuggets, shredded bark, cocoa shell mulch, etc.)	Air trapped within loose materials provides a cushioning effect. An adequate depth of material must be provided to have this effect.	Low initial cost. Ease of installation. Attractive. Less abrasive than sand. Good drainage. Does not attract cats and dogs.	Environmental conditions can reduce shock absorbency. Susceptibility to burning. Subject to microbial growth when wet. Cannot be installed over existing hard surfaces. Can get thrown around. Concealed animal excrement and sharp objects.
A. Bark Nuggets (not tested by CPSC)	As above.	Bark nuggets from 1/2 to 1 inch screen size are a principal wood product used for surfacing under play equipment. (not tested by CPSC)	Softness accelerates its decomposition process. Some children are allergic to bark dust. Initial cost and maintenance requirements make it an expensive alternative.
B. Wood Chips (random-sized wood chips, twigs and leaves collected from a wood chipper)	As above.	Preferable to bark nuggets: lower cost, ease of maintenance. Easier to police for broken glass. Readily available.	Suitability depends on the wood source (see Chapter 11, Section 3.2b).

RECOMMENDED DEPTH	MAINTENANCE REQUIREMENTS	ACCESSIBILITY	PLAY VALUE
Min. 12 inches (depends on equipment height)	Requires replacement and continuous maintenance to maintain appropriate depth and remove foreign matter.	See specific materials.	Provides useful "props" to support dramatic play. Children can manipulate the material itself. Some types of organic loose materials increase playground accessibility for individuals with disabilities.
Min. 12 inches (depends on equipment height)	As above.	Inaccessible.	Provides useful "props" to support dramatic play. Children can manipulate the material itself.
Min. 12 inches (depends on equipment height)	As above.	Wheelchair accessible once matted down; challenging for ambulatory disabled who may experience balance problems on uneven surfaces.	Provides useful "props" to support dramatic play. Children can manipulate the material itself. Provides some degree of playground accessibility for individuals with disabilities.

SUMMARY OF SHOCK-ABSORBING SURFACING MATERIALS FOR USE IN PLAY EQUIPMENT FALL ZONES

MATERIAL	SHOCK ABSORBING CHARACTERISTICS	ADVANTAGES	ISSUES TO CONSIDER
II. INORGANIC LOOSE MATERIAL (sand, gravel, stone dust, crushed stone, shells, rubber buffings, chopped tire, etc.)	Conforms to the shape of the falling child, spreading the area of impact while increasing its duration. The rubber products also trap air to provide cushioning.	Initial cost. Ease of installation. Not ideal for microbial growth. Generally nonflammable (except rubber products).	Environmental conditions can reduce shock absorbancy. Can be swallowed, blown or thrown. Spreads outside the containment area. Conceals animal excrement and sharp objects. Cannot be installed over existing hard surface.
A. Sand Fine sand, sieved by ASTM Standard Method C136-84a with yield: 100% passing #16, 98% passing #30, 62% passing #50, 17% passing #100, 0-1% passing #200.	As above. Particles should be round and as uniform in size as possible. Select sand composed of hard, round particles between 1/16 inch and 3/16 inch diameter.	Low cost (major cost is transportation). Preferable and more popular than pea gravel.	Small particles bind together when wet. Particles larger than 3/8 inch can cause serious eye injury when thrown. Species of original stone affects longevity. If used under play equipment, additional sand areas must be provided for play. Attractive to cats and dogs.
B. Chopped Tire	A shock absorbent material which also traps air between the particles to provide a cushioning effect.	Six inches will provide and retain significant shock-absorbing ability.	Spreads outside its containment area. Surface deteriorates with wear. Subject to vandalism. Is flammable. Unpleasant, "rubbery" smell.
III. SYNTHETIC COMPACT MATERIALS (rubber mats or tiles, synthetic turf on foam mats, rubber sheeting on foam mats, poured-in-place urethanes, and rubber compositions)	Consists of a shock absorbing material such as rubber.	Low maintenance. Colors. Clean. Consistent shock absorbency. No displacement. Generally low life cycle costs. Good footing. Accessible. Harbors few foreign objects.	Initial cost, replacement after useful life. Vandalism. Seams, loss of color, water drainage, slip-resistant surfacing. Meets CPSC impact-attenuation guidelines. Ease of maintenance. Attractive and complementary to the appearance of the playground. Warranty and estimated life of the material.

RECOMMENDED DEPTH	MAINTENANCE REQUIREMENTS	ACCESSIBILITY	PLAY VALUE
Min. 12 inches. (depends on equipment height)	Requires replacement and continuous maintenance to maintain appropriate depth and remove foreign matter.	See specific materials.	Manipulative play value. Generally, they do not increase access to play areas for disabled, except chopped tire.
Depends on equipment height: 12 inches minimum; 18 to 36 inches for sand play area.	As above.	Inaccessible to wheelchairs or ambulatory disabled; should not be eliminated from play areas because of its play value.	High value for manipulative play, especially when access to water (faucet or water element) is also provided.
4–8 inches. (depends on equipment height)	As above.	Wheelchair accessible; inaccessible for ambulatory disabled who may experience balance problems when walking on this surface.	Provides for increased play area access for individuals with disabilities. Chopped tire may have some manipulative play value.
Ranges from 1–6 inches thick; desired thickness depends on the equipment height and product resiliency.	Generally minimal.	Accessible.	Provides increased access for individuals with disabilities.

12. LANDFORMS/TOPOGRAPHY

Landform is often underutilized as a play opportunity in site design. A mix of landforms and vertical elements can provide a variety of experiences in three-dimensional space, including varied circulation within and between spaces and varied interaction of the body in space (rolling, crawling, sliding, balancing, jumping). Especially, it can provide design opportunities for integrating fixed equipment into the landscape (NPFA, 1978a). Through careful manipulation of topography, access can be provided without the use of special ramps. Low mounds can increase the sense of challenge without increasing the fall height.

Planning Criteria

Play Value. Landforms and topography provide for large muscle activities, spatial experience, and spaces for "refuge." Stimulation of orientation skills, hide-and-go-seek games, viewing, rolling, climbing, and sliding. Opportunities for dramatic play and imagination can be supported by landforms.

Programming. Landforms support building activity, points of suspension, and cantilevers.

Play Leadership. Landforms have good potential for supporting hiding/chasing and trailing games. They present opportunities for building sites in adventure play programs.

Safety. Steep slopes and sudden drop-offs must be avoided. Guardrails may be needed on paths and ramps.

Risk Management. Plan for regular maintenance. Changes in level, steps and ramps must be highly visible with no hidden surprises.

Accessibility. Accessible routes should be provided. "Summit" points need to accommodate wheelchairs and provide support for people with other disabilities.

Integration. There is good potential for interaction when children help each other negotiate the challenge of varied topography.

Management/Maintenance. Height, slope, groundcover, and protective barrier criteria need to be specified to avoid erosion on earthformed mounds.

179   *Landforms can be used to define gathering places.*

180   *Mounds support hide-and-go-seek and chasing games.*

181   *Grassy hills are excellent for rolling games.*

12.1   Range of Design Choices

Slopes, varied topography, and landforms satisfy many play needs. They should be retained when they exist on a new site. If they do not exist, they should be created. However, earth moving and related site improvements (e.g., drainage) can be expensive. Opportunities will therefore vary depending on existing site conditions and budget.

The design approach can range from importing material to creating a mound on a flat site, to complete regrading of the site to create a continuously varied ground surface with topographic features.

12.2   Topographic Features

Topographic features can be designed into the site to add interest and a variety of play opportunities as illustrated below.

a.   **The Hill and Hill Circle** (Bunin et al., 1980; Gordon, 1972)

A grassy hill, surrounding a tree, is graded gently for crawlers as well as for climbers to ascend to a plateau summit, roll down on the grass, or slide down on a protected, enclosed fiberglass slide. The hill circle, surrounding the base of the tree, provides a quiet nook for children. It has a circular bench to sit on in a shaded area for individual play, group interaction, and socializing.

12.3   Minimum Provision (Seattle, 1986)

a.   Provide a grassy hill, natural or constructed, as part of each play area (NPFA, 1986).

b.   Provide a minimum of one or two earth berms, 4 feet to 5 feet high (200 to 400 sq. ft.) with varying slopes of 1:3, 1:4, and 1:5 for each play area.

c.   Typical earth-form slopes shall not exceed:

- 3:1 for mowable grass areas;
- 2:1 for cut or fill slopes with erosion-control matting and special nonmowable ground covers.

d.   During the construction of a play area, remove all rocks and debris larger than an adult fist to a depth of 12 inches.

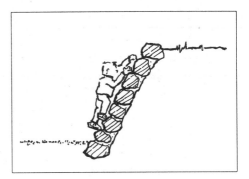

182   *Rock-face climbing wall stimulates large muscle coordination and sense of achievement.*

183   *The bridge stimulates social interaction, spatial orientation and sense of discovery.*

184   *Jumping "cliffs" can be provided, with proper attention to ground surface treatment for safety.*

12.4   Drainage of Play Areas   (Seattle, 1986)

All open areas should slope to drain, with the exception of loose surface areas under children's play equipment. Positive drainage can be reinforced by:

a.   Percolation layer.

b.   Tightline to storm system.

c.   Perforated line.

12.5   Surface Slopes for Drainage   (Seattle, 1986)

a.   Provide a 0 to 2% slope for resilient surfacing, provided with underdrainage.

b.   Provide a 2% minimum slope and cross-slope for asphalt surfaces.

c.   Provide a 1% minimum slope for concrete surfaces.

d.   Provide a 2% minimum slope for open lawn areas.

e.   Avoid crossing play areas with drainage swales which might cause children to fall.

12.6   Drainage Collection Systems   (Seattle, 1986)

Subsurface drainage is required for all surfacing beneath children's play equipment.

A play area drainage system has to be considered in conjunction with the entire park drainage system in order to determine specific methods. A combination of surface and subsurface drainage must be considered for all sizes.

185 *Stepping stones and logs stimulate large muscle coordination and balancing skills.*

186 *To attain a sense of challenge and achievement, grass hills at heights of 4 to 5 feet for toddlers and 9 to 13 feet for older kids are recommended.*

187 *A slide can be incorporated into a slope to prevent injuries from falls and make the slide more accessible. Sand at the bottom cushions the landing.*

188 *Hill and hill circle.*

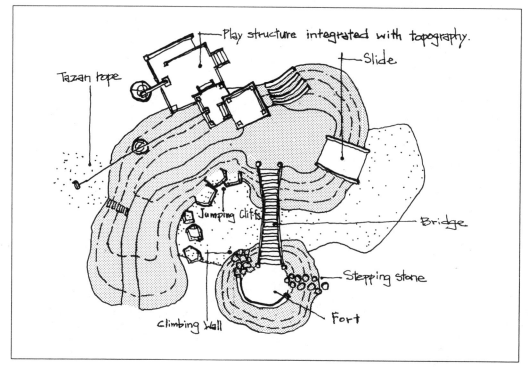

Play structure integrated with topography.
Slide
Tazan rope
Jumping Cliffs
Bridge
Stepping stone
Climbing Wall
Fort

189 *Topographic form used as a design element to connect and unify fixed features of the site.*

13. TREES/VEGETATION

Trees and vegetation should be established to satisfy the need for shade, wildlife habitat, sensory variety, loose parts, softly edged spaces, space separation, hideaways, and a friendly atmosphere. It is imperative that children have opportunities for interacting with vegetation in their daily environment so that they grow up with an intuitive sense of value for the natural environment.

Planning Criteria

Play Value. Vegetation is an intrinsically interesting setting that stimulates exploratory and discovery behavior, dramatic play, and imagination. It provides subtle visual complexity and is ideal for hide-and-seek games. Tree-climbing is a universally favorite activity. Trees add a highly significant positive ambience to play settings through their variable mix of sun/shade, color, texture, fragrance, and softness of enclosure. Vegetation offers enormous play potential. There is no substitute for vegetation as a major source of play props: leaves, flowers, fruit, nuts, seeds, and sticks.

Programming. Vegetation can be used to support many different program activities requiring spatial diversity and a stimulating atmosphere. Trees are good for building in, for hanging things on, for swinging on. Vegetation supplies a variety of play resources that children can harvest for themselves (Allison, 1975; Johnston, 1990; Moore, 1986b; Moore & Wong, in press; Schools Council, 1974). Vegetated settings are essential for environmental education programs, especially on school grounds (Adams, 1990).

Play Leadership. Play leaders need to be knowledgeable about play opportunities that can be supported by vegetation and trees.

Safety. Choose appropriate tree species and place them so that problems of dropping limbs and "kitten-up-a-tree" (child climbs up, can't come back down, and gets stuck) are avoided. Do not place trees so near structures that children can climb from one to the other, unless the structure is deliberately designed around the tree.

Risk Management. Choose appropriate species and locations, avoiding toxic and allergy-related species. Regular inspections of health are required. An annual pruning regime needs to be established.

Accessibility. For children with physical disabilities, the experience of being in trees needs to be replicated by choosing appropriate low-branching and weeping types, by not pruning off low-growing vegetation, and by integrating vegetation into accessible settings. A conflict can occur with low-hanging branches over pathways. Trees that a child using a wheelchair can roll into or under should be placed away from pathways. Otherwise, they may present hazards for the visually impaired.

Integration. Trees provide opportunities for child-to-child play and for shared experience, especially with regard to play props. Vegetation is one of the most important elements for integration because it can be enjoyed and shared equally by all.

Management/Maintenance. A program of regular maintenance is needed. Public policies need to recognize the value of vegetation and trees as a community and childhood resource. Local listings should be developed that identify the most appropriate regional species for different purposes, such as play, wildlife habitat, and visual enhancement. Species that support all three purposes clearly have high priority for installation. Listings of unsuitable toxic species should also be highlighted.

Note: MIG Communications will publish a planting guide for children's outdoor environments in 1992 or early 1993.

190 *Plants and children grow together.*

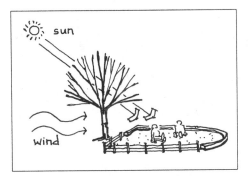

191 *Trees are an excellent modifier of microclimate.*

192 *Vegetation marks the passing of the seasons.*

13.1   How Trees and Vegetation Improve Play Settings

Trees and vegetation have no substitute as play setting elements. Children are especially attracted by a mix of natural and people-made elements (Mason, 1982; Moore & Schneekloth, 1989). Emphasis should be on the integration of plantings into play settings, rather than creating segregated "nature areas."

a.   **Variety of Play Opportunities.** Vegetation settings greatly extend the range of play activity: collecting plant parts, climbing and playing in trees, hide-and-seek games, and exploration.

b.   **Climatic Modification.** Vegetation is an effective modifier of climate because it is so varied and, therefore, provides a greater range of climatic choice than structures made by people. Trees are the best way to provide shade. Spreading, deciduous species that shed their leaves to let winter sunlight through are especially good (but have maintenance implications).

c.   **Seasonal Variation.** Vegetation marks the passing of the seasons and introduces children to a sense of time and natural processes.

d.   **Improved Surface Runoff and Erosion Control.** Broad-leaved deciduous trees can reduce the direct impact of heavy rain and extend the runoff period. Surface root systems bind the soil and help resist erosion.

e.   **Variety of Enclosure.** Size, shape, and enclosure of play settings are greatly enhanced by being wholly or partly achieved with vegetation. A more varied spatial and textural setting is achieved with a complexity and subtlety beyond that possible through people-made elements alone.

Vegetated enclosures give a "boundary-depth" with more character than a rectilinear fence. Vegetated space divisions produce a great variety of shapes and forms, thereby increasing territorial variety and extending the possible range of games and social interaction.

f.   **Sensory Variety.** Quality of the movement experience is greatly improved by vegetation (in conjunction with topography). Planting can be used along paths to create a sequence of texture, smell, light, shade, and color. "Specimen" plants are important orienting elements.

193 *Planting adds soft, ambiguous enclosures and "boundary" depth to play areas.*

194 *Raised planting improves the quality of movement experience, especially for children in wheelchairs.*

Plants can teach about texture, fragrance, and color (Seattle, 1986):

1) Vary texture of leaves: evergreen with deciduous; shiny with rough; serrated with smooth edges; thin with thick.

2) Vary form, size, and shape of plants used near children's areas.

3) Select plants for seasonal changes: evergreen vs. deciduous; color through the seasons; early leaves, late flowers; flowers and fruit.

4) Consider opportunities for color in trees, ground covers, vines, annuals, and perennials.

5) Select plants for fragrance.

6) Select plants for craft and culinary potential.

7) Select for auditory stimulation. Some plants, especially in the fall, produce interesting sounds when the wind blows through their dry leaves. Plants like bamboo and pine trees produce sounds year round.

g. **Indoor—Outdoor Transitions** can be softened with vegetation—especially for people whose eyes adjust slowly to changing light levels and glare.

h. **Manipulative Play Material (Play Props)** (Moore, 1989c). Plants are a valuable source of play material. Small horizontal surfaces (tables, benches, ledges, logs, rocks) should be provided to support this activity.

195 *Specimen trees can be landmarks for orientation.*

196 *Vegetation provides a great diversity of texture in play settings.*

197 *The fragrance of flowers is valuable to children with sight disabilities.*

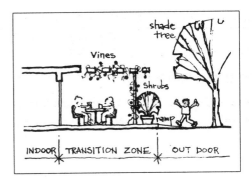

198   *Indoor–outdoor transitions.*

199   *Vegetation is a manipulative play material.*

Leave woods and natural areas in a rough state; avoid the tendency to "clean up," except for thorny material and dead branches and twigs which are at eye or neck height (Seattle, 1986).

i.   **Craft and Culinary Activities.**   A range of annuals and perennials can support specific activities such as cooking, dying, and doll-making (PLAE, 1981–87).

j.   **Comfortable Social Setting.**   Many children find natural environments more comfortable for social activity. Objects having a clear identity, such as trees, large rocks, and ponds, function as landmarks and produce a strong visual impact on the user. Mature shrubs make excellent hideouts and refuges (Kirby, 1989).

k.   **Wildlife Habitat.** Vegetation provides, through establishment of plant communities, a range of habitat conditions for wildlife that cannot be matched by people-made settings.

It is important for children to observe wildlife (Leedy, 1982; Schicker, 1986). Select plants with fruits, cones, and seeds to attract birds, squirrels, and other wildlife (Seattle, 1986).

Bird houses can be built so that children using wheelchairs can get a closer look.

l.   **Open-endedness.** Vegetation of all types provides props and settings for imaginative play. Trees and large shrubs provide flexible open-ended situations that children can build onto.

200   *Shrubs provide excellent hideaway places.*

201   *Vegetation is a habitat for wildlife.*

202   *Trees become "woods" and "forests" to children.*

203 *Plants to play around.*

204 *Trees to play under.*

205 *Impact of vegetation on users.*

m. **Play Area Identification.** Visually distinctive plantings or particular "specimen" plants can provide identity to a play area even though no manufactured equipment is present. Such identity plantings can signal "permission" to play.

n. **Community Playground Aesthetic Value** (Los Angeles, 1987).

The overall design must be pleasing and attractive to the whole community. People of all ages respond to flowering shrubs, deciduous trees, rockeries, flower pots, herb gardens, etc.

13.2   Child—Plant Interaction

Opportunities should be provided for children to interact with plants using all their senses. Children/plant places extend in scale from a few blades of grass poking through a crack in the asphalt, to a large natural resource area. Whether small or large, simple or complex, the idea in supporting children-plant interaction is to maximize user impact while minimizing environmental impact.

13.2.1 Factors That Affect User Impact

The impact of plants on the users of a space is influenced by:

a. **Age and Sex of Users.** Younger children appear to appreciate plants more readily than older children. Girls seem more appreciative than boys (Moore, 1986a).

b. **Environmental Values of Users.** The degree to which children appreciate and understand plants depends on their cultural situation, family circumstances, and their degree of participation in environmental education activities.

Ensure that local schools are involved in play area development and that environmental education is included in the curriculum.

c. **Season and Climate.** Inclement weather reduces the amount of contact between children and plants. Regions with heavy winters have this disadvantage. Seasonal change, on the other hand, is an important dimension in the plant world, which children need to experience.

d. **Type of Plant.** Some plants are more attractive to children than others because of their sensory qualities and play potential. Bamboo, for instance, is universally liked. All manner of flowering plants are attractive.

Injurious and toxic species must be avoided.

206   *Vegetation and trees can be incorporated into programmed activities.*

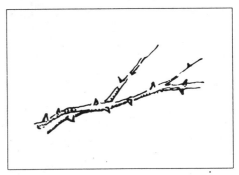

207   *Injurious and toxic species must be avoided.*

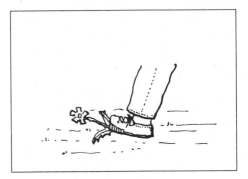

208   *Environmental impact of users on vegetation should be minimized.*

e.   **Density/Diversity of Plants.** Volume and variety of plants are important factors. An increase in either will increase the complexity and number of possible interactions.

f.   **Habitat Conditions.** Effective user impact will be increased if protective structures (fences, etc.) are designed to also allow maximum contact.

13.2.2 Factors That Affect Environmental Impact

The impact of children on designed vegetated settings is conditioned by several factors, including:

a.   **Age and Sex of Users.** Older kids, especially boys, are more aggressive.

b.   **Environmental Values of Users.** Attitudes towards vegetation reflect the cultural values of the community.

c.   **Season and Climate.** Inclement weather reduces the amount of human activity.

d.   **Maturity of Plants.** Larger, older plants are able to withstand impact better than smaller, younger plants.

e.   **Type of Plant.** Plants vary tremendously in their attractiveness to children, the amount of abuse they can withstand, and their recovery time. Some plants, such as willow, have an attractive play potential and are naturally hardy (Moore, 1989c).

f.   **Habitat Conditions.** Plants are adaptable to specific conditions. Some are more broadly adaptable than others. Habitats can be more or less suitable for a given plant, depending on soil conditions, drainage, irrigation, exposure, and associations with other plants.

g.   **Habitat Perception.** New, unconventional, or bizarre planting will attract undesirable attention. A freshly planted tree, standing on its own, surrounded by asphalt, looks out of place. Kids will perceive it that way and very likely will damage it. A group of trees, growing together with associated plants, looks very different and more natural, and will stimulate different behavior.

h.   **Habitat Protection.** The degree to which plants are physically protected by permanent barriers from direct impact is crucial. Staking, tying up, and other management efforts to help the plants assume their natural position are important.

209 *A rock surrounded by a small amount of dirt provides a minimal niche for plant growth.*

210 *Raised planters and staking provide a hierarchy of protection for plants, children's play, and wheelchair access.*

211 *Edges of buildings provide naturally protective interfaces for plantings.*

Each plant must be surrounded by several "lines of protection." For example, a small shrub may be tied to a stake; it may also grow in a planter and thereby be protected from traffic flow; the planter itself may be sheltered by being placed against a building or in a fenced-off area. There are many ways of implementing this principle.

i.   **Density/Diversity of Plants.** The ability to withstand impact is a function of both density and diversity.

j.   **Differentiation.** Any object projecting from, resting on, or close to the ground will create a small, protected niche within which plants and associated life forms can flourish.

13.3   **Design of Child-Plant Interactions**

a.   **Protective Interface.** A design objective of any open space occupied by both children and plants is to achieve high user impact with low environmental impact.

Protective elements should divert children's kinetic energy sufficiently to avoid irreversible plant damage. Therefore, they need to:

1)   Allow children to move in three-dimensional space;

2)   Allow plants to grow in three-dimensional space;

3)   Allow children to have intimate contact with plants (high user impact);

4)   Protect plants from excessive damage (low environmental impact).

Protective elements should be designed as multipurpose supporters of both plants and play by combining the principles of **separation** and **interpretation**:

1)   **Separation.** Separation of people zones from plant zones, vertically and/or horizontally, is the main way of reducing environmental impact.

2)   **Interpenetration.** Interpenetration of people and plant zones is the main way of increasing user impact. This can be done more easily on the horizontal plane, although vertical interpenetration is also possible (e.g., a climbing structure designed around a tree).

c.   **Climbable trees.** Climbable trees are an example of vertical interpenetration. Platforms can be constructed to assist this function, more safely, with less environmental impact.

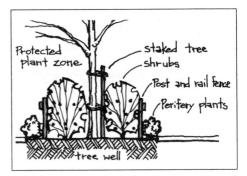

212 *Simple post-and-rail fences provide effective separation between people and plants.*

213 *Beanpole teepee (carpeted with sand), a simple form of child-plant interaction.*

214 *Tree climbing gives children a sense of achievement.*

13.4   Native and Exotic Species

A mix of both native, or naturalized, and exotic plants should be used in play settings. Native plants provide hardy background planting. They are usually more resilient. Exotic species add variety and interest.

13.5   Maintenance (Seattle, 1986).

It is important that plantings are maintained to avoid potentially hazardous branches and twigs at children's eye levels.

a.   For protection of both child and plant:

1)   Plant 2-inch minimum caliper trees or larger.

2)   Use heavy tree guards or stakes around plants until established.

3)   Avoid small lawn areas where they will provide access to roof tops.

4)   Avoid plants known to be poisonous in or near children's play areas.

b.   For barrier plants:

1)   Discourage foot traffic with denser branching or a thornless shrub substructure.

2)   Use soft-branching plant material where children may fall into it or run through it.

3)   Use low maintenance plant material.

4)   Use plants tolerant to foot traffic.

5)   Use multitrunked and multibranching plants.

6)   Use quick-growing and "self-perpetuating" plants which heal after breaking.

7)   Use hedge-like, thicket plants for small defensible areas.

215 *Low-slung, ramped platforms can provide an accessible treehouse setting.*

c.   **Because all trees can be climbed:**

1)   Select trees which develop strong trunks and horizontal branches, and are fast-growing, thornless, and low maintenance for children's areas.

2)   Provide resilient surfacing under trees, and trim or prune existing trees for safety.

3)   Use trees and shrubs with fruit, cones, or pods to provide props, but do so judiciously. Do not use such species in locations where "shedding" could be hazardous (e.g., on main pathways) or a severe maintenance issue.

14. GARDEN SETTINGS

Gardens are one of the best ways of enabling children to interact with nature, to learn about the ecological cycle, and to cooperate with peers. They are excellent settings for integrating children with and without disabilities.

Planning Criteria

Play Value. Gardens provide for social interaction, fine motor skills development, and sensory stimulation.

Programming Potential. There is excellent potential, with spin-offs into nutrition, food chain, nonfood uses of plants, economics of food, cross-cultural awareness, and third world food problems (Moore & Wong, in press).

Play Leadership. Leaders need training in how to use gardens.

Safety. Tools need to be locked up. Gardens need to be enclosed.

Risk Management. There must be supervision, signs, checkout for tools, and a fenced enclosure.

Accessibility. Provide raised beds, U-shaped to allow easy reach to center, with easy access to water (e.g., levers) and recoilable hoses. Compost boxes must be low to the ground for wheelchair access. Provide rolling bins for fertilizer.

Integration. Gardening is a good group activity, good for child-to-child assistance.

Management/Maintenance. Policy is needed to support the importance of gardening; extra training for staff and maintenance people should be provided.

216 *Gardening stimulates cooperative work between children.*

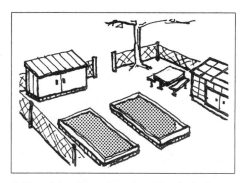

217 *A basic enclosed garden includes raised beds, compost boxes, storage, etc.*

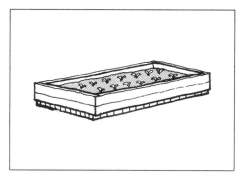

218 *Raised beds provide order and a practical working arrangement.*

219 *Children's gardens must be enclosed.*

220 *Height and width of planting beds should allow wheelchair access.*

221 *Low-rise beds can be accessible to children out of wheelchairs.*

222 *Straw makes a comfortable, tidy groundcover in gardening areas.*

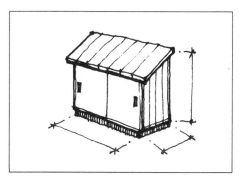

223 *Lockable, secure storage is essential in a garden setting.*

224 *Accessible tables are essential for working and social interaction.*

225   *Gardens provide a good vehicle for special events.*

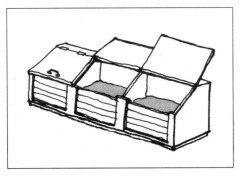

226   *Tri-compartment compost box with lids and removable boards provides the most practical means of composting. Compartments must be low to the ground to allow for wheelchair access.*

14.1   Guidebooks

For further information on children's gardens, consult:

a.   *A Child's Garden* (1978), available from Ortho, 575 Market Street, San Francisco, CA 94105.

b.   *Grounds for Learning: A Practical Guide to Schoolground Use and Development* (1990), by Dennis Cox, Ian McMaster and John Obuch.   Dellasta: Victoria, Australia. Copies are available from Natural Resources Conservation, 593 Springvale Road, Springvale South, Melbourne, Victoria, Australia.

c.   *City Farmer*, available from the National Federation of City Farms, The Old Vicarage, 66 Fraser St., Windmill Hill, Bedminster, Bristol BS3 4LY, England. Tel. 0272.660663.

d.   *The Outdoor Classroom: Educational Use, Landscape Design and Management of School Grounds*, in *Building Bulletin 71*, Department of Education and Science (1990). London: Her Majesty's Stationary Office.

15. ANIMAL SETTINGS

Animals stimulate a caring and responsible attitude towards other living things. They provide therapeutic effects and offer opportunities for learning about biology.

Planning Criteria

Play Value. Animals can have a particularly powerful therapeutic effect on children. A source of wonder and fascination, they are living things that children can interact with, talk to, and invest in emotionally.

Animals provide companionship in nonthreatening ways and almost always come back for more contact. This can be critical for a child with limited self-esteem who has little contact with other living things (Schneekloth, 1985).

Caring for animals can produce a sense of responsibility and pride in children. Having animals around provides an opportunity to learn to care for other living things. But it is important that these lessons be learned under the guidance and direction of caring adults (Schneekloth, 1985).

The strong motivation to care for animals makes them a powerful socializing medium for children. Documented childhood memories of animal care are very strong (Moore, 1986c). Animal care stimulates a sense of personal competence, self-esteem and autonomy (*Children's Environments Quarterly*, Vol. 1, No. 3, 1984).

Programming. Animals may relate to many program themes and can be a theme in themselves. They provide an excellent tie to children's literature (Moore, 1984) and a connection to conservation education.

Play Leadership. Leaders need good knowledge of animals appropriate for use in play programs (HAPA, 1978; PLAE, 1981–87).

Safety. There are risks of bites, scratches, disease, and insect pests.

Risk Management. Animals need proper housing and care. Parents and children must be made aware of animal needs and informed of the risks of interaction.

Accessibility. Some species have substantial potential for close contact and interaction with children, e.g., rabbits, hamsters, guinea pigs, gerbils, and tortoises. Fish in their natural habitat and in aquaria have good potential, too. Ponies have a powerful potential for children with disabilities.

Integration. Excellent potential for shared experience between children of different ages and abilities and between adults and children.

Management/Maintenance. Policies are needed that protect both animals and users, including a rotation plan for larger animals. Different animals need housing in different ways. Requirements for adequate care vary. Sheep and goats are a potential agent of maintenance by being allowed to graze grass areas.

In one adventure playground in England, a young mentally retarded man became the animal caretaker. It was a source of great pride for him. He eliminated the need for teachers to always be present while still allowing the children the chance to interact with living things.

227 *Caring for animals instills responsibility . . .*

228 *. . . and promotes respect for other living things.*

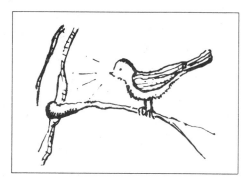

229 *Bird song provides a positive acoustic ambience.*

15.1 Appropriate Types of Animals

a. **Nonharmful insects and insect-like organisms** should be considered an important aspect of the play setting. The vast majority of insects are beneficial to the human race, do not bite, do not eat valuable materials, and do not spread disease. They are an inevitable part of any vegetated setting. Caterpillars, butterflies, moths, ladybugs, beetles, pillbugs, spiders, millipedes, and snails are particularly attractive to children (Moore, 1984).

b. **Birdlife.** There are specific habitat requirements: high places for nesting, sources of nesting materials, and food-producing plants. It is difficult for children to make close contact with birds (except if caged); nonetheless, birds add a positive ambience to play settings (movement, color, song). Birds in large, naturalistic caged settings are a possibility.

c. **Small animals, amphibians, and reptiles.** Typical species include salamanders, squirrels, toads, mice, moles, snakes, lizards, etc., that are adapted to specific habitat conditions. Gerbils are a popular caged animal. Tortoises are fascinating, and easy to care for.

d. **Fish, frogs, and pond life.** These are very attractive to children and have minimum habitat requirements (see Chapter 16, Water Settings).

e. **Domesticated and farmyard animals.** Rabbits, guinea pigs, and hamsters are the most popular and easiest to care for. Several others are appropriate (chickens, goats, sheep, pigs, ponies, and donkeys) and have become a traditional aspect of the playground scene in some countries (Broadway, 1979; *Childhood City Newsletter*, 1981).

15.2 Habitat Requirements for Attracting Wildlife to Play Settings

Two habitat requirements are essential: shelter and sustenance (food and drink). In many cases, vegetation fulfills both requirements (Schools Council, 1974). The presence of vegetation will support a dramatic increase in the population level and diversity of organisms, particularly insects—herbivorous ones first, then their carnivorous predators (Moore & Wong, in press).

Pioneer vegetation provides basic habitats for populations of small organisms (insects, arachnids, millipedes, sow bugs, etc.) that in turn provide a food source for larger animals (amphibians and birds) that walk, crawl, or fly to the site from surrounding areas. In order to encourage this colonization process and the building up of a biotic pyramid, a census of wildlife living around the site, in neighbors' gardens, and on vacant lots is useful. Staff from the local university, high school, or parks department can help give advice, carry out the census, and/or work directly with the children.

Three complementary strategies are possible in attracting wildlife to a play setting:

a.   Create basic habitat conditions and see what happens;

b.   Once a census has been made of what's around, create habitats attractive to specific organisms;

c.   Introduce organisms directly and see what happens.

Specific ideas for making the site more attractive to wildlife include (Moore & Wong, in press):

1)   **Diversity of vegetation**—the primary habitat. Include volunteer wild plants, ground covers, wall covers, shrubs, trees, etc. Pay attention to specific food-producing plants.

2)   **Dark undersides** and cavities are necessary for all kinds of "crawlers" and insects. Place logs, rocks, and other heavy objects on the ground, with cavities beneath.

3)   **Chip pile.** An excellent habitat for "burrowers." A load of chippings from the parks department or city street tree crew dumped in a quiet corner of the playground with reasonable drainage will support a rich community of organisms. Children will spend hours hunting through the surface of the pile to see what they can discover.

4)   **Compost Heap.** Set aside a corner where prunings and weeds can be piled to decompose. Within a short time it will become a hive of activity and a resource for anyone who wants to lift off the top layer and take a look. Eventually, compost will be useful for mulching garden areas.

5)   **Wood Pile.** Wood piles provide a great habitat for insects and other organisms. Logs must be tied together so that they don't get scattered around.

230   Aquatic habitats support many animals that fascinate children.

231   Rabbits and other domesticated animals are particularly appropriate for integrated play settings.

232   All animals are adapted to particular habitat conditions; some have more specific requirements than others.

233   *Undersides of rocks and logs provide ideal wildlife niches.*

234   *Large, decomposing logs provide an excellent habitat for small organisms.*

6)   **Large Logs.** Large, heavy, decomposing logs provide useful self-contained ecosystems. Full or partial shade is important to keep logs moist.

7)   **Water Places.** Ponds provide self-contained ecosystems (see Chapter 16, Water Settings). Wildlife can be encouraged by carefully designing the bottom and edge conditions and by creating landings, islands, and marshes.

Birdbaths are also worth considering.

15.3   Birdscaping

Local species of birds can be attracted by creating environmental conditions which support avian life: food, cover, and nesting sites.

Basic bird needs are not a complicated enterprise. Remember that a diversity of vegetation ranging from large tree canopies and small trees to a shrubby understory jungle punctuated by weedy, seedy wild annuals and perennials can create a bird oasis even if it is relatively close to busy city traffic and heavy child impact.

15.4   Guidebooks

The School Outdoor Resource Area. Schools Council (1974), London: Longman.

Nature Areas for City People, by Jacklyn Johnston. The London Ecology Unit, 1990. Available from the London Ecology Unit, Bedford House, 125 Camden High Street, London, NW1 7JR, U.K.

The Outdoor Classroom: Educational Use, Landscape Design and Management of School Grounds, in Building Bulletin 71, Department of Education and Science (1990). London: Her Majesty's Stationary Office.

16. WATER SETTINGS

Water features and aquatic environments are highly valued by children (Moore, 1986a); they support a variety of terrestrial and aquatic wildlife and add a substantial aesthetic dimension to any recreation setting.

Planning Criteria

Play Value. The play value of water is tremendous because of its multisensory character: sounds, textures, changes of state, and feelings of wetness. Water is a primal element and holds endless fascination for young children. It excites and relaxes. Children seldom miss opportunities for water play, whether they are in the bathtub, in puddles, or in swimming pools (Schneekloth, 1985). Water is also a valuable addition to other play elements, particularly sand.

Programming. Aquatic settings support a vast range of play and learning opportunities: exploring, fishing and wildlife activities, dam building and engineering works, "panning for gold," flotation, and boat building (Moore, 1987).

Play Leadership. Leaders need knowledge of how to use water as a program resource. Sensitivity to parental reactions to children getting wet is important.

Safety. Setting standards for water features is difficult. It is said that children can drown in 1 inch of water, but facts about actual water-related mishaps are hard to find. Sharp drop-offs must be avoided. Careful edge treatment is essential. Edges must be physically defined. Bottoms must be gently shelved. Maximum water depth must not exceed 14 inches. Bottom covering must be slip-proof. Water must circulate or recirculate and must be sufficiently oxygenated to maintain adequate water quality.

Risk Management. Regular water quality tests are needed. Watch for empty bottles and broken glass. Stress parental awareness of risk management and procedures to reduce parental anxiety.

Accessibility. Edge treatments are critical to accommodate vision-impaired users. Wheelchair transfer places are needed to enable children with mobility impairments to get close to the water or to make contact with it: lean-over spots, decks, stacksacks full of sand, etc. Develop inflatables to allow children to float on water.

Integration. Water encourages shared activities and interaction.

Management/Maintenance. Policies are needed to address the use and value of water to children, maintenance of aquatic features, and the different options available.

235 *Still water feels calm, reflects the sky and surrounding elements, and is contemplative.*

236 *Running water feels animated, and stimulates interaction and experimentation among children.*

16.1   Water on Handicapped Adventure Playgrounds (HAPA, 1978, slightly edited)

All HAPA playgrounds have artificial streams, some with waterfalls, running beneath wooden bridges into shallow ponds, not more than 14 inches deep. The water is supplied with a pump system causing it to circulate continuously once the pond is full enough. The movement of the water helps to keep the pond and stream clean and clear. Good filter systems keep the drains free from leaves, mud, and sand. Emptying and sweeping out the bed of the stream and pond gives as much pleasure to children as playing in the water when they are full. A bridge is fun as a place to cross-over or as a place from which to simply sit and watch. It is also interesting to paddle underneath or to sail under on a raft or boat. A bridge should be built high enough over the water for these purposes, but it must also be accessible for everyone. Ground-level water features should be provided for children using prone boards.

16.2   Purposes of Water in Play Settings

Water settings range in scale from a dew-covered leaf, to a fully developed pond system, to an elaborate fountain structure. They embody three related functions:

a.   Life support oriented towards program purposes, wildlife habitats, and aesthetic appreciation.

b.   Play support emphasizing physical contact with water as a play material (sand, water, and plant part combinations are particularly powerful).

c.   Cooling-off for hot weather (possibilities range from hoses to spray pools).

16.3   Physical Properties of Water Relevant to Design

a.   Water is essential to all biological life.

b.   Water is an incredibly attractive play material, which is a child's way of experiencing all life's dependency on water.

c.   Water can be combined with earth or sand in a spectrum of aquatic conditions from clear water, to mud, to damp earth, to intermittently wet sand.

d.   Water flows downhill on the line of least resistance until it reaches the lowest level.

e.   Water can be sprayed upward—vertically or at an angle—under normal faucet pressure.

237 *Water cascade.*

238 *Hose-filled ponds and streams are a simple means of providing temporary waterplay features.*

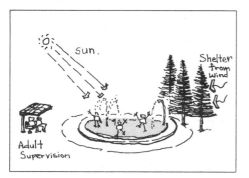

239 *Basic waterplay and cooling-off settings need sun, shelter from the wind, and adult supervision.*

f.   Water is subject to change in state from liquid to solid to gas.

g.   In order to evaporate, water takes its latent heat from its surroundings.

h.   Some materials float, some sink.

16.4   Types of Aquatic Features

Wherever possible, preserve existing natural water features. Natural streams, creeks, ponds, and puddles enhance play. Consider them within the context of overall park design.

The most common aquatic features are:

a.   Marshes

b.   Ponds

c.   Pools

d.   Streams and creeks

e.   Channels

f.   Fountains

g.   Hose-filled ponds or streams

h.   Water tables and trays

16.4.1 Waterplay Areas (Seattle, 1986)

Waterplay areas are powerful playground attractors. Water can be used by the child in many ways: to splash, pour, mix with sand and dirt, float boats, etc. Acoustic qualities are attractive and valued.

Wherever feasible, provide water as a play element.

Waterplay areas can be wading pools, spray pools, play pools, streams, bubblers, sprinklers, troughs, or even a running hose bib in a sand box; the possibilities are endless.

Safety is a primary concern. Contexts vary from "body contact" waterplay features to natural resource features. Water depth must be carefully considered, on physical and programmatic circumstances. Far more research is needed concerning specific design standards for water features. As drowning is a risk, caution must be exercised.

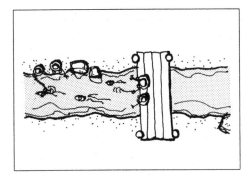

240 *Bridges are very attractive to children and provide a simple means of getting close to water.*

241 *Stepping stones allow close contact with water.*

242 *Child-operated water pump.*

The following are critical considerations:

- Areas around water features must be nonskid and well drained.
- Water areas must be sunny and protected from the wind.
- Plumbing and pump systems for water features must be simple, with a minimum number of moving parts.
- Forms and construction methods for water features must be simple and robust.
- Provide for adult supervision in waterplay areas.

16.4.2 Hose-Filled Temporary Ponds (CMHC, 1979)

A simple play stream or an elaborate recirculating and filtering system can be devised, depending on use, funds, and climate.

a. A stream may be of any size and shape providing it drains to the lowest point.

b. The depth of water should be 6 inches maximum. Careful judgement should be exercised according to the age and abilities of the children.

c. The stream bottom should be either reinforced concrete or asphalt.

d. The edge of the stream should be lined with flat smooth stones laid in mortar.

e. A footbridge may take any shape.

f. The drain should be located at the lowest point. It should be connected to a dry well or sewer depending on local conditions and requirements. A screw-in plug attached to the bottom with a chain is a standard plumbing house fixture; a screen mesh at the top of the drain should be provided.

g. Islands of wild grass or sand can be added design features.

16.5   Design Criteria for Water Settings

a. **Varied Movement**. Both horizontal and vertical movement exemplify the innately liquid character of water.

b. **Continuity**. Water works as a continuous system at many scales, in both natural and people-made systems. Elements, functions, and forms should be juxtaposed and integrated into a total system, albeit at a small scale.

c. **Channel Character**. Streams can be wide or narrow, shallow or deep, fast or slow, rough or smooth, straight or curved.

243 *Wandering channels allow more water access.*

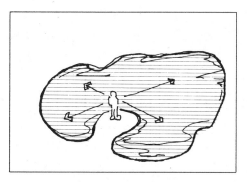

244 *Headlands give an overview and island sense.*

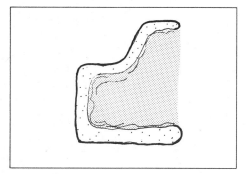

245 *"Vernal" puddles fill with rainfall.*

d. **Edge Character.** Both streams and ponds can have a wide variety of edges from hard to soft, deep to shallow, fenced to unfenced, etc.

e. **Balanced Impact.** Design strategies should maximize user-impact and minimize environmental impact:

1) Protection of the land-water interface can be achieved by fences, barriers and rocks. Rocky shorelines, stepping stones, or platform projections are all good impact reducers, because they help keep feet clear of the fragile meeting of land and water.

2) Marshes are particularly impact-resistant, provided they retain a couple of inches of water—most kids really don't like getting muddy.

3) Waterplay elements located away from life-support elements will help draw high energy play activity away from fragile resources.

f. **Interpenetration.** Forms can be designed that support close contact between users and water. They include wandering channels, deltas, headlands, stepping stones, inlets, and bridges.

g. **Multiuse.** Water features should be designed for use when empty (roller skating, wheeled-toy play) or for winter use (skating, sliding) in cold climates.

16.6   Hard Surface Settings

Play areas often contain large areas of asphalt that in effect are giant catchment basins.

a. **Hoses** can be used to explore the subtle variations in surface and slope in an apparently uniform asphalt terrain. Rates of flow can be measured in different places to assess relative gradients. Natural lines of drainage can be plotted for future reference.

b. **"Vernal" Pools or Puddles** can be small, permanent modifications to the flow of water, if located away from main foot traffic. They provide a modest waterplay setting. Over time, silt and debris will collect against the "dam," providing a microhabitat for small plants and organisms. Studies can be made of the changes.

Paved areas can be designed to create puddles but should be limited to a specific area. Puddles should have a maximum depth of 1 inch and a maximum area of 1 square yard per event (Seattle, 1986).

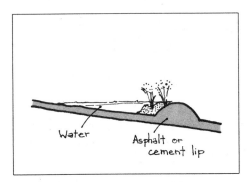

246 *Small plants grow out of accumulated silt.*

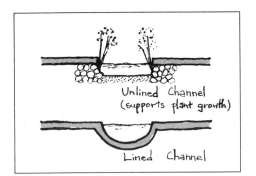

247 *Potholes and channels provide water access, too.*

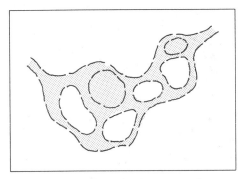

248 *Deltas are a simple means of providing a "hard" water system.*

c. **Potholes and Channels** can be designed into asphalt areas in various shapes and sizes, coincident with natural drainage lines (which may be discovered in hose experiments). Channels can be straight or curved. In a short period of time, plants will invade and create a modest aquatic habitat.

d. **Deltas and Pools.** By making excavations bigger, deeper, and/or more complex, a more varied system can be created.

16.7 Diversified Hard and Soft Settings

A number of play elements can be cut out or built into asphalt surfaces to make a diverse setting, including willow thickets, minimarshes, pools, and channels.

16.8 Soft Settings

Soft settings can be developed in nonasphalted areas. They can be more subtle, complex, and extensive. The system illustrated here contains two ponds, a marsh, an island, a stream, and a bridge (the Environmental Yard, Berkeley, California).

A scaled down version of this kind of setting would be feasible, if adequately protected. The choice of features and their juxtaposition are highly dependent on the disposition of the site, topography, and drainage pattern. Many alternatives are possible.

16.8.1 Water Circulation/Recirculation Ponds

Ponds are fascinating to children.

Ponds should have gently sloping sides to allow children to play safely. They should be a maximum of 14 inches deep. Water should be kept clean and changed regularly; an efficient drainage and filter system is essential. By installing an electric pump, the water can be made to circulate and flow along a stream into the pond. A stream of running water provides marvelous opportunities for play, such as making dams and water falls. Rafts and boats can be floated on the pond. St. Francis Park in Portland, Oregon, has an outstanding example of a recirculating waterplay setting.

If natural rainfall is insufficient to keep ponds topped up, they will need to be connected to the public water supply, regulated by a float valve assembly. Recirculation systems are required for larger installations.

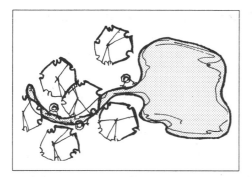

249 *Inlets provide additional shoreline and an intimate waterplay setting away from the large pond.*

16.9 Pools, Fountains, Cascades and Sprays

These features provide play-oriented water activity and also promote diversity. Many designs are possible.

a. **Pools** (Seattle, 1986)

1) Locate in sunny, highly visible areas.

2) Pools must have a shelter house nearby for:

- safe storage of chlorine and chemicals;
- supervision visibility and safety;
- storage of waterplay equipment and props.

3) Pools must have adult supervision when water is being used.

4) Provide benches at pools in both sun and shade locations.

5) Spray areas and areas of shallow running water are preferable to standing water.

6) Use a fine spray mist that is comfortable in all-weather situations.

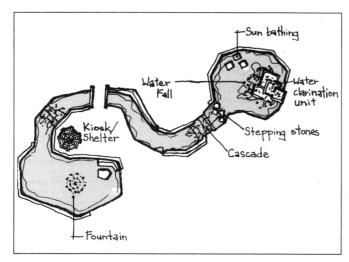

250 *Prototypical recirculating aquatic system with full water treatment.*

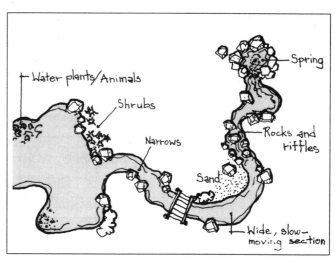

251 *Prototypical "soft," recirculating aquatic setting.*

252   *Waterfalls are a stimulating feature for people of all ages; sheer drops, however, can be hazardous.*

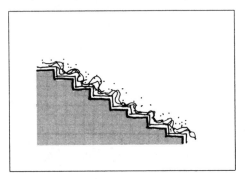

253   *Cascades avoid the sheer drops of waterfalls but achieve a similar effect of falling water.*

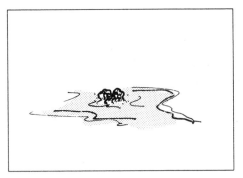

254   *Rocks and riffles provide added interest to running water.*

7)   Spray areas and water collecting areas must have nonslip surfaces.

8)   Provide several depth areas in all pools: shallow parts for tots and parents; deeper parts for older children. Undulating bottom surfaces provide an exciting variety of water spaces. The slope toward the center of the pool should be less than 1:12.

9)   Provide several drains and water sources for any kind of pool. This lessens the time needed to fill and drain the pool and provides play opportunities for more children.

10) Place fill and drain valves in locked boxes above grade or in a shelter if immediately adjacent to pool.

11) Provide a hillside, on-grade water slide wherever possible with a convenient hose bib or water source for continuous running water when in use.

12) Provide many different sources of spray which can be easily installed by a play supervisor:

- quick coupling, stand-pipe hose attachments;
- surface spouts;
- hose bibs, hoses, nozzles, fire hydrants.

b.   **Fountains** (Seattle, 1986)

Consideration should be given for other types of water spray such as fountains and waterfalls.

16.9.1 Water Entrapment (Seattle, 1986)

In programmed play settings, where feasible, allow water to be manipulated with stoppers and other moveable water entrapment devices along water courses.

16.9.2 Aeration and Stagnation (Seattle, 1986)

All water in public contact must meet all applicable health and safety standards and be aerated, chemically treated, or replaced as necessary to prevent stagnation.

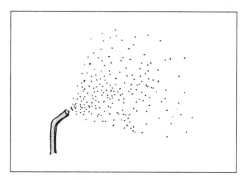

255 *A fine "mist" spray provides a simple cooling-off function.*

256 *Fountains provide an important aesthetic dimension to playgrounds.*

257 *Water tables provide access to water for children using wheelchairs. There are many design alternatives.*

16.10 Watertables (Gordon, 1972)

Water is a most intriguing material to young children, yet it often lies beyond the restricted reach of children using wheelchairs or of hands that control crutches and are not free to touch, feel, and make contact. Watertables can make this basic material more accessible to children. Watertables should be designed at graded heights to allow for children of different sizes.

Watertables should meet sanitation standards and be at heights accessible to a variety of user groups (Seattle, 1986). To allow for wheelchair access, clearance of 27 inches should be provided under the watertable with a clear floor or ground space of 36 inches by 55 inches for forward approach. Ideally, to allow for adequate forward reach, the upper rim of the watertable should not be higher than 30 inches above the floor or ground surface. However, the difference in these dimensions (3 inches) means that the water will be too shallow for adequate play value (the bottom of the table structure could be almost 3 inches thick). The only way to accommodate forward approach is to lower the 27-inch clearance limit (say, to 24 inches as for drinking fountains) and assume that people in wheechairs have removable arm rests.

17. SAND SETTINGS

Sand, along with water, is the most popular play material because of its softness and malleability. When combined with water, it has even more potential.

Planning Criteria

Play Value. Sand is an excellent medium for creative play and social interaction. It is easy to move and mold. It can be dug, sifted, sculpted, poured, thrown, and drawn upon. It is the ultimate "loose part."

Programming Potential. In some ways, very structured activities are unnecessary because of sand's inherent play characteristics. Combined with water, sand has good potential for construction play.

Play Leadership. Leaders need to appreciate the potential of sand for varied play experiences.

Safety. Sand is commonly used as a safety surface, although it is not accessible. Other potential problems include broken glass and animal feces. When sand is spilt on concrete or asphalt, it can create a slippery surface.

Risk Management. Adequate containment is important. Regular inspection and maintenance is needed. Do not locate sand areas next to residential backyards where domestic animals might be attracted. Sand will go rancid if covered from light.

Accessibility. This is a difficult problem which can be solved to some degree by providing ramps or by rolling out plastic carpet over the sand surface to support wheelchairs. (This should not be considered a solution for providing access to play equipment, only for providing access to sandplay areas.) Be aware that sand in bearings of wheelchairs can cause problems. Multilevel sand areas at wheelchair height are perhaps the best solution to provide accessible sand play.

Integration. Sand offers good potential for parallel play. Cooperative play and social interaction can result from children playing in close proximity in sand areas.

Management/Maintenance. Pro-sand policies are required. In many instances it may be preferable to use tan bark or wood chips as a surfacing material. Even when sand is used as a surface under play equipment, separate sandplay areas should be provided.

17.1   Sand on Playgrounds

Sand can serve both as a play material and as a safety surface. *Sandplay* areas should be explicitly designated.

A playground sand area should be like a beach—deep, wide, and near to water. It should be near a path and have a ramped approach so that children on wheels can get in easily and not fall in by mistake. Playing with hoses and buckets of water in the sand is fun and easily managed if there is a supply of water nearby. If the sand area is at least four feet deep with good drainage below and no covering over it, it will be perfectly hygienic. Rain, air, and sunshine keep it so. If it is exposed to falling leaves in autumn or to cats and dogs at nighttime, a fine-meshed cover can be put over it (HAPA, 1978). Rolled canvas covers can also be used.

17.2   Sand Playability Criteria

a.   **A small grain size** will allow the material to be molded and to "stick together."

b.   **Low dust content** will minimize the "dirty" aspects of material sticking to clothes and limbs, and reduce the risk of dust being blown into children's eyes.

c.   **Moldability** makes sand easy to "smooth out" and incorporate fine detail when sculpted.

d.   **Cakiness** allows material to remain stuck together after molding.

e.   **Digability** makes digging with hands or small implements easy.

f.   **Specification** for sand areas or boxes shall (Seattle, 1986):

1)   Be a balanced mix of particle sizes ranging from coarse sand (not more than 1.5 mm) to very fine;

2)   Pack well when moist;

3)   Be well-washed, clean, free of dirt, clay, silt oxides or iron, or other contaminants.

g.   **Depth** of sand in larger sandplay areas shall be between 18 and 24 inches (Seattle, 1986). The sandpit shall be deep enough (about four feet) for children and leaders to dig using proper garden spades (HAPA, 1978).

258   *Sand should be 4 feet deep (HAPA)/ 18 to 24 inches (Seattle).*

259   *Sandplay areas need shade in summer and sun in winter. They should be sheltered from cold wind.*

17.3   Design Principles

Sandplay areas are one of the most commonly misdesigned elements in playgrounds and parks. Sound design principles include:

a.   **Ambient microclimate.** This is essential for extensive sand play. Shade in hot weather and sun in cool weather should be provided with shelter from prevailing winds. All sand play areas should be sited to receive sun for part of the day for natural cleansing (Seattle, 1986).

   4)   Shelter from prevailing winds.

b.   **Enclosure.** Sand material must be kept in place to thwart children from disturbing or running through the creative sand play of others. Enclosures provide a psychologically calm atmosphere. Shelf-like play surfaces can be designed in, along with places to sit or "perch" with peers. Enclosures must be made wide enough to support such activities.

   1)   If using concrete, provide an apron with a minimum of 18 inches around the sandpit on all sides, flush with grade for sweeping sand back into the pit (Seattle, 1986).

   2)   Provide lids for sand areas when practical. Lids, preferably screen material, must allow light and air circulation for natural cleansing (Seattle, 1986).

   3)   Sandpits should be designed with a minimum 3-foot wide sand walk-off apron. The apron surface should slope 2% to 3% into the sandpit to permit sand to flow back into the pit (Los Angeles, 1984).

   4)   The perimeter enclosure of sandpits should be level. Sandpits should have positive drainage systems, preferably a storm drain, and daylight. Level sandpits are required because sand flows and tends to seek its own level (Los Angeles, 1984).

c.   **Accessibility.** Sand pits should be designed to facilitate transfer of children from wheelchairs to the playing surface. Alternatively, sheets of rubber can be laid across sand surfaces to provide wheelchair access.

Provide handrails along the perimeter to help youngsters maintain balance as they go into and out of the area independently (Gordon, 1972).

d.   **Size.** Sand areas must be large enough for many children to play without getting in each other's way.

260   *Enclosures to sandplay areas can incorporate "play shelves" and barriers against the spread of sand.*

261   *Sand areas must be accessible to children and adults.*

262   *Shelves provide sitting places and...*

263   *...a support for sand play with loose parts.*

264   *Natural elements such as rocks and vegetation add interest and additional play opportunities.*

e.   **Play Surfaces.** Sand tables, rock, or stone worktops and shelves provide necessary support.

f.   **Toy Play.** Children like to play in sand with small toys—especially pocket-sized trucks, animals, and vehicles—or they find other props including on-site vegetation. This activity is supported by providing a variety of work and play surfaces.

g.   **Adequate Drainage.** This is necessary to avoid waterlogging. The best methods will depend on site conditions.

Provide controllable drainage to allow for programmed moisturizing of sand for compaction (Seattle, 1986).

h.   **Vegetation.** Vegetation growing within or immediately adjacent to sand areas greatly enhances the range of dramatic play by supplying plant parts (Moore, 1986b). Many types of plants are feasible, from grass and wild plants to mature trees.

i.   **Water Supply.** Water is essential for sand play. A spring-loaded or dripping, tamper-proof faucet works best. Hoses may also be used.

Provide a limited-flow water source next to sand areas, such as hand water pumps or trickling water troughs, to allow for sand and water play. Locate drinking fountains away from sandplay areas (Seattle, 1986).

j.   **Boundary Enclosure.** A variety of places for individual and small group activities should be provided. Sand areas should be sized and shaped to encourage smaller groups of 1 to 4 children to play together; these sub-areas can be linked to create a larger sand area, accommodating more children overall (Seattle, 1986).

k.   **Separation.** Sandplay areas must be separated from active play equipment (Seattle, 1986).

Keep sandpits far enough away from any building, to prevent tracking sand onto floors (Los Angeles, 1984).

265   *A water supply should be located adjacent to sandplay areas.*

266   *Separation of sandplay areas from zones of high activity is necessary.*

267   *Elevated sand surfaces let children using wheelchairs interact with peers.*

l.   **Age Groups.** A variety of sandplay opportunities should be provided. Sand for toddlers should be at a shallow sand bench or table to allow stand-up play (Seattle, 1986).

Sand play for 4-year-olds and older can be at ground level. Several smaller areas are better than a giant one. Children play in groups of one to four, making tunnels, canals, castles, and mountains.

17.4   Sandpits (CMHC, 1979)

Control of sand overspill is helped by a center "table." Another deterrent is to round the outside edge of the pit with a half log, curved side up, attached to the wood timber sides. If bricks or concrete are used, this curved edge is easily accomplished. Cobblestones or flat paving stones around the sandpit help take sand off the feet and improve the appearance (but can be difficult for children using wheelchairs to traverse). The depth of sand below the edge also prevents blowing; however, it may need a step down for little children and a ramp for children using wheelchairs.

Hedges or another type of wind screen may be necessary for some sites.

If cats are a problem, nylon netting that allows rain and purifying sun through can be stretched over the sand when not in use (never cover completely as sand will go rancid). A handy rake or scooper permanently stored nearby is a simpler solution. Sand must have water available and be kept damp. Storage close at hand for sand toys is necessary.

17.6   Raised Sand Areas

Sandboxes should be provided both at ground level and above ground level for wheelchair users without transfer skills.

A raised sand area can be built into a berm. The raised end should provide 27 inches vertical clearance and 18 to 24 inches between the edge of the box and the base.

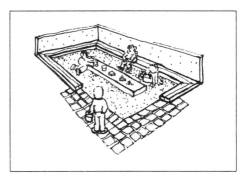

268 *Prototypical sandplay area with a table in the center.*

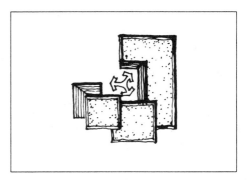

269 *Multilevel sandtables provide the greatest range of accessibility.*

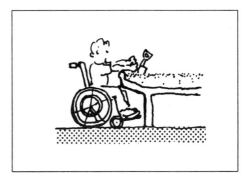

270 *Sandtables can accommodate children using wheelchairs.*

271 *The corners of sandtables allow children to play together.*

17.5   Elevated Sandtables

An elevated area containing sand or water can provide access for wheelchair users (children, parents, or caregivers). Flat areas are also useful for toy cars, crafts, etc.

They should be located on platforms of varying heights with the table positioned at the joining of two platforms. This position allows one table to accommodate wheelchairs of different heights. A fully accessible, forward approach will face the same dilemma as for watertables (see Chapter 16, Section 10).

18. PLAY PROPS AND MANIPULATIVE SETTINGS

Props should be recognized as an essential part of any play environment. They help children manipulate their environment to stimulate imaginary and dramatic play. There are two major categories: 1) a wide variety of small natural and synthetic "found objects," such as insects and small mammals, sticks and stones, bottle tops and popsicle sticks, logs and rocks, plant parts, sand and dirt; and 2) larger manufactured items such as modular systems, wheeled toys, and dress-up clothes. Play props provide an immediate low-cost method of enhancing existing play settings.

Manipulative settings range from found objects in fixed settings to elaborate adventure playgrounds where children continually construct and alter their play environment.

Planning Criteria

Play Value. Play props and manipulative settings provide critical support for social, imaginative, and creative play (PLAE, 1981–87). They promote:

a. Fine motor skill development, which is as important as gross motor skill development.

b. Social-emotional development stimulated by intimate social interaction.

c. Cognitive skills inherent in manipulating the physical environment to solve child-initiated problems.

d. Independent living and self-management skills by giving children a sense of control over their environment.

e. Social-organizational skills, providing children an opportunity to work together to implement their own projects.

f. Self-concept development which is supported by children's increased opportunities to differentiate themselves from their surroundings by using props.

g. Language skills providing experiential richness and social interaction, thus stimulating a greater diversity of verbal expression.

Programming Potential. Play props are essential to creative programming.

Play Leadership. All play leaders should be skilled in the creation and use of play props and manipulative play settings.

Safety. Very small loose parts can be dangerous to small children who may suck on and swallow them.

Risk Management. Adequate storage facilities are needed to keep unused loose parts out of the active play environment. Children should checkout and return items as part of a monitored distribution program. Hazardous items should be discarded.

Accessibility. Many props are more or less accessible.

Integration. Play props offer tremendous opportunities for integration. They encourage children to work together.

Management/Maintenance. Policies are needed to recognize the importance of play props and support their use. Checkout systems are also needed. A low cost, local source for simple play props should be identified and assessed.

Areas where play props are used must be designed carefully and screened to avoid unsightly appearance to passersby.

Many manipulative settings and most larger props require supervision and effective play leadership.

272   *Manipulative settings offer more play value.*

273   *Play settings with loose materials stimulate interactions between children of different abilities.*

274   *Fixed-but-moving parts, such as gates, must be recognized as play objects.*

18.1   The Value of Manipulative Settings

An effective play environment should allow for combinations of fixed features and loose props. Fixed, open-ended features provide a beckoning "stage," stimulating children to build onto them. Children use an undulating wall, fence, or ground surface to run toy cars along; they build a shelter between two shrubs; or use pieces of vegetation to make "pizza" on a park bench.

Play props are especially important in unsupervised settings. When the stimulus of play leadership is missing, children must rely on their own inventiveness to manipulate and shape their personal environment. Play props can be used in any number of inter-changeable ways, at many scales, ranging from an individual child playing with a few twigs, a softdrink can, or dirt, to large scale group construction of "forts" and "club-houses," to dramatic play using dress-up clothes or races using wheeled toys.

Children must be able to manipulate and interchange parts of their environment. It is a fundamental aspect of normal development, and essential for children with disabilities who depend on touch for much of their environmental information. Play settings should contain a continuum of fixed and movable parts including:

a.   Small "found objects" (plant parts, sand, cartons)

b.   Larger manufactured parts (large blocks, tires, boards, etc.) with adequate leader-ship and storage.

c   Fixed-but-moving parts, such as (small scale) latches, door knobs, hooks, gears and handles; and (large scale) gates, turnstiles, windows, and doors.

d.   Fixed parts, such as structures, and bounded areas which provide for perma-nence and stability (adapted from Schneekloth, 1985).

18.2   Empowerment: Children Making a Place of Their Own (adapted from AEC, 1980)

Responsive elements allow a child to learn properties of the physical environment and develop skills in manipulating it.

A physical environment that responds to a child's manipulations encourages exploration and discovery. Amorphous materials, like sand, water, and mud, invite activity and interaction. Play props can be manipulated, put together, and torn apart. They are the ingredients that children use to make their own environments.

Play props might be wood and tools, large pieces of lightweight styrofoam, fabric, old tires, or modular blocks. Children might make their own forts, cities, or teepees, and then tear them down for the next project. Play props allow children to test their relationship to the physical environment and learn relationships between cause and effect in a safe, free-play situation.

Place-making is empowering for everyone, but especially for children, as they are rarely given the opportunity to build with anything larger than blocks. The opportunity for children with special needs is even rarer, because there is often an exaggerated concern for their safety and protection. The confidence and ability to adapt one's physical environment is an important step toward independent living.

When children identify an area as their own, they will take better care of it than if it were a public space (Moore, 1989a).

18.3   Types of Manipulative Settings

There are six main types of manipulative settings. They provide varied play potentials and a continuum of control by the child: **found objects** or ad hoc props in existing settings; **purpose-made props** such as those created by children or leaders during structured activity programs; **modular systems** designed for user applications; **large wheeled vehicles** that users can manipulate at will; **adventure playgrounds** created from scratch, where all parts and their dispositions are decided by the users; and **natural settings** that can be integrated into all five of the preceding types.

a.   **Found Objects in Fixed Settings.** Play settings usually contain small play props. These include:

1)   Small objects and materials. All manner of sticks, stones, dirt, and dead leaves can be used in two ways:

- As "tools" they enable the child to interact more fully with another material, e.g., to scratch dirt with a stick, throw a rock in a pond, or bang a piece of play equipment to make a noise.
- As "props" in dramatic fantasy play, e.g., stones as "money," dead leaves as "soup," or a piece of wood as a "microphone."

Often such materials are swept away, the setting becomes too tidy, and the play value is lost. In adult eyes, they are so small that their play value is overlooked. But for young children they represent valuable play materials.

275 *Pebbles, stones, shells, sticks, and small toys are essential loose parts.*

276 *Sand and dirt—the most common loose play items.*

277 *The use of most manufactured objects must be carefully monitored.*

A major problem of having play props in an asphalted, fixed equipment, or structured area is that they look out of place, and so small-scale that they appear to be litter. Vegetated areas help disguise play props so they look less obtrusive and become part of the setting.

2) **Small Manufactured Toys.** Children bring or have supplied on-site their own small toys (cars, trucks, dolls, etc.) to use as props. Small wheeled toys of all sizes are particularly important.

3) **Sand, Dirt, and Water.** These materials may be used individually or in combination with each other, and with small objects.

4) **Ephemeral Objects.** These include manufactured items such as cardboard boxes, plastic cartons, softdrink cans—"bits and pieces" which find their way onto the site by accident (or by design). Part of their attraction is the surprise factor. But such materials quickly deteriorate, needing careful management and disposal.

Natural materials are also valuable, such as scrap lumber, logs, and truckloads of clean leaves for making leaf piles in the fall (often available from the local parks and recreation department).

Recycled material can sometimes be sanded, painted, or varnished to prolong its life. Large storage cupboards may be necessary to protect the more attractive items from being taken away. Replacing, repairing, and constantly adding new loose material is worth the effort in terms of child development and sustained play value.

5) **Heavy loose parts.** Some items are too heavy to be moved off the ground, although they can be moved around by groups of children working together. Large blocks of lumber are a good example. Because of their weight, they are not likely to be scattered all over the site, so they are easier and less time-consuming to maintain.

The heaviest loose parts should only be movable by adults and can serve such purposes as space definition.

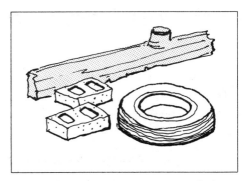

278 *"Stuff" includes all manner of larger, longer-life props.*

279 *Dress-up clothes of all types are essential for dramatic play.*

280 *Swedish Blocks and Playchest.*

b.   Purpose-Made Props

These include objects with a fixed form (puzzles) and manufactured parts with a flexible or modular form (lightweight panels or blocks). Adequate storage and supervision is essential (Seattle, 1986).

1)   **Dress-up Clothes.** A large chest of dress-up clothes (collected together and replenished from time-to-time) is an essential resource for dramatic play programming.

2)   **Foam Mattress** (Gordon, 1972). For children with restricted movement who are unable to walk or to sit alone without support, a foam mattress can be extremely valuable. Using the mattress, a child can be prone but still experience the sensation of open space, can see the sky instead of a ceiling, can become aware of clouds and of a tree responding to winds, and can observe the play of other children.

3)   **Inflatables.** Inflatables have a great potential for use by children with and without disabilities. This type of equipment use requires further research. Inflatables are forms which contain air. They can be easily blown up or deflated for easy storage. This type of equipment requires supervision.

c.   Modular Systems

Manufactured play props, like giant tinker toys or outdoor modular blocks, can be provided under supervision.

Adult-size ladders can be sawn in half. Adult-size sawhorses can be used by older children, but some smaller sizes are suggested. Barrels, sturdy boxes, and large containers can also be added (CMHC, 1979).

Play settings can be designed to be added to when the play leader arrives with a kit of parts. Movable walls can be suspended from permanent structures. Other props can be added by children.

1)   **Swedish Blocks and Storage Playchest** (CMHC, 1979). These blocks are similar to kindergarten blocks but are designed for outdoor use. The addition of boards and other loose material extend their play value. The playchest is sturdy and houses 145 blocks; it also serves as a playhouse, store, spaceship, or other play object. The double-hinged top lies flat against the back to discourage use except for locking up. The blocks are expensive initially, but they fascinate children of all ages and are indestructible. Quan-

281 *Using simple materials, children can construct their own village.*

tity is very important—you can never have too many. Specifications are listed below.

- The chest
  - 1500 mm (5 ft.) long, 900 mm (3 ft.) deep, 900 mm (3 ft.) wide.
  - Must be treated with exterior finish and could have a padlock.
  - Double-hinged lid flat against back when not in use.
  - Drain holes in the bottom.
  - Raisers approximately 38 x 90 mm. (1-1/2 x 3-1/2 in.)
  - Drop-down front for clambering in and playing "store." Support with chains and heavy duty hinges.
- The blocks
  - Cut lengths of 65 x 140 mm (3 x 6 – nominal) hardwood:
    - 12 @ 1200 mm (4 ft.) long
    - 24 @ 600 mm (2 ft.) long
    - 169 @ 300 mm (1 ft.) long.
  - Round all edges. Finish blocks with mixture of good, heavy duty, hardwood floor sealer plus colored oil stain.

2) **Hollow Blocks** (CMHC, 1977). These are specially recommended for preschool play groups where the size of the group is controlled. Sizes are units of one another and form modular systems. The sizes, shapes, and weights were designed by Caroline Pratt, U.S. educator, to fill specific developmental needs. With the addition of boards, ladders, and other miscellaneous props, a play group may need no other equipment. Shallow storage means easy access and clean-up. Where vandalism is not a problem, they can be stacked against a wall by size and left out all year. They are great fun in the winter.

3) **Movable Adventure Village.** Developed by PLAE, Inc., this building system uses standard 3/4-inch thick-walled PVC pipe and fittings. Cardboard and cloth infill panels complete the package. It is ideally suited to use with a traveling playbus program. Within a few minutes, in a local park or shopping center, a group of children and play leaders can erect a "village" environment that can then become a setting for a thematic workshop such as "Wild West," "Living on the Frontier" or "Adventure Village."

282   *Wooden boards and boxes are favorite play props.*

283   *Plastic pipes and fittings are a type of modular system.*

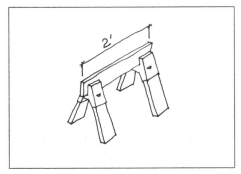

284   *Sawhorses can be made with standard brackets.*

d.   **Large Wheeled Vehicles.** (HAPA, 1978)

It is very important for children who are physically disabled to have the means for independent mobility.

New methods for allowing independent exploration are being invented. Various commercially produced vehicles including large bicycles, hand-propelled tricycles, and garden trucks can be useful. HAPA has specially-designed wheeled toys.

When buying wheeled toys, make sure they are robust enough to withstand intense use. Note that something designed for a particular child may not be suitable for others. Solid tires are preferable to inflatable and industrial wheels are stronger than toy ones.

Special electrically operated vehicles can be bought or made for children with severe physical disabilities. These are naturally very popular with many children so it is best that such vehicles are kept locked away until needed.

Battery-driven, hand-propelled, and push vehicles should be considered, including old prams, baby walkers, supermarket trolleys, bicycles, and garden trucks. A bean bag or a specially designed wooden corner seat placed in a trolley or truck, for example, can help children be more mobile.

e.   **Adventure Playgrounds** (Allen, 1968; Bengtsson, 1970; Shier, 1984). A concept from Europe, adventure playgrounds are similar to other manipulative settings, but with one critical difference—they are staffed by trained play leaders.

Play leadership describes the multirole relationship between children, adults, and the community, requiring special training and experience. In some countries it exists as a separate profession (animation, social pedagogy) alongside allied education and recreation professions.

A skilled play leader increases the scope of adventure play by:

1)   Providing tools (hammers, saws, nails).

2)   Managing construction materials.

3)   Disposing of materials that have lost their usefulness.

4)   Inspecting children's constructions and play sites for safety.

5)   Involving children nondirectively in constructive activity.

285 *Special wheeled vehicles adapted to children with disabilities offer valuable play experiences.*

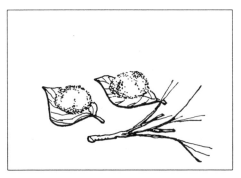

286 *Plant parts make excellent play props.*

287 *Adventure Playgrounds with trained play leaders are the most developed form of manipulable play settings.*

6) Being a role-model, friend, and confidant to children.

7) Maintaining liaison with community groups and individuals to facilitate communication and interaction—specifically through voluntary participation and contribution to the playground in time, money, or materials.

An adventure playground may also contain an enclosed building for storage, shelter, meetings, and social events.

Adventure Playgrounds are the most developed example of responsive play settings, but because of the difficulty of managing and maintaining them, they are rare. Ways should be found to incorporate adventure play elements into designated play settings.

f.   **Natural Settings.** Natural materials provide many opportunities for children to manipulate their environment. Rocks, pebbles, leaves, sticks, twigs, and branches can be built into boats, forts, castles, and costumes. They can be stacked, linked, piled, poured. Children's imaginative use of these objects is boundless (Seattle, 1986). Children have such a strong affiliation with vegetation as a play resource that it is vitally important to ensure a good supply (see Chapter 13, Trees/Vegetation for further details).

Natural settings provide good support for manipulative play. Low maintenance vegetation areas should be set aside in playgrounds and parks for this purpose.

Settings of any size containing dirt, water, trees, and flowering plants can provide a setting for manipulative play, if designed and managed appropriately. In park landscapes, such play functions may not be recognized. This inevitably results in conflict between management and children, when plants get broken and/or dirt is dug up and scattered around.

Suitable materials include plants such as bamboo and willow. "Prunings" from streets and parks may be available from the city parks department. If this is not done, children may deliberately harvest other plants and run the risk of being labeled "vandals." Larger pieces of vegetation are suitable for constructing self-designed shelters, forts, huts, and clubhouses.

1) Select plant materials near play areas which recover quickly from being pulled and broken (Seattle, 1986).

2) Organize maintenance crews to provide piles of natural play props in some play areas on a seasonal basis: piles of autumn leaves, a yard of extra dirt, a half-load of tree clippings. Expect to do a "sweep-up" later (Seattle, 1986).

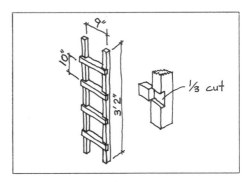

288   *Short ladders make useful play props, but need careful supervision.*

In areas of 1500 sq. ft. or larger, a considerable variety of manipulable play can be provided. The area should be dirt-surfaced and enclosed with a strong, high fence. An accessible gate (42 inches wide) and a "squeeze-through" entrance (9 to 12 inches wide) should be provided, plus a larger 8-foot gate for vehicle access.

Suitable building materials for use by children include scrap lumber, prunings from the city parks department, cardboard boxes, and packing crates. Corners, edges, and other areas which are small enough to be spanned with available materials are ideal sites for building a shelter.

Props which find their way onto the rest of the playground can be periodically returned to the compound. Every so often materials should be replenished and unusable materials discarded.

18.4   Setting Management

Manipulative settings and play props must be carefully designed and managed by adults who understand the importance and function of manipulative play. Parent education must be stressed. One of the best ways to promote the concept of props and loose parts is through programs that use them to demonstrate their potential for integration. Community artists have a critical role to play here.

Play props always present management issues—real and imagined. Specific settings must be created to provide for loose parts, so they can be both available and manageable. Adequate storage must be provided, especially for manufactured props. (In West Germany, storage sheds are provided in parks and managed by paid, retired people.)

Playground and park settings must be viewed as dynamic, ever-changing environments that respond to user needs.

19. STAGE SETTINGS

To support group productions, performances, and a sense of community, children and adults need a well-defined, slightly elevated, accessible stage space and adjacent audience space.

Planning Criteria

Play Value. A stage supports dramatic play, performance activities, and presentations of self and teamwork.

Programming Potential. Stages are places for informal gatherings, community events, festivals, and performances.

Play Leadership. Leaders should understand the role of performance and be trained to use the full potential of staging facilities.

Safety. Drop-offs at the edge of the stage must be avoided.

Risk Management. Signs are required to indicate proper use.

Accessibility. Ramps or other access must be provided onto the stage and accessible seating must be included in the audience viewing area.

Integration. Stages allow children to feel "on stage," both as an audience and as performers.

Management. Stage facilities offer excellent opportunities for community-wide participation in parks and play settings. Such participation should be encouraged and facilitated. Policies and schedules should be established to coordinate the use of stage facilities.

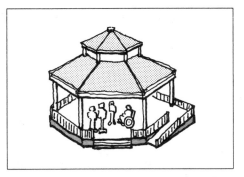

289 *Traditional spaces such as gazebos make excellent staging places.*

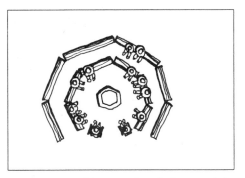

290 *Accessible campfire circles or mini-arenas provide a basic staging area for average-sized groups.*

291 *In this accessible stage for up to 15 children, wooden posts are nailable and support all manner of "scenery" and shade props.*

19.1 **Types of Staging Areas**

a. **Verandas, Gazebos, Terraces, and Decks.** These traditional indoor-outdoor elements serve an important social purpose. Many variations can be designed. In fact, in most climates, partially enclosed, covered spaces must be provided in order to make effective use of the outdoors.

Such structures have great potential as staging areas and can provide a major support for program activity. Picnic tables inside such structures can provide convenient work settings. Storage should be incorporated.

b. **Campfire Circles/Mini-Arenas.** Depending on the number of concentric rings provided, large groups can be accommodated. A fireplace is not essential, but should be given serious consideration.

There are several ways to construct campfire circle forms to accommodate groups of up to 25. If there are more than two or three rings, they should be "raked" to assist visual and acoustic contact. Circles can be made of utility poles, railroad ties, or lengths of tree trunk. Accessibility for wheelchair users should be taken into account.

c. **Group Program Spaces.** The primary function is to provide comfortable places where groups of children and leaders can meet for program activities. The maximum feasible group is about fifteen.

Spaces can be designed to serve functions such as eating and hanging out for older kids and teenagers. They can be places where neighbors and parents can meet informally, especially if adjacent to preschool facilities.

d. **Stages and Arenas.** Groups larger than 15 or so need special consideration. Spaces are needed that cater to groups ranging in size from 25 to a couple hundred or more, to accommodate dramatic art, mime, music activities, and large community gatherings. Spaces of this size must be located away from traffic noise and visual distractions. Large arenas or stages consume space and have a high cost relative to their social utility, yet the availability of such a facility can have a substantial effect on interaction and development of children and the community at large.

e. **Amphitheaters** (Bunin et al., 1980). Steps and narrow aisles in amphitheaters can be troublesome barriers for wheelchair users. Designing an accessible amphitheater will benefit all patrons by allowing them to choose their seats with minimum effort and maximum safety. The amphitheater illustrated in Figure 294 is

292   Stages can be altered to fit pro-gram needs.

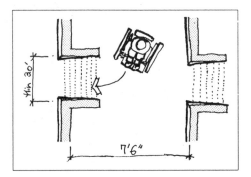

293   Aisles should accommodate wheel-chair access.

raked steeply enough to require steps, but is also graded and ramped to provide wheelchair access to four of the five seating levels and the stage. The design can be adapted easily to fit site conditions and programming needs.

1)   Provide firm, wide paths leading to the amphitheater and support facilities (restrooms, parking, concessions).

2)   Ensure that pathway surfaces are slip resistant whether they are wet or dry.

3)   Whenever possible, grade the site to provide access at several different seating levels without the use of steps or ramps. Otherwise, provide ramps (in addition to stairs) that are at least 44 inches wide (preferably 88 inches wide) with a slope of 1:20 or less. If a 1:20 slope is not feasible, a slope of 1:16 is permitted. The maximum horizontal run for any slope is 20 feet (CAH, 1992). See Chapter 6, Section 16 for details on ramp requirements.

4)   Provide wheelchair seating in as many different viewing areas as possible. The number of accessible seating spaces required depends on the total number of seats in the facility.

f.   **Groups of Picnic Tables.** Half-a-dozen or so picnic tables can be assembled into a group program area. Placing them under lightly shaded, sun-filtered trees ensures microclimatic comfort.

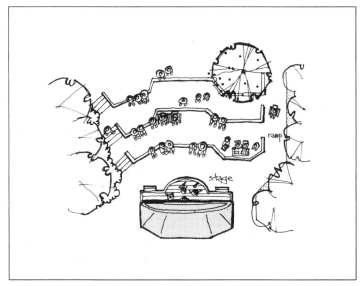

294   Prototypical amphitheater accessible to wheelchairs.

20. GATHERING, MEETING AND WORKING PLACES

To support social development and cooperative working relationships, children need small, comfortable gathering places where they can meet and work together in small (2 to 7), medium (7 to 15) and large (15+) groups (Moore, 1989a).

Planning Criteria

Play Value. Gathering, meeting and working places are critical for social interaction.

Programming Potential. They provide support for programming activities.

Play Leadership. They support leadership functions.

Safety. Table surfaces must not be located under a climbable element and must be nonflammable.

Risk Management. Table surfaces should be placed in partial shade at appropriate heights for wheelchair use and should be washable for hygiene.

Accessibility. Table surfaces must be open.

Integration. Gathering, meeting and working places support social interaction.

Management. Different types and sizes of spaces are required for different-sized groups and different purposes. It should be possible to reserve these spaces in public parks. Work tables should be wider than standard picnic tables and have a continuous, smooth surface. Corners should be rounded, heights varied, and benches flexible to accommodate varied group configurations.

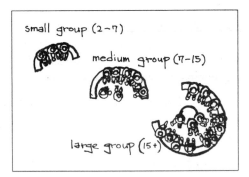

295 *Spaces should be provided for groups of different sizes.*

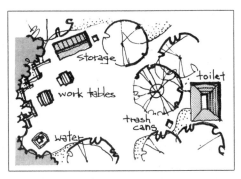

296 *Prototypical, multipurpose meeting and working place with work tables, water, trash cans, storage, and toilets nearby.*

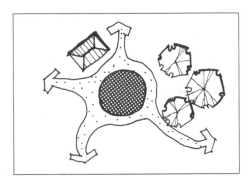

297 *Some meeting places may be located at points of high access and visibility.*

20.1   Importance of Places for Meeting and Working

Social interaction is basic to playing and learning. If appropriate meeting places are provided, social relationships can be extended to greater breadth and depth. Gathering, meeting and working places must be able to accommodate groups that range from a couple of children sitting on a log to large working groups (Moore, 1989a).

Many playgrounds consist of poorly designed groupings of equipment set in sand. They are uncomfortable for children and adults alike, and foster boredom and aggression rather than positive social development. Play areas need to accommodate many types of activity and "non-activity." Children need privacy at times. Quiet, secluded places should be provided where children can gather, where imaginations can have free reign.

The distinction between "work" and "play" is not made by young children in their informal activity. Although play is often like work in character, "work" to a child usually means activities which are organized and directed by adults.

Comfortable, practical places are essential if adults and children are to work together successfully outdoors. These places must be designed as multi-purpose "gathering spots" that can accommodate meeting, working and playing at different times for different people. These places must accommodate:

- Children taking time-out from playing (this is particularly important for children with limited stamina).
- Children sitting and relaxing alone, with a friend or an adult.
- Adults sitting and talking to each other or watching over children they are responsible for.

20.2   Design Principles

a.   **Location.** Some meeting and working settings should be located at points of high accessibility, at main path crossings, or at entrances. Others should be located in the reverse circumstances, so that small groups can meet and work in private.

A prime area for meeting and working activity is at the point of transition from inside to outside. It is usually important to locate work places adjacent to storage facilities, so that tools and materials are close at hand. Proximity to a sink or other water supply is often necessary. For programming convenience, working places can be located next to staging areas.

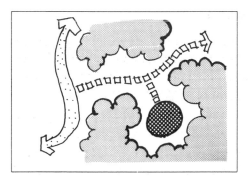

298   *Other places may be in quiet, private retreat-like surroundings.*

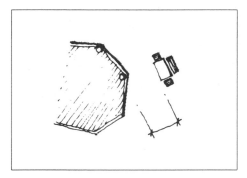

299   *Work table adjacent to staging areas adds convenience.*

300   *Ambient microclimate is an important consideration in designing meeting and working places.*

b.   **Microclimatic Comfort.** Protection from the wind is always necessary. Summer shade and winter sunshine are necessary in most temperate and Mediterranean climatic zones. In wet climates, protection from rain must be provided. This means that a choice of "open," "covered," and "enclosed" places is necessary.

c.   **Social Support.** There are many ways to design places so that they facilitate and support social interaction (Moore, 1989a).

d.   **Diversity of Body Support.** Site elements should be designed so that they are anthropomorphically correct, properly dimensioned and proportioned to support the human body. However, in outdoor settings, over-design should be avoided. People in general, and children in particular, use outdoor furniture in many "undesignated" ways, reflecting subtleties of social interaction. Therefore, a diverse choice of furniture options should be provided. The anthropometric requirements of children with disabilities add further to the need for diversity.

e.   **Multilevel Structures.** Different levels should be designed into meeting and working places to support different body positions and a broader range of social interaction. Many fixed structures such as fences, play structures and stairways can be designed as places for people to sit and interact.

There should be many different places to sit, rest and lie down in each play setting. Conventional benches with backs and arms are needed at entrances and along paths. In addition, there should be platforms and edges that are easy to sit on, dry places on the ground to sit and lie down, and soft areas for sitting and lying.

Some sitting places should have special benchrests and grab bars. There should also be benches that can be straddled for children who need to prop themselves on their elbows.

f.   **Sense of Enclosure.** Physical enclosure should provide a feeling of privacy, but not so strongly that children feel claustrophobic. The pleasure of privacy is often increased by retaining visual contact with one's surroundings. A range of settings should be provided that have a varied sense of enclosure, from very private to open.

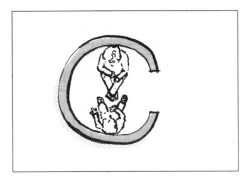

301   *Intimate enclosures stimulate close social contact.*

302   *Multilevel structures support different body positions and a variety of social interaction.*

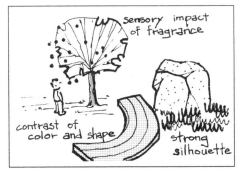

303   *Meeting and gathering places need a sense of identity.*

g.   **Identity.**   Areas which are visually identifiable can foster a feeling of affiliation and recognition, and contribute to a "sense of place."   Clear, strong identities make it easy to choose a rendezvous point.   Being able to say, "see you on the round bench" or "on the rocks" or "by the cherry tree" avoids confusion and frustration.

A well-differentiated environment containing a hierarchy of "named" places is essential for effective behavior management and for clarity of communication between inside and outside.   Play leaders must be able to give clear geographic instructions in changing from one activity to another.

Identity can be designed through use of:

1)   **Contrast:**   between place and background; of color, texture and form.

2)   **Strong, clear shape:**   a geometrical or semi-geometrical form.

3)   **Sharp silhouette:**   strong, vertical planes, especially "skylines."

4)   **Sensory impact:**   "accent", or "identity;" plants having a strong smell; texture; movement in the wind; plants that have strong fall colors or bear fruit.

20.3   **Types of Meeting, Working and Gathering Places**

a.   **Built-in, Ancillary Places.**   Places that serve other main functions (such as stairways, rails, low walls, and structures) can be designed to accommodate social interaction, "hanging out" and private daydreaming.

The most action-oriented play structure can become a quiet social sanctuary at off-peak times.   For example, fences can be designed so that they are comfortable to sit on.   Comfortable seats and "perches" can be used to create an informal people-plant setting that is relaxing and potentially educational.

b.   **Small Group Settings.**   Places are needed that function primarily as social and work-related places for small groups (solos, duets, trios, and quartets).

The most simple work settings are off-the-ground surfaces: benches, tables, and seats with places to lodge materials, clipboards, etc.

c.   **Logs, Rocks and Found Objects.**   Simple sitting and working spots can be created using heavy objects in the 100- to 300-pound range (e.g., logs or rocks that can be moved by a group of adults but not by children).   Found objects can be used individually or grouped according to the social purpose in mind.

304 *Meeting spaces can be built into play structures.*

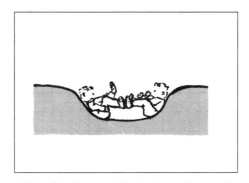

305 *Small group (duet, trio and quartet) meeting spots are important.*

306 *Work tables—a basic meeting and working facility.*

307 *Logs, rocks, and other readymades.*

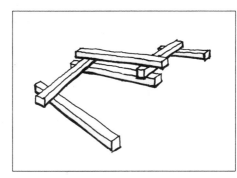

308 *A simple gathering place made from large timbers . . .*

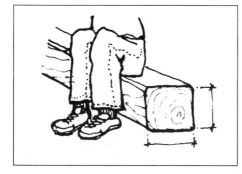

309 *. . . provides seating at a comfortable height.*

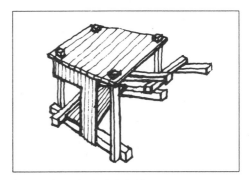

310 *A temporary "clubhouse."*

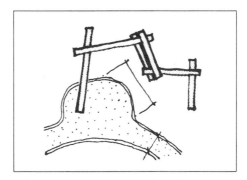

311 *Places should be accessible to wheelchair users from a main path.*

312 *Physical layout can be introduced to a blind child through use of a 3D model.*

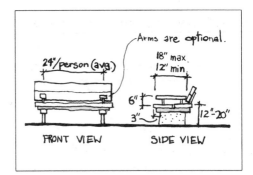

313   *Standard park bench with arms and back.*

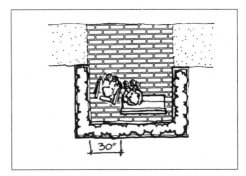

314   *Spaces beside benches for wheelchairs.*

315   *Small platform for sitting and working on.*

d.   **Self-Made Places.** Children can make temporary social settings for themselves, if given:

1)   An adequate supply of building materials and loose parts.

2)   Suitable "building sites."

3)   Understanding leadership (see Adventure Playgrounds, Section 14.3e).

e.   **Designed Gathering Places.** Settings for meeting, gathering and working can be made from a variety of materials.

20.4   **Seating (Seattle, 1986)**

a.   Provide seating at every significant play event in the play area.

b.   All benches for adults should have backs and armrests to increase comfort. Armrests are also helpful for getting into and out of seats and benches.

c.   Group the benches in various configurations for sitting alone or in groups.

d.   Choose materials which do not retain heat or cold. Avoid rough materials or those that may splinter (Robinette, 1985).

e.   Different age groups have different seat-height requirements (CAH, 1992):

- Eight to 12 inches for toddlers and preschoolers.
- Twelve to 17 inches for school-age children.
- Eighteen to 20 inches for adults.

f.   Seat surfaces less than 12-inches wide are uncomfortable for many adults. Likewise, widths greater than 18 inches can become awkward for people of average height.

g.   A clear "heel space" extending at least 3 inches under the front of the bench seat will make it easier to rise from a seated position.

h.   Seat surfaces should be pitched to shed water.

i.   Provide a clear space beside each bench for a wheelchair or stroller. This space must be level and at least 30 inches wide by 40 inches deep. It must also have accessible surfacing and be adjacent to an accessible path.

j.   Seating areas should be located adjacent to (but not obstructing) pathways and developed trails. Seating areas are particularly valuable along inclines.

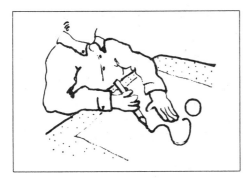

316 *Provide smooth tabletops with rounded corners and no recesses.*

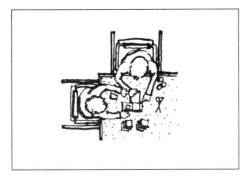

317 *Table corners are good for pairs of children to work.*

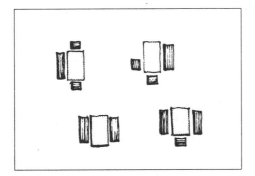

318 *A mix of work table configurations.*

k. Texture changes should be provided across walkways adjacent to seating areas to cue the blind on the location of benches.

l. Benches that contrast in color from surroundings are more easily distinguished by people with visual impairments.

20.5   Work Tables

a. Provide tables with seating at every play area to accommodate eating, games and crafts. A covered table makes the play area usable even in misty or rainy weather (Seattle, 1986).

b. The top surfaces of all work tables should be no higher than 34 inches above the ground. For children using wheelchairs, the upper surface of the table should be no more than 30 inches above the finished ground surface. At least 27 inches clearance should be provided on the underside of the table (CAH, 1992).

c. To accommodate people using wheelchairs, ensure that at least one side of every table is clear of fixed seats or benches. For spaces that will be used by adults in wheelchairs, provide a clear level space at least 30 inches wide and 24 inches deep beneath the table (and at least 48 inches deep overall). There must be at least 27 inches of clearance between the ground and the underside of the table surface at this location. For spaces that will be used by children in wheelchairs, provide a clear knee space that is 36 inches wide and 24 inches deep beneath the table (55 inches deep overall), with 27 inches of clearance between the ground and the underside of the table surface (CAH, 1992).

Be sure that the surfacing under and leading to the work table is accessible.

d. Round-off or chamfer all exposed corners or sharp edges.

e. Keep table tops smooth, with no recesses that might hold water or food particles.

f. Bench and table materials should be comfortable to touch in hot and cold weather.

g. Accessible tables should be located on level sites adjacent to a firm, stable-surfaced path (Bunin et al., 1980).

h. There should be 5 feet of clearance on the sides of the table that are accessible, and 4 feet of clearance on all other sides.

319   *Vary table heights for different-sized children.*

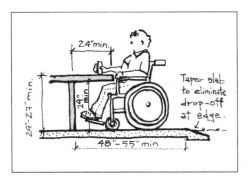

320   *Minimum table dimensions vary for adults and children in wheelchairs.*

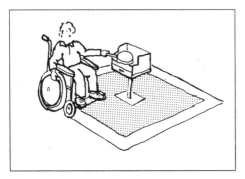

321   *Use a distinctive paving texture around grills as a warning to children and people with visual impairments.*

20.6   Fireplaces and Grills

Fire is needed for a variety of program activities: candle-making, leather-branding, pottery work, etc.

Children, like many adults, are fascinated by fire. However, they have few opportunities for learning how to handle fire safely. They need to learn about its uses for heating and cooking, its dangers, and ways to control it. Fire is also very soothing, much like water, in its ability to draw out our thoughts and create opportunities for quiet reflection (Schneekloth, 1985).

Provide a special place that can safely accommodate fire. Make sure that children know the rules regarding how and when fire is permitted. Let the children cook, burn trash and leftover materials, sit around and tell stories, and enjoy the fire's warmth.

Any fire on a playground must be under the constant supervision of an adult. But for children who rarely have the chance to see an open fire, the experience of gathering sticks and building, managing and extinguishing bonfires can be interesting and instructive. Cooking on campfires and barbecues is always popular. It is easy to make a raised fireplace using bricks and a metal grill so that children in wheelchairs can join in frying sausages, hamburgers and pancakes (HAPA, 1978).

a.   Grills are preferable to fireplaces. Cooking surfaces should be positioned no more than 30-inches above the ground surface if they are to be used by children in wheelchairs. Cooking surfaces for fire pits should be at least 18-inches above the ground. In addition, there should be a clear, level space that is 36-inches wide and 55-inches deep adjacent to the grill. Grills and fire pits should be located on an accessible surface and there must be an accessible walk to the area.

b.   Use rotating grills; place them downwind from camping and seating areas. Handles should not conduct heat and must be easy to grasp.

c.   Use a distinctive paving texture around grills and fireplaces as a warning to children and people with visual impairments.

d.   The front of the grill should be flush with the front of the fireplace.

322   *Design water sources to ensure comfortable reach dimensions for children using wheelchairs.*

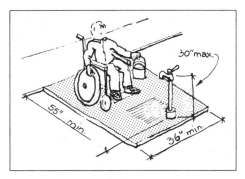

323   *Provide a clear level space that is at least 36 inches wide and 55 inches deep.*

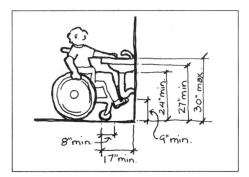

324   *Sink clearances must allow for a person using a wheelchair.*

20.7   Water Sources

Outdoor sinks and water spigots should be accessible to meeting and working areas and must be designed so that they can be used by a person in a wheelchair or a small child.

a.   The water source must have a clear, level space that is at least 36-inches wide and 55-inches deep to allow for use by a person in a wheelchair (CAH, 1992). If the water source is counter-mounted, 19 inches of the clear space can be located beneath the counter.

b.   The water source must be on an accessible surface adjacent to an accessible pathway. Use materials that will not become soft or slippery when wet. Do not use gravel.

c.   For outdoor sinks, there must be adequate knee space to allow for a person using a wheelchair. There must be 27 inches from the ground surface to the underside of the apron or counter, a 36-inch clear width, and a clear depth of at least 17 inches to allow a wheelchair user to pull far enough under the sink to reach and operate the controls (CAH, 1992). Pipes and the sink bowl may encroach on this space if they do not protrude to within 8 inches of the sink front or counter edge and 9 inches of the ground. If faucets are mounted on the side of the sink, there must also be 32 inches of clear floor space on the side upon which the faucet is mounted (CAH, 1992).

d.   The top surface of the sink rim or counter must not be higher than 30 inches above the floor.

e.   Faucets should be lever or push-button. They should be mounted on the face of the front apron or on the rim or counter surface no greater than 14 inches from the leading edge of the apron. Controls should require no more than 3 pounds of operating force. Force vectors on push-button controls must be less than 90 degrees.

f.   If drains are located on the ground surface, openings between the gratings must be less than 1/2 inch.

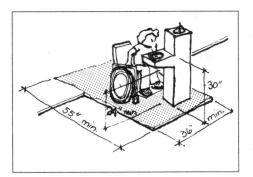

325 *Drinking fountains should be mounted on a wall or post and have a cantilevered design.*

20.8   Drinking Fountains

Drinking fountains must be designed and located so that they are usable by a person in a wheelchair. Keep in mind that many people with disabilities require water frequently. Also, if a drinking fountain is designed so that it is accessible to a child in a wheelchair, it will also be accessible to an adult in a wheelchair as well as able-bodied children.

a.   **Location.** Drinking fountains should be mounted on a wall or a post and should have a cantilevered design that provides space below the fountain for a wheelchair. The fountain should also be protected by an alcove, wing walls or railings that extend to the ground. Alternatively, the ground surface must be textured 12 inches beyond the fountain edges in all directions.

b.   **Clear Space.** There must be a clear level space that is 36 inches wide and 55 inches deep at the front of the fountain. This space must be on an accessible pathway and have an accessible surface that does not become slippery when wet.

c.   **Knee Space.** Drinking fountains used by children must have clear, unobstructed knee space that is 24 inches high (between the bottom of the apron and the floor surface), 17 inches deep and 36 inches wide.

d.   **Spout Location.** Spouts on drinking fountains and water coolers used by children must be no higher than 30 inches, measured from the floor or ground surface to the spout outlet (CAH, 1992). It must also be within 6 inches of the front edge of the fountain and should project water in a stream that is parallel to the front of the fountain and at least 4-inches high.

e.   **Spout Controls.** Controls used by children must be push-bar and electronic type and hand-operable. The push bar must be mounted on the front or on the front and side.

f.   **Drains.** If there is a drain in the floor surface beneath the fountain, its openings must be less than 1/2 inch.

20.9 Trash Receptacles (Bunin et al., 1980; Nordhaus et al., 1984)

a. Trash receptacles should be located adjacent to meeting and working areas on a hard surface pad adjacent to an accessible pathway.

b. The opening must be within comfortable horizontal reach from a wheelchair and located 3 feet or less above the ground surface. If there is a lid or other opening device, it must be operable without twisting or tight grasping. Spring-loaded mechanisms must not require more than 5 pounds of operating force.

c. Use trash receptacles which have rounded corners and are free from sharp edges.

d. Locate cans adjacent to, but not obstructing, trails and pathways to avoid hazards for the visually impaired.

e. In areas where scavenging animals pose a problem, use a cover mechanism that will allow trash to be thrown away with a single arm motion.

f. Locate litter receptacles at the points where children are likely to enter or leave a play area, whether a marked formal entry or not (Seattle, 1986).

20.10 Outdoor Telephones

The accessibility requirements for telephones set forth in the ADA Guidelines (*Federal Register*, July 26, 1991) are rather complex; they vary depending on whether the phone can be approached from the side or from the front. It is best to consult those guidelines directly to determine the design requirements for a particular telephone. Following are some considerations particular to telephones in environments that may be used by children.

a. If a telephone is intended for use by children, the highest operable part of the telephone must be not more than 36 inches above the finished floor. The required forward reach should not exceed 12 inches.

b. Telephones must be located on an accessible surface adjacent to an accessible pathway and must have a clear, level floor space at least 30 inches by 48 inches. Telephones should be located so that they are visible from active areas of use.

c. Telephones should be identified with graphic signs that can be read and understood by children and people with vision disabilities.

d. If the telephone will be used at night, adequate lighting should be provided.

326 *Centrally located outdoor telephones are a critical asset for play settings, especially as a safety device.*

e.   Shelves should be provided at the phone location as a convenience for parents who may be carrying heavy bags or infants.

20.11 Toilets

Toilets are a valuable asset for gathering and working places. Toilets, like telephones, are subject to a number of accessibility requirements under the ADA Guidelines (*Federal Register*, July 26, 1991). It is best to consult the Guidelines directly for information on the specific requirements of a particular type of facility. The following measurements and considerations should be used as supplements for toilets that are located at play areas and will be used primarily by children.

a.   **Location.** Toilet facilities should be provided at or near to all public play facilities. They should be located so that they are easily visible and directly accessible from the main areas of the play environment. Pathways and any ramps leading to the toilet facilities must comply with the accessibility requirements outlined in Chapter 6.

b.   **Signs.** Toilet facilities should be identified with graphic signs that can be read and understood by children and people with sight disabilities (see Chapter 7, Signage).

c.   **Access.** Toilets should remain unlocked during normal hours of play area use.

d.   **Clear Area Requirements.** Toilet facilities should be designed so that they are completely accessible. Different toilet room configurations have different measurement requirements (see the ADA Guidelines, *Federal Register*, July 26, 1991). However, no matter what the configuration, there should be adequate clear space (30 inches by 48 inches, minimum) to accommodate a person using a wheelchair. If a person using a wheelchair must maneuver within the space, there must be a circular clear area 60 inches in diameter.

e.   **Toilet Height.** If toilets are to be accessible to children using wheelchairs, they must meet different height requirements from those of adults. The following measurements apply to toilet seat heights (measured to the top of the toilet seat) for children (CAH, 1992):

- Pre-kindergarten: 11-1/2 to 12-1/2 inches
- Kindergarten to third grade: 12 to 15 inches
- Fourth grade and older: 15 to 17 inches

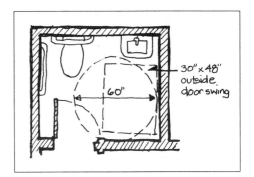

327   *A 30-inch by 48-inch clear area must be provided. A 60-inch clear area is necessary if a person using a wheelchair must maneuver within the space.*

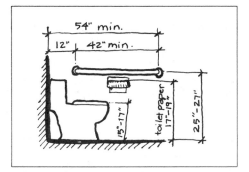

328 *Children's environments have different dimensional requirements from those of adults.*

f.   **Grab bars.** Grab bars are essential to help people using wheelchairs to transfer onto the toilet seat. The ADA Guidelines (*Federal Register*, July 26, 1991) provide specific measurements for grab bars in adult environments. The following measurements should be applied to environments used by children (CAH, 1992):

- Side bar heights (measured from the floor to the top of the side bar):
  - Pre-kindergarten: 18 to 20 inches
  - Kindergarten to third grade: 20 to 25 inches
  - Fourth grade and older: 25 to 27 inches
- A back bar is not required for pre-kindergarten age children. For other ages, the side bar height should be used unless the tank/flush valve does not allow a mounting height that low, in such cases the back bar should be mounted at the lowest height possible that permits free hand movement along the bar.
- Distance from the center-line of the toilet bowl to the wall on which the side grab bar is mounted:
  - Pre-kindergarten: 11 inches
  - Kindergarten to third grade: 11 to 15 inches
  - Fourth grade and older: 15 to 18 inches
- Grab bar diameters:
  - Pre-kindergarten: 1 inch
  - All others: 1 to 1-1/4 inches

g.   **Flush Controls.** Flush controls should be mounted on the wide side of toilet areas within 20 to 30 inches above the floor, depending on the age of children.

h.   **Dispensers.** Toilet paper dispensers used by children should be installed at the following heights above the floor:

- Pre-kindergarten: 14 inches
- Kindergarten to third grade: 14 to 17 inches
- Fourth grade and older: 17 to 19 inches

The leading edge of the dispenser should be parallel to the front of the bowl.

20.12 Electrical (Seattle, 1986)

All electrical conduit and wiring should be underground in and around a children's play area.

Provisions for utility metering, transformers and other electrical equipment should be located in locked vaults or utility rooms away from children's play areas.

20.13 Lighting (Seattle, 1986)

The decision to include lighting in the play area must be made carefully. A lighted play area may give the illusion of safety and security after dark and invite children to play in an unsafe area.

Lighting is most appropriate at drop-off and pick-up points and at restroom buildings.

20.14 Bike Racks (Seattle, 1986)

Provide bike racks at every play area. For an indication of how many will be needed, consider the play area's attractiveness for 6 to 12 year olds.

Locate bike racks in several places throughout each play area to minimize the chance of bikes falling into the path of play. If bikes are likely to create hazardous conditions in the play area, due to crowded conditions or the presence of younger children, place the bike racks at the play area entrance with a sign indicating that bikes are not allowed inside the play area (see Chapter 9, Section 1.6c-4).

329 *Nighttime lighting is an important consideration in site planning.*

21. STORAGE SETTINGS

Facilities are needed to store play equipment and materials, loose parts and maintenance materials and equipment.

Planning Criteria

Play Value. Although not expressly intended, storage places are often settings for social interaction.

Programming Potential. Storage areas provide essential program support.

Play Leadership. Leaders must be able to manage storage facilities effectively.

Safety. They must be lockable and nonclimbable.

Risk Management. Careful checks must be made for toxic and inflammable materials.

Accessibility. It is critical that users have easy access to storage facilities, including employees, play leaders, supervisors, and children.

Integration. Not applicable.

Management. Policies which recognize the importance of secure storage facilities are needed. For example, the provision of "rentable" facilities for groups who deliver programs.

330 *Playstore: an attractive place serving many needs for security and storage.*

21.1   Function of Storage Facilities

Storage space should be designed as an integral part of an environment to facilitate all activities that go on within the space. Unfortunately, some manufacturers do not see a sufficient profit margin in the supply of storage. But this can be overcome by making it a multipurpose, integral play setting component.

Proper storage space helps to reduce clutter that can limit activities. Accessible storage areas that are clearly defined, labeled, and properly placed will encourage children to initiate, carry out, and clean-up after their own activities (AEC, 1980).

Some children with disabilities use special equipment, such as canes, walkers, wheel-chairs, or crutches. Storage for these items should be accessible to a child who might be crawling, standing, or sitting. It should also be unobtrusive, so that it does not make the space look as if it is only for children with disabilities and unnecessarily increase the stigma attached to special equipment.

21.2   Outdoor Storage Cupboard

Size and arrangement will depend on the number of objects to be stored and the number of users. Storage cupboards can be incorporated into the design of playhouses or climbing structures for maximum accessibility. The outside of a storage unit can be made playable. It can be designed so that when it is empty it can be used for play, but should not have play as its primary use.

Storage units should not be too deep; this encourages junking and makes it difficult to see what is inside. The aim is to make play materials as accessible as possible. If the store opens wide during play time, children will be able to select toys and put them back when done, making it easier to maintain and supervise. Air holes should be provided in case a child gets locked in.

Walk-in storage can be designed, but shelves must not be too deep and the passage must be kept uncluttered. Good storage can make all the difference in the "playability" of a playground.

a.   Overall dimensions will vary, depending on storage needs. Storage needs are almost universally underestimated. A minimal unit might measure 3 feet, 6 inches deep by 6 feet wide.

b.   Doors should be lockable. Pull-down or roll-down garage doors should be considered. Indeed, a garage type space is a good model to meet storage needs.

c.   Shelves need sturdy support for heavy play equipment.

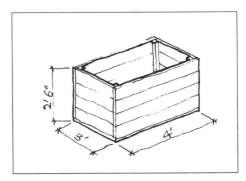

331   *Storage box.*

21.3 Storage Box (CMHC, 1978)

This box, combined with loose material and blocks, appeals to children's imaginations. Open side to the sky, it becomes a cave or hold of a ship; covered by boards, it is a secret place; with a trap door, a second story can be added; turned on its side with the addition of blocks, it may be a quick playhouse; open side down with short ladders or block steps, it is a lookout platform; and on its end, an even higher lookout.

Exact dimensions are not important although the size should allow the box to be tipped and managed by three year olds. If it is too big, requiring adult help, the imaginative possibilities are limited; if it cannot be moved at all, the play value is lost. A group of 20 children should have at least two such boxes. The aim should be to provide as many as space and budget permit.

21.4 Field Houses

Auxiliary spaces are needed outdoors as resource centers and program bases. Storage is an integral aspect. On most recreation sites, some kind of field house is necessary for the effective use of the outdoors. Several alternatives are possible. Buildings may be provided by the conversion of existing buildings or the construction of new ones. A third alternative is to import a prefabricated portable building. Some manufacturers include them as catalog items.

In most cases the building should be located near the geographic or activity center of the site.

Once constructed, a field house can be used as a protected garden space; or it can be lined with polyethylene to make a greenhouse; or roofed over to make a covered work-shop or storage area; or lined with plywood to make a place for animals or a tool shed. It should be convertible from one use to another.

21.5 Storage Compounds

To store large items of equipment and bulky materials such as sawn lumber, a chainlink fenced enclosure can be used. An advantage of chainlink fencing is that it is almost indestructible—a property that can be used to great advantage in building high-security, indoor-outdoor places.

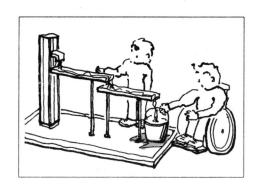

PART C:

PFA Guidelines in Action

22. PFA GUIDELINES IN ACTION: REBUILDING A PUBLIC PLAYGROUND AT FLOOD PARK, SAN MATEO COUNTY, CALIFORNIA

22.1 Overview

Flood Park was constructed in the 1930's as a WPA project for the citizens of San Mateo County. For fifty years it served the recreational needs of its constituents, operated by the San Mateo County Parks and Recreation Division of the Department of Environmental Management. In 1982, a new Master Plan for the park's future development was approved. When some of the community groups using the park raised concerns over the scope and direction of the plan, the County Board of Supervisors commissioned a study to address the needs of park users with respect to "whole access," that is, the accessibility of the park's facilities to all users. Project planners and designers were Moore Iacofano Goltsman, Inc. and Lawrence Wight & Associates.

The goal of the Flood Park Barrier Free Access Design Project was to improve accessibility to the park's facilities and amenities for all people, with attention to the specific needs of three user groups:

a. Children with and without disabilities.

b. Adults with disabilities.

c. The elderly.

22.2 Community Needs Assessment

a. **Community Workshop.** In October 1985, a community workshop was held to bring together the park's various constituent groups. Flyers were distributed and telephone contacts were made with recreation and community service organizations to publicize the workshop.

Participants defined the term "people with special needs" as those whose needs were not presently being met. They included:

1) Developmentally disabled.

2) Emotionally disabled.

3) Physically disabled (both temporarily and permanently).

4) Those with stamina limitations: the very young, the active elderly, and the frail or institutionalized elderly.

5)   Economically and culturally disadvantaged.

6)   New residents (such as immigrants).

7)   Hearing impaired (both from birth and adventitiously acquired).

8)   Visually impaired.

In a further workshop segment, participants defined a "whole access" environment as one which:

1)   Allowed physical and programmatical access to all user groups.

2)   Provided safety, security, and support.

3)   Offered all users maximum independence.

4)   Facilitated access to all of the park's "natural" experiences.

b.   **Walking Tour.** The group was given maps and instructions for a specially prepared walking tour of the Flood Park site. Eleven stations, including the play areas, were set up to serve as observation points for an environmental assessment. At each station, participants were asked to jot down constraints and possibilities for whole access and general comments about the park's facilities and amenities.

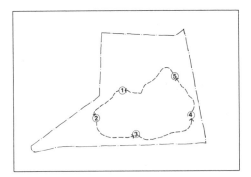

332   Walking Tour Map

c.   **Community Workshop Results.** Participants' observations identified the following issues to be addressed:

1)   Physical accessibility: surface materials, slope, pathway width, proximity of activity areas to vehicle loading areas, use of restroom facilities.

2)   Program accessibility: use of activity areas by people with a wide range of disabilities; promotion of activities that permit participation by people with and without disabilities; maximization of experience of the natural settings for all park users.

3)   Communication accessibility: development of a map and signage program to provide information about the historical aspects and locations of the park's facilities; provision of telecommunication devices for the hearing impaired.

d.   **Children's Design Workshop.** A second workshop, for children of the Flood Park community, was held a week later, sponsored by PLAE, Inc.

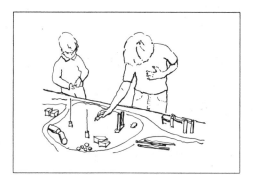

333   *Children's design model.*

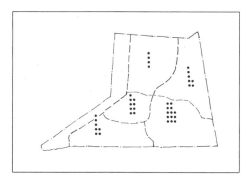

334   *Behavior Map*

The goals of the workshop were to demonstrate how park facilities might be utilized and to gather information directly from children about what types of elements they would like to see in the play areas.

A 4 foot by 8 foot model of the playground with basic outlines of pathways, buildings, and existing play structures was set up. Two tables loaded with model-making parts (corks, straws, marshmallows, packing material, spagnum moss, rocks, toothpicks, netting, sticks, modeling clay, yarn) were set up, and children were encouraged to create models of their own play settings. Twenty children, including a minibus of children with disabilities, participated.

e. **Children's Workshop Results.** The children proposed many imaginative play setting designs, ranging from practical to whimsical. Flags, pennants and banners were planted atop various structures, adding a circus feeling to the playground. Water features were prominent, with a stream flowing into a small pond where boats sailed. Another pond was for jumping in. Elevated structures with ramps were popular. The most complex play structure design was a net hidden by trees, shrubs and flowering bushes.

Adding a festive atmosphere to the event, multicolored, helium-filled balloons surrounded the model. Toward the end of the workshop, children attached notes to the balloons about their designs and asked other children who found the balloons to send in more ideas.

f. **Use Analysis.** A complete analysis of the site was made, incorporating observations about current uses, vegetation, facilities, equipment and behavioral mapping data.

g. **Accessibility Survey.** An accessibility survey was conducted to identify physical barriers in each use area. This information was compiled into a series of maps and analyzed for future park development.

h. **Preliminary Design Alternatives.** Design alternatives were prepared based on the community workshop findings, analytical data and the accessibility survey, and presented for review by staff, parks commissioners and the Board of Supervisors.

i. **Master Plan.** A play area master plan incorporating PFA guidelines was produced and a phasing plan developed. The site and a selection of setting designs are presented on the following pages.

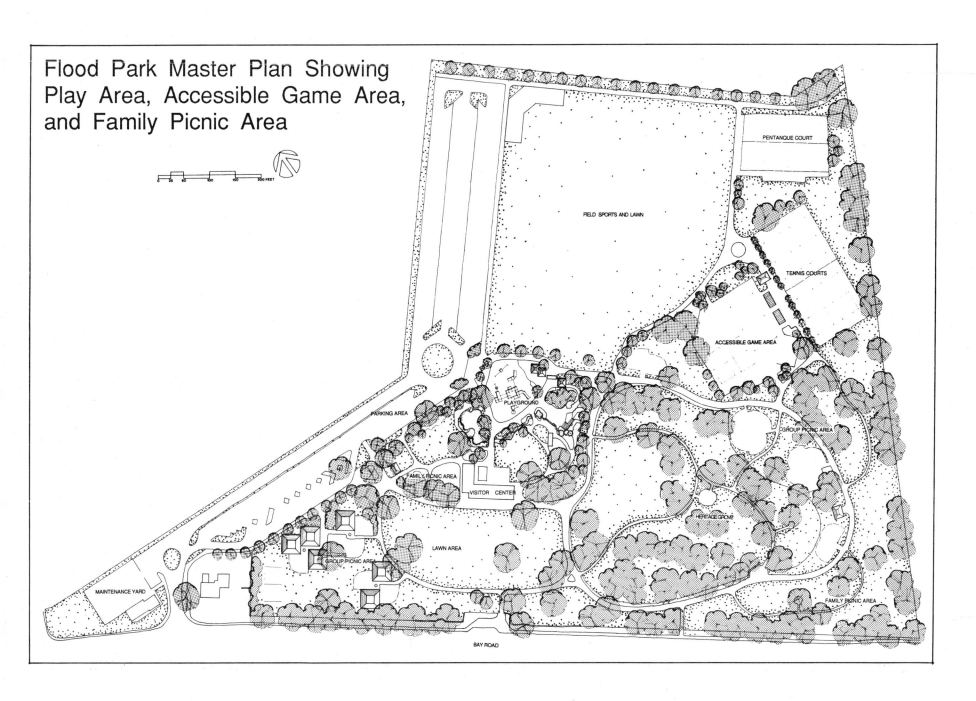

Flood Park Master Plan Showing
Play Area, Accessible Game Area,
and Family Picnic Area

PENTANQUE COURT

FIELD SPORTS AND LAWN

TENNIS COURTS

ACCESSIBLE GAME AREA

PARKING AREA

GROUP PICNIC AREA

PLAYGROUND

FAMILY PICNIC AREA

VISITOR CENTER

HERITAGE GROVE

LAWN AREA

GROUP PICNIC AREA

MAINTENANCE YARD

FAMILY PICNIC AREA

BAY ROAD

Flood Park Play Area Showing
Location of Play Settings

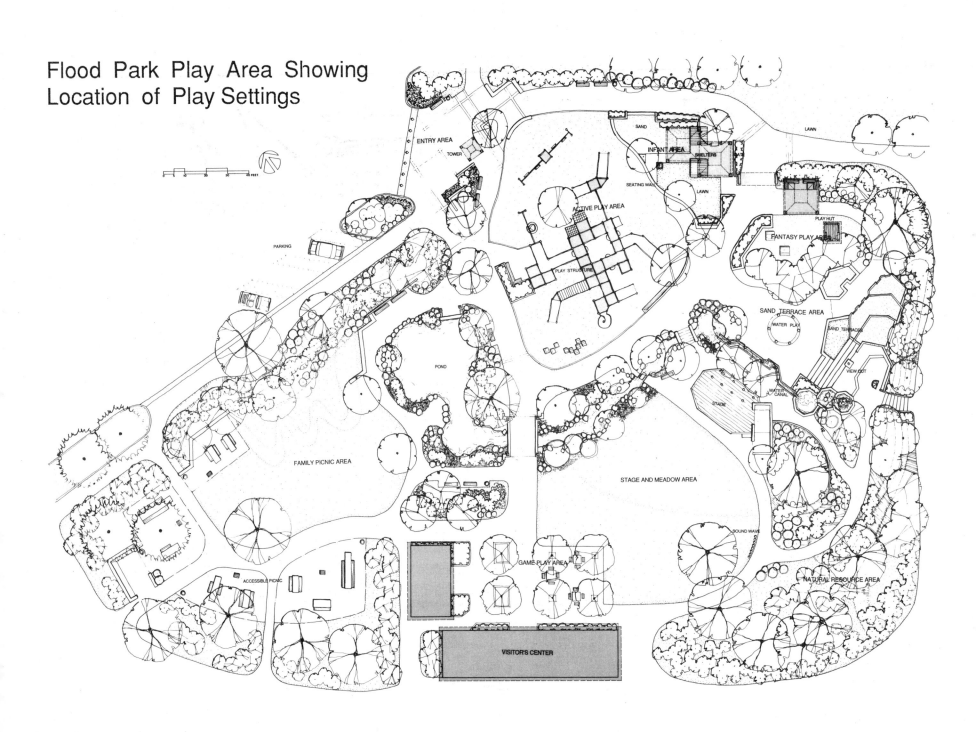

ENTRY AREA

LAWN

SAND

TOWER

INFANT AREA

SHELTERS

SEATING WALL

LAWN

PARKING

ACTIVE PLAY AREA

PLAY HUT

FANTASY PLAY AREA

PLAY STRUCTURE

SAND TERRACE AREA

WATER PLAY

SAND TERRACES

POND

VIEW OUT

WATER CANAL

STAGE

FAMILY PICNIC AREA

STAGE AND MEADOW AREA

SOUND WAVE

ACCESSIBLE PICNIC

GAME PLAY AREA

NATURAL RESOURCE AREA

VISITOR'S CENTER

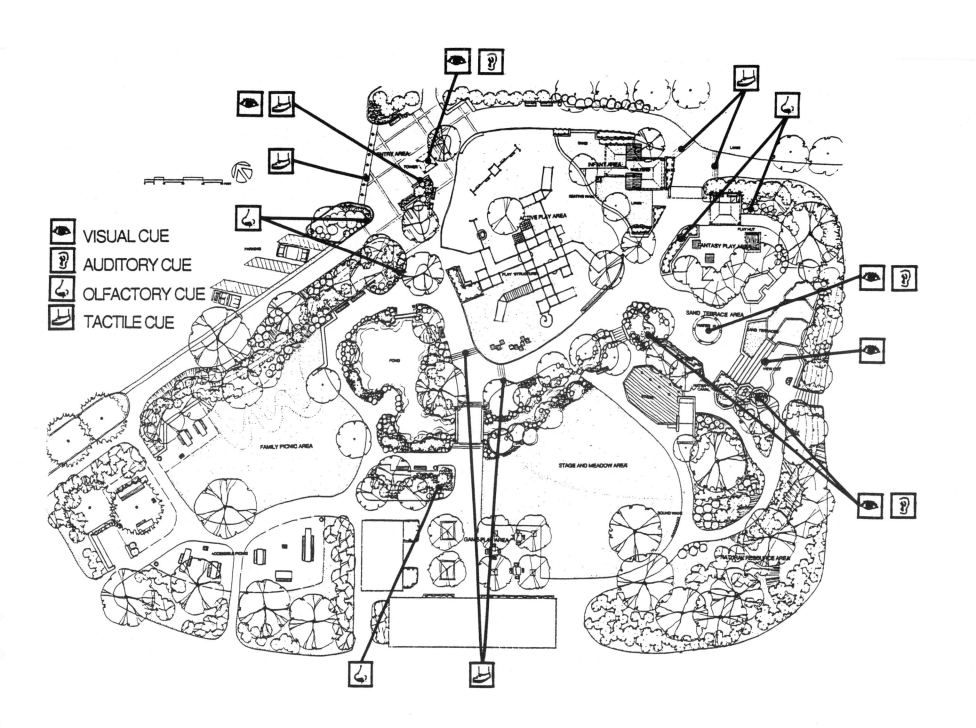

VISUAL CUE

AUDITORY CUE

OLFACTORY CUE

TACTILE CUE

Flood Park Play Area Entry Setting

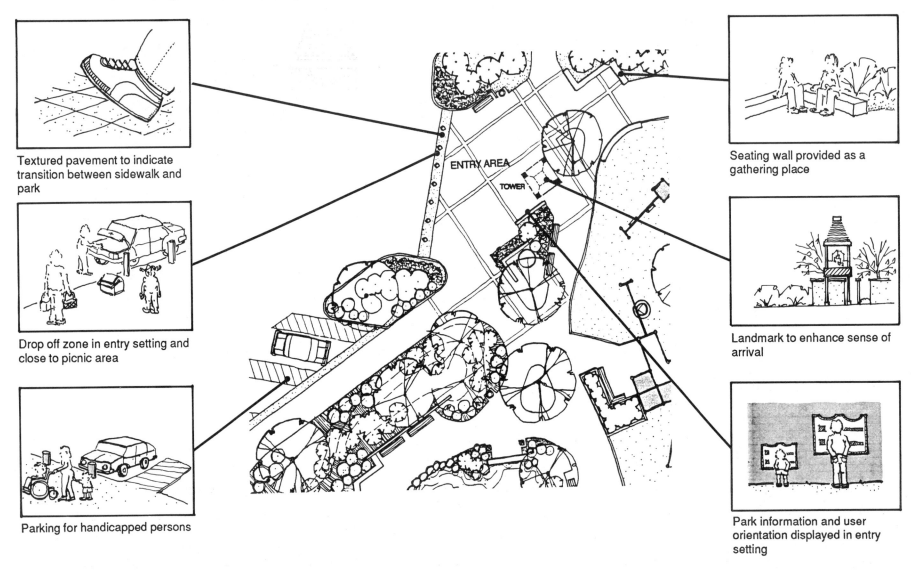

Textured pavement to indicate transition between sidewalk and park

Drop off zone in entry setting and close to picnic area

Parking for handicapped persons

ENTRY AREA

TOWER

Seating wall provided as a gathering place

Landmark to enhance sense of arrival

Park information and user orientation displayed in entry setting

Entry Setting in Elevation

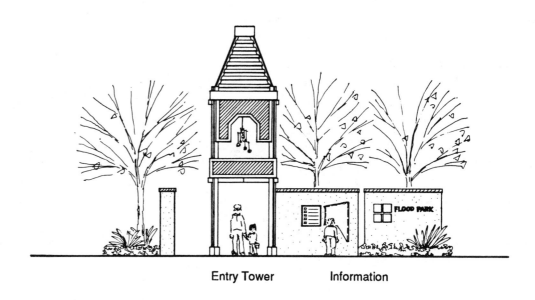

Entry Tower   Information

Section through Infant Play Setting

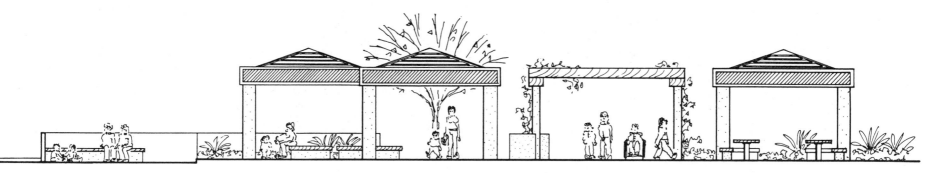

Infant Play Area Shelter   Pergola   Fantasy Play Area Shelter

Manufactured Equipment and Sand Settings

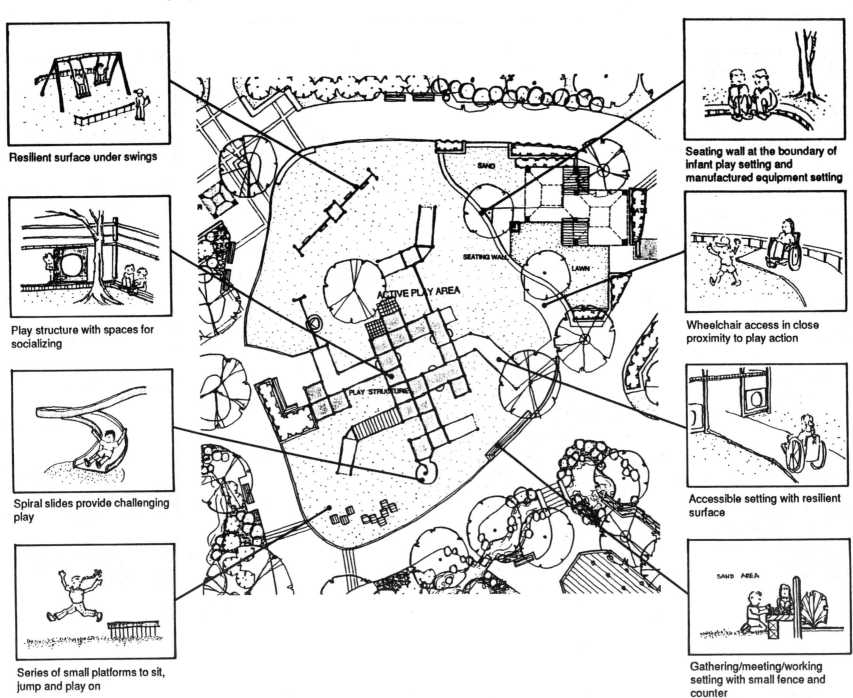

Resilient surface under swings

Play structure with spaces for socializing

Spiral slides provide challenging play

Series of small platforms to sit, jump and play on

Seating wall at the boundary of infant play setting and manufactured equipment setting

Wheelchair access in close proximity to play action

Accessible setting with resilient surface

Gathering/meeting/working setting with small fence and counter

Infant Play Setting

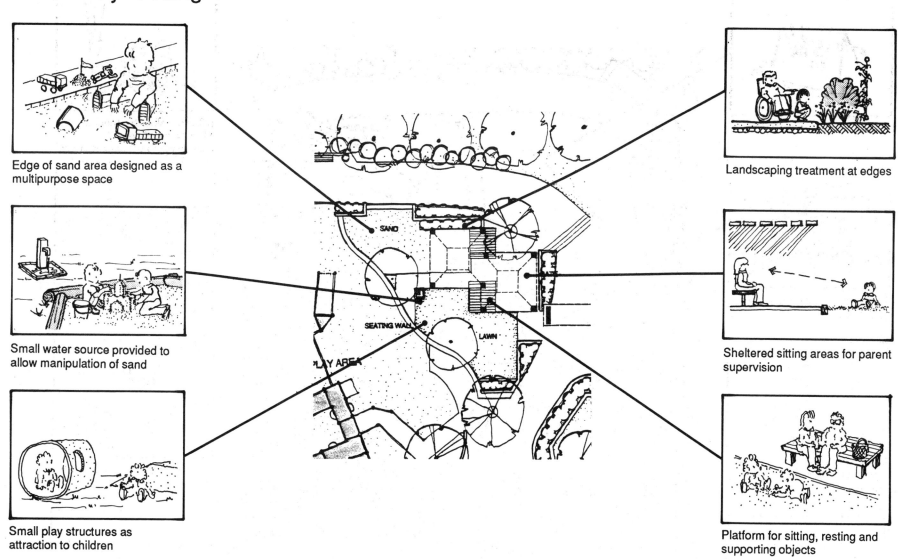

Edge of sand area designed as a multipurpose space

Small water source provided to allow manipulation of sand

Small play structures as attraction to children

Landscaping treatment at edges

Sheltered sitting areas for parent supervision

Platform for sitting, resting and supporting objects

SAND

SEATING WALL

LAWN

PLAY AREA

Fantasy Play Setting

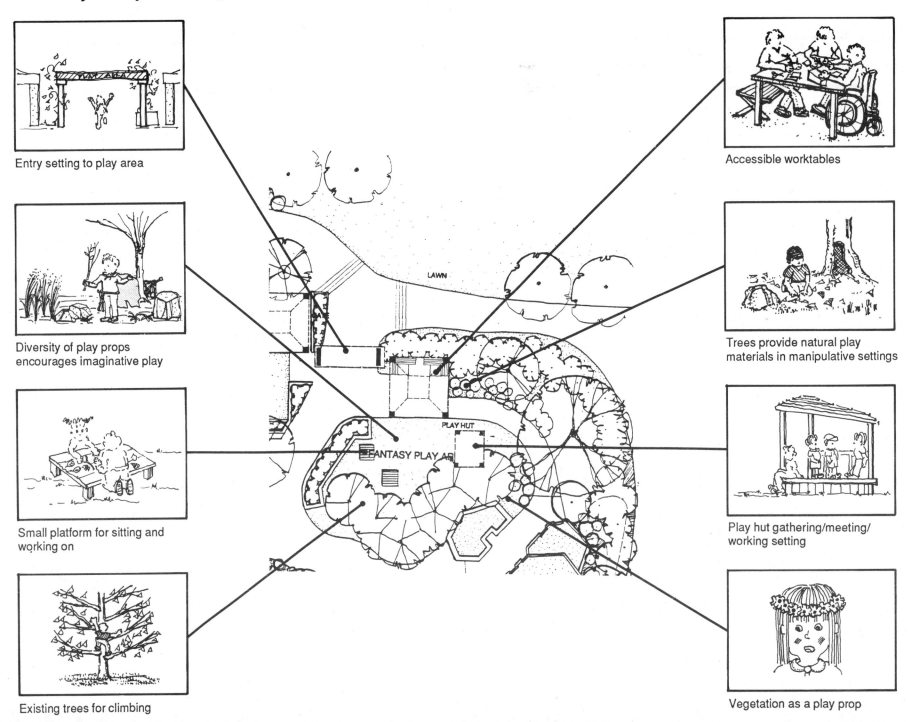

Entry setting to play area

Diversity of play props encourages imaginative play

Small platform for sitting and working on

Existing trees for climbing

Accessible worktables

Trees provide natural play materials in manipulative settings

Play hut gathering/meeting/ working setting

Vegetation as a play prop

LAWN

PLAY HUT

FANTASY PLAY AR

Sand Setting

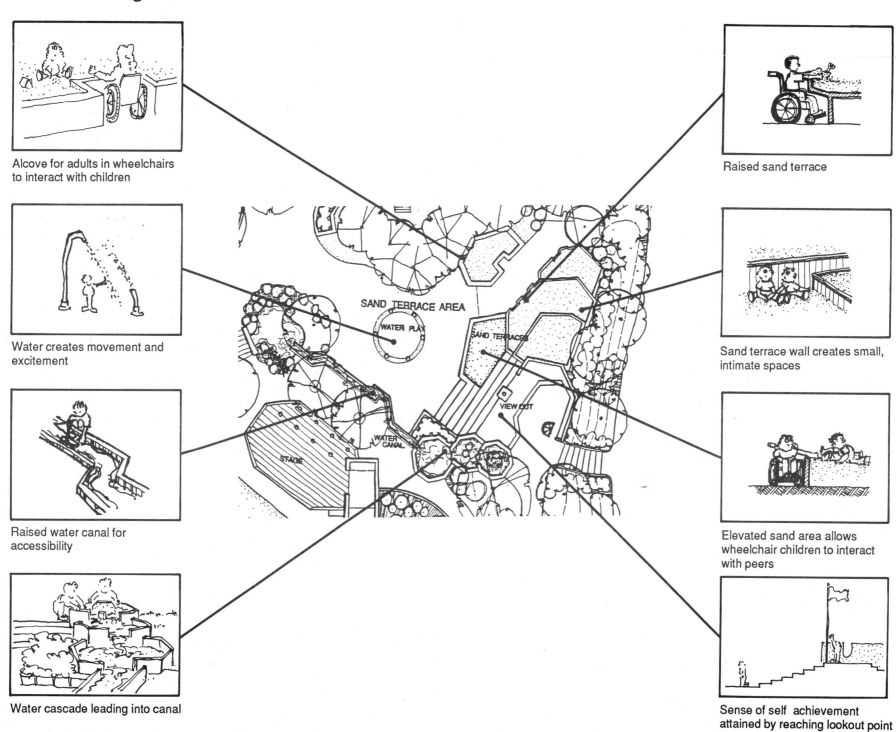

Alcove for adults in wheelchairs to interact with children

Water creates movement and excitement

Raised water canal for accessibility

Water cascade leading into canal

Raised sand terrace

Sand terrace wall creates small, intimate spaces

Elevated sand area allows wheelchair children to interact with peers

Sense of self achievement attained by reaching lookout point

SAND TERRACE AREA

WATER PLAY

SAND TERRACES

VIEW OUT

STAGE

WATER CANAL

Section through Sand Play and Water Settings

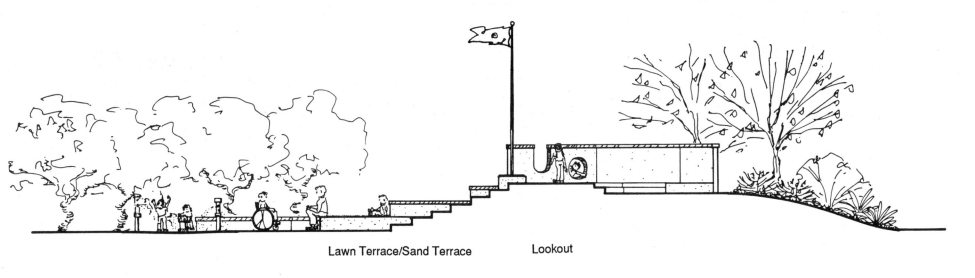

Lawn Terrace/Sand Terrace   Lookout

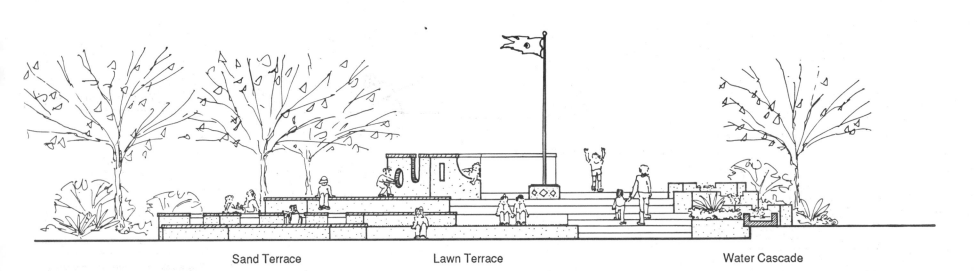

Sand Terrace   Lawn Terrace   Water Cascade

Staging and Multipurpose Meadow Settings

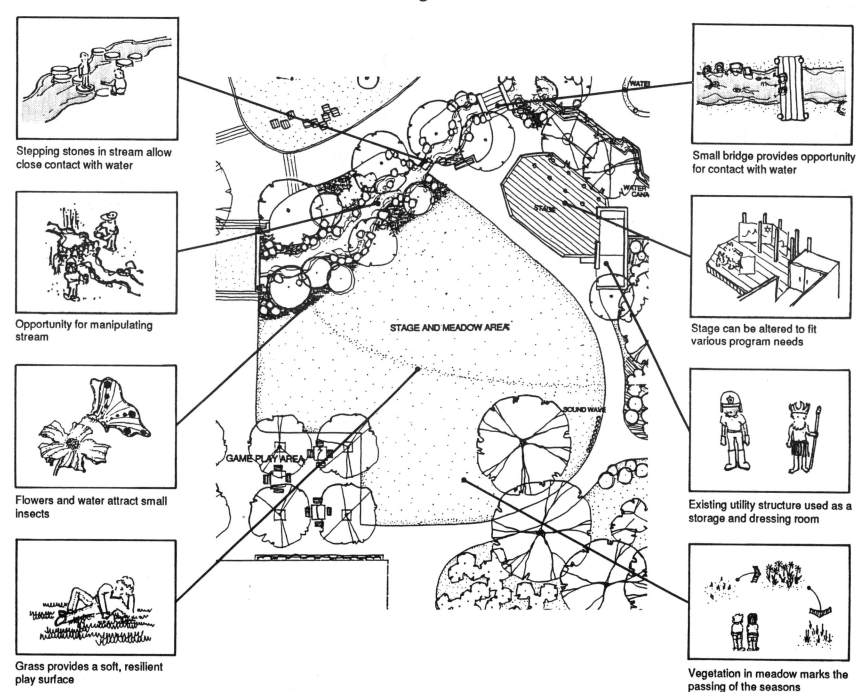

Stepping stones in stream allow close contact with water

Opportunity for manipulating stream

Flowers and water attract small insects

Grass provides a soft, resilient play surface

Small bridge provides opportunity for contact with water

Stage can be altered to fit various program needs

Existing utility structure used as a storage and dressing room

Vegetation in meadow marks the passing of the seasons

STAGE AND MEADOW AREA

GAME PLAY AREA

SOUND WAVE

WATER CANA

STAGE

WATE

Gathering/Meeting/Working Setting at Visitor's Center

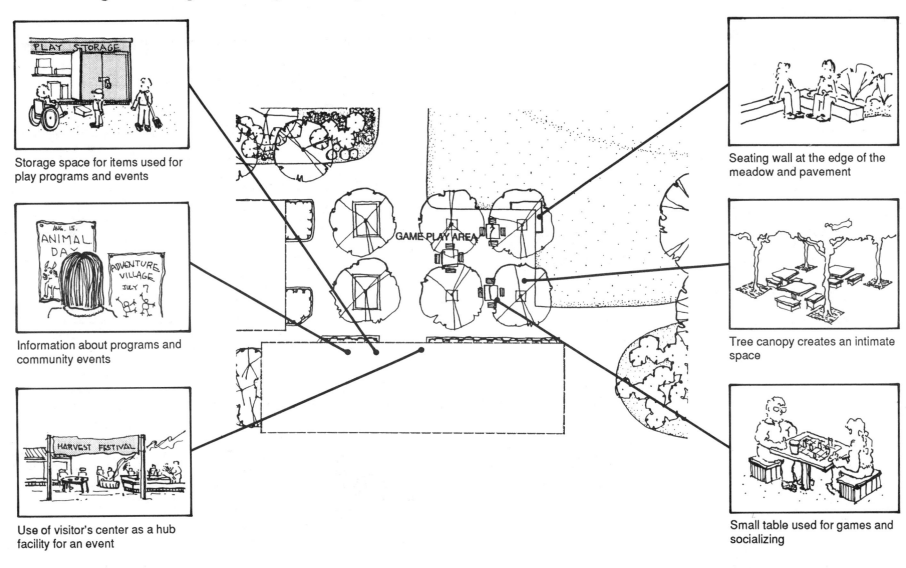

Storage space for items used for play programs and events

Information about programs and community events

Use of visitor's center as a hub facility for an event

GAME PLAY AREA

Seating wall at the edge of the meadow and pavement

Tree canopy creates an intimate space

Small table used for games and socializing

Multiuse Family Picnic Setting

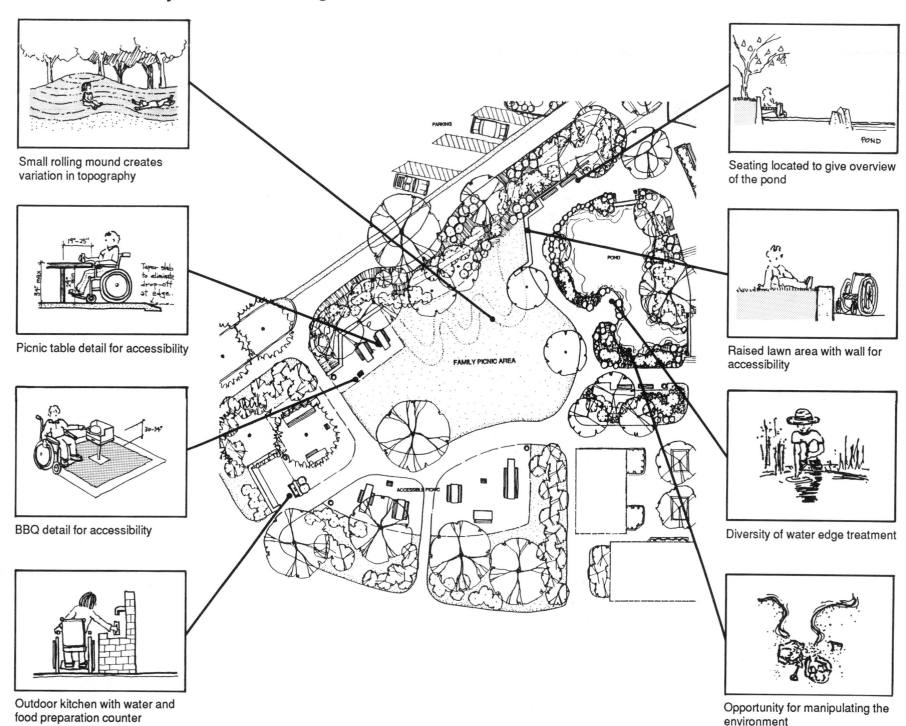

Small rolling mound creates variation in topography

Picnic table detail for accessibility

BBQ detail for accessibility

Outdoor kitchen with water and food preparation counter

Seating located to give overview of the pond

Raised lawn area with wall for accessibility

Diversity of water edge treatment

Opportunity for manipulating the environment

PARKING

POND

FAMILY PICNIC AREA

ACCESSIBLE PICNIC

Multipurpose Accessible Games Setting

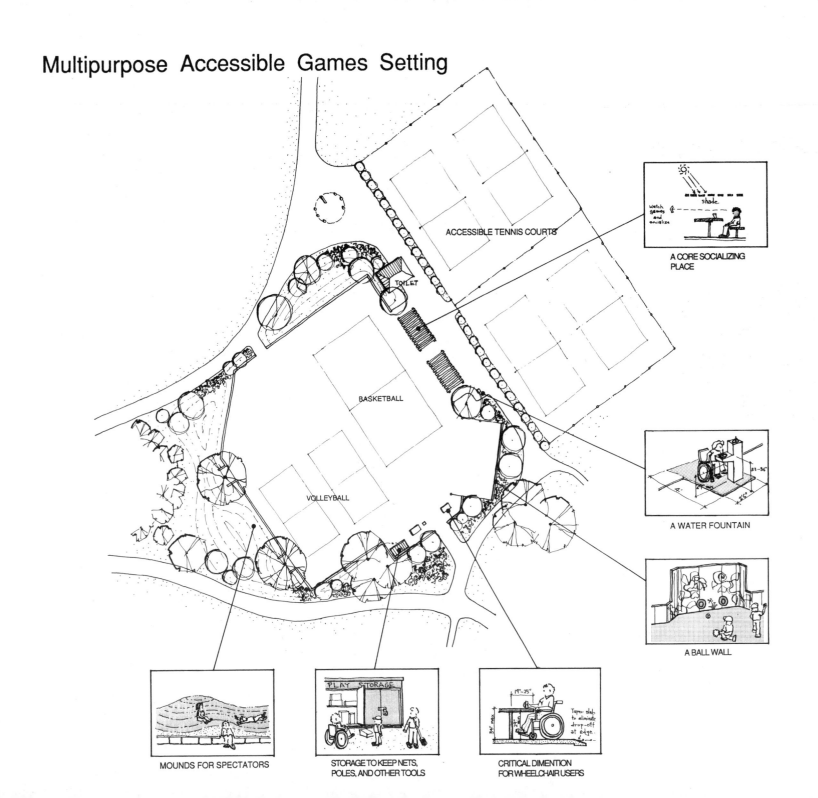

ACCESSIBLE TENNIS COURTS

TOILET

BASKETBALL

VOLLEYBALL

A CORE SOCIALIZING PLACE

A WATER FOUNTAIN

A BALL WALL

MOUNDS FOR SPECTATORS

STORAGE TO KEEP NETS, POLES, AND OTHER TOOLS

CRITICAL DIMENTION FOR WHEELCHAIR USERS

Play Station Locations

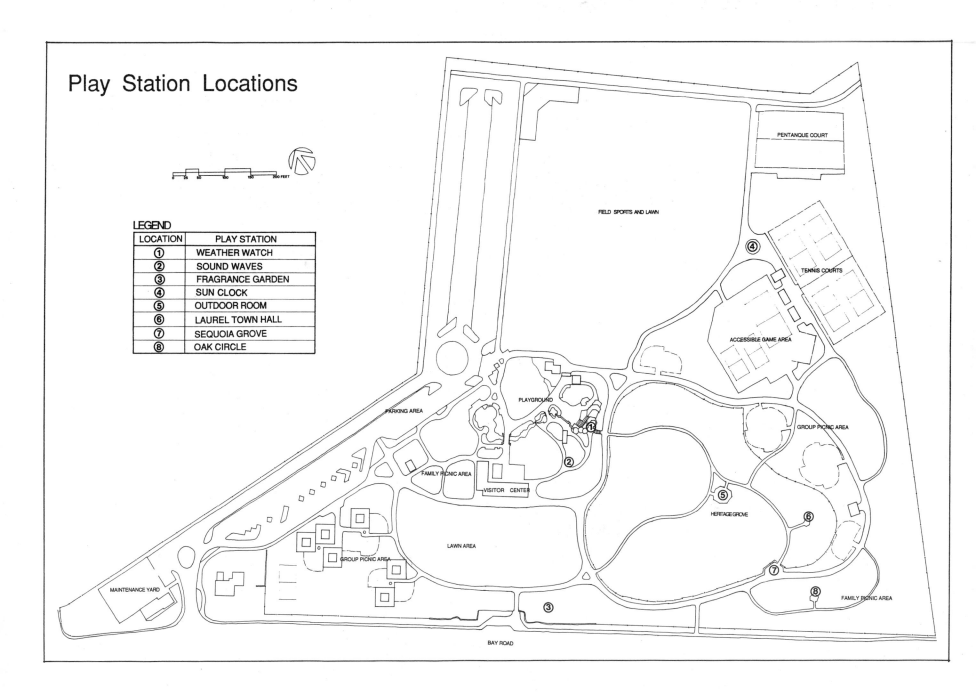

0   25   50   100   150   200 FEET

PENTANQUE COURT

FIELD SPORTS AND LAWN

④

TENNIS COURTS

ACCESSIBLE GAME AREA

PARKING AREA

PLAYGROUND

①

②

GROUP PICNIC AREA

FAMILY PICNIC AREA

VISITOR CENTER

⑤

HERITAGE GROVE

⑥

LAWN AREA

GROUP PICNIC AREA

⑦

⑧   FAMILY PICNIC AREA

③

MAINTENANCE YARD

BAY ROAD

Play Station

WEATHER WATCH ①

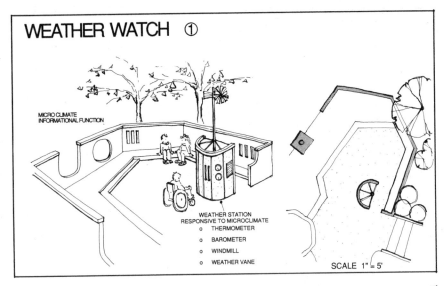

MICRO CLIMATE
INFORMATIONAL FUNCTION

WEATHER STATION
RESPONSIVE TO MICROCLIMATE
o   THERMOMETER
o   BAROMETER
o   WINDMILL
o   WEATHER VANE

SCALE 1" = 5'

SOUND WAVES ②

SOUND WAVE PIPES WILL BE MANUFACTURED LIKE A GAMALAN.
THERE ARE THREE TONES WHICH ARE HARMONICALLY
COORDINATED, SO THEY ONLY CREATE BEAUTIFUL SOUNDS.

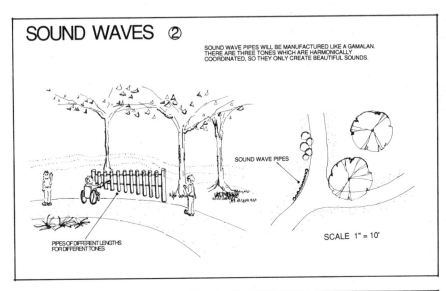

SOUND WAVE PIPES

PIPES OF DIFFERENT LENGTHS
FOR DIFFERENT TONES

SCALE 1" = 10'

FRAGRANCE GARDEN ③

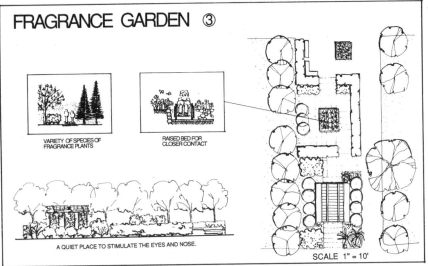

VARIETY OF SPECIES OF
FRAGRANCE PLANTS

RAISED BED FOR
CLOSER CONTACT

A QUIET PLACE TO STIMULATE THE EYES AND NOSE.

SCALE 1" = 10'

SUN CLOCK ④

SCULPTURES AROUND THE SUN CLOCK COULD EACH BE
DESIGNED AND DONATED BY LOCAL GROUPS. SCULPTURE
WOULD BE TOTEM-LIKE SYMBOLS OF THE COMMUNITY.

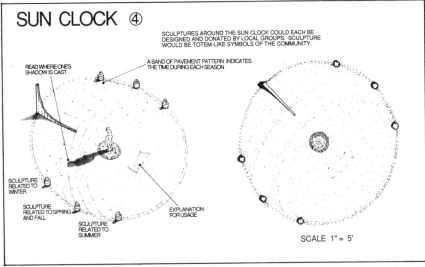

READ WHERE ONE'S
SHADOW IS CAST

A BAND OF PAVEMENT PATTERN INDICATES
THE TIME DURING EACH SEASON

SCULPTURE
RELATED TO
WINTER

SCULPTURE
RELATED TO SPRING
AND FALL

SCULPTURE
RELATED TO
SUMMER

EXPLANATION
FOR USAGE

SCALE 1" = 5'

Play Station

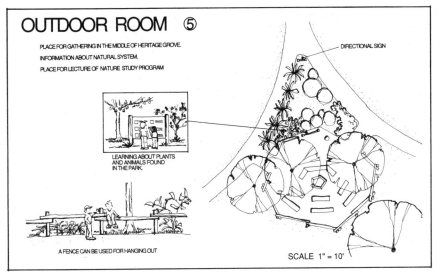

OUTDOOR ROOM ⑤

PLACE FOR GATHERING IN THE MIDDLE OF HERITAGE GROVE.

INFORMATION ABOUT NATURAL SYSTEM.

PLACE FOR LECTURE OF NATURE STUDY PROGRAM

DIRECTIONAL SIGN

LEARNING ABOUT PLANTS AND ANIMALS FOUND IN THE PARK.

A FENCE CAN BE USED FOR HANGING OUT

SCALE 1" = 10'

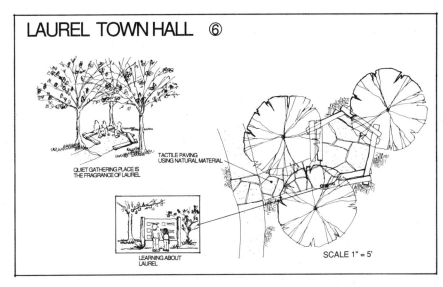

LAUREL TOWN HALL ⑥

TACTILE PAVING USING NATURAL MATERIAL

QUIET GATHERING PLACE IS THE FRAGRANCE OF LAUREL

LEARNING ABOUT LAUREL

SCALE 1" = 5'

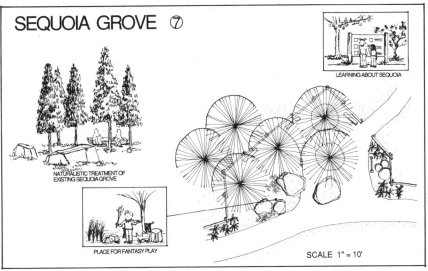

SEQUOIA GROVE ⑦

LEARNING ABOUT SEQUOIA

NATURALISTIC TREATMENT OF EXISTING SEQUOIA GROVE

PLACE FOR FANTASY PLAY

SCALE 1" = 10'

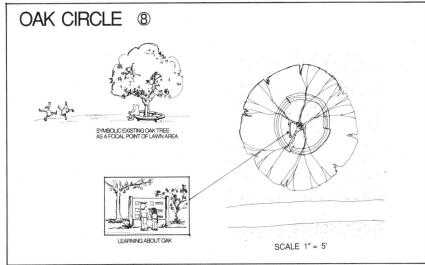

OAK CIRCLE ⑧

SYMBOLIC EXISTING OAK TREE AS A FOCAL POINT OF LAWN AREA

LEARNING ABOUT OAK

SCALE 1" = 5'

Accessibility Levels, Pathway Materials and Slope

ACCESSIBLE LEVEL	PAVING MATERIAL (EXAMPLE)		SLOPE	
ACCESSIBLE ⬆	CONCRETE	PAVERS ON CONCRETE	SLOPE 1:20 (5%)	CROSS-SLOPE 1:50 (2%)
	ASPHALT			
	PAVERS ON SAND	DECOMPOSED GRANITE	SLOPE 1:16 (6.2%)	CROSS-SLOPE 1:30 (3.3%)
	WOOD DECK	WOOD CHIPS		
CHALLENGING ⬇	UNTREATED SOIL	GRASS	SLOPE 1:12 (8.3%)	CROSS-SLOPE 1:20 (5%)
INACCESSIBLE	SAND	LOOSE GRAVEL	STEPS	

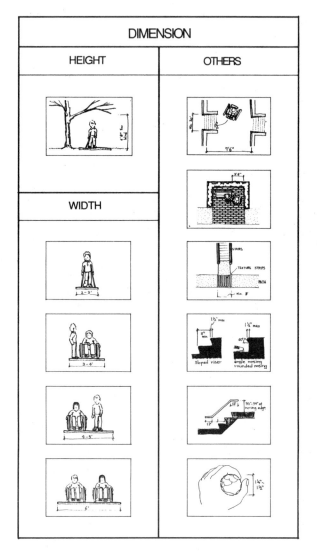

DIMENSION	
HEIGHT	**OTHERS**
WIDTH	

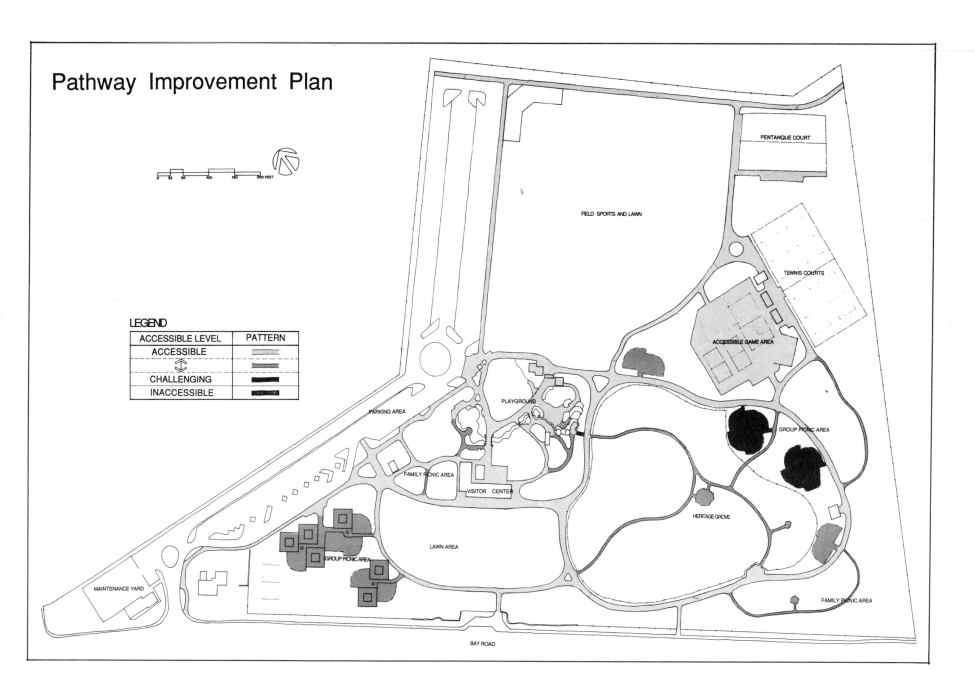

Pathway Improvement Plan

0 25 50 100 150 200 FEET

LEGEND

ACCESSIBLE LEVEL	PATTERN
ACCESSIBLE	
CHALLENGING	
INACCESSIBLE	

PENTANQUE COURT

FIELD SPORTS AND LAWN

TENNIS COURTS

ACCESSIBLE GAME AREA

GROUP PICNIC AREA

PLAYGROUND

PARKING AREA

FAMILY PICNIC AREA

VISITOR CENTER

HERITAGE GROVE

LAWN AREA

GROUP PICNIC AREA

MAINTENANCE YARD

FAMILY PICNIC AREA

BAY ROAD

22.3   Play Setting Evaluation and Design Criteria

Based on the results of the Flood Park community workshops and a design program of play settings, reflecting the opportunities and constraints of the site, a plan checklist (with the additional criteria of maintenance and cost) was developed. This checklist then became a decision making tool to weigh the trade-offs required for each setting before moving into the design development phase. The checklist is presented on the following pages and *can* be adapted as a design programmaing tool for other play settings.

FLOOD PARK PLAY AREA PLAN CHECKLIST

SETTING TYPE	PLANNING CRITERIA					
	Play Value	**Program Potential**	**Safety**	**Mgt/Maint.**	**Access/Integration**	**Issues**
Pedestrian Entrance. • Tower. • Map. • Signage. • Seating. • Vegetation.	Orientation. Historical. Tactile map of park. Understand aqua-duct connection to Hetch Hetchy Resevoir.	History Play Station.	Bollards to separate pedestrians from cars. Map protected with shade.	Vegetation. Signage upkeep.	Tactile map, signage with raised letters, tower as landmark with wind chimes as audio cue. Full wheelchair access.	Tower right-of-way. Art work commission.
Pathways • Major. • Minor. • Trails.	Wide enough for circulation & wheeled toy play.	Self programmed.	Fire truck access. 5' narrow paths. Edge detailing, signs/seating off pathway.	Clear pathways, good repair. Vehicle policy.	Level pathways. Change in ground texture at cross roads and at signage & seating. Seating max. every 100'.	Bicycles, skateboards, cars on paths. Cart checkout?
Climbing Area • Manf. Equip. • Slides. • Swings. • Linked structures.	Active play, large muscle, graduated challenge for ages 3—12, easier smaller events on one side.	Preprogrammed play events.	Protected fall zones within & around equip. Seating for adults to supervise. Sand under large equip. 12" deep.	Sand off paths. Clean sand daily. Safety checks, monthly detailed inspection of equipment.	Grab bars and rails, textured platforms at height changes, all after a corner or with defined texture accessible, tire swing with resilient surfaces, including entrance of structure.	Relocation of existing equipment.

FLOOD PARK PLAY AREA PLAN CHECKLIST

SETTING TYPE   PLANNING CRITERIA

	Play Value	Program Potential	Safety	Mgt/Maint.	Access/Integration	Issues
Infant/Toddler Area • Sand Play. • Water Play. • Sensory Path. • Equipment. • Signage. • Seating. • Vegetation.	Exploratory, environmental awareness, manipulation, motor skills, social skills.	Parental guidance.	Soft surfaces, no glass or other harmful items. Gates on entrance/exit. Appropriate vegetation. Nontoxic materials.	Sand contained. Animal droppings cleaned daily. Check for harmful substances.	Adjacent to large play area so parents can view children .Older and younger children can see each other. Multisensory cues.	
Fantasy Play Area • Picnic/worktable. • Clubhouse. • Small stages. • Vegetation.	Dramatic skills, social skills, role play, quiet play.	High potential. Child programmed.	Careful selection of grasses & natural ground covers. Observable from a distance.	Wild grass, rough cut, no large power mower.	Dirt pathway, clubhouse with wind chimes in roof for audio cue. Accessible club house.	
Sand Play Area • Raised sand amphitheater. • Sand shelves.	Fine motor & social skills. Dramatic, creative manipulative play.	Self programmed.	Edge detailing. Sitting steps 24" wide, hard sur-face. Shelf visible 6" above sand.	Keeping sand in boxes. Sand swept off steps.	Seat access at different heights in center of activity area. Edge detailing provides cues. Wheelchair access. Universal play activity.	

FLOOD PARK PLAY AREA PLAN CHECKLIST

SETTING TYPE	PLANNING CRITERIA					
	Play Value	Program Potential	Safety	Mgt/Maint.	Access/Integration	Issues
Play Mound • Seating. • Topography. • Vegetation.	Overview. Quiet play.	Child programmed. Flood Park Flag contest.	Retaining wall. Edge details.	Erosion potential. Ground cover carefully. maintained	Multiple means of access. Landmark helps to orient, gives overview of area. Good from infant to senior, across disabilities. Slope 1:20.	
Water Play • Spray.	Sensory stimulation. Social skills.	Child programmed.	Potable water. Nonslip surfaces.	Clear drains.	Fully accessible, lever handles.	
Water • Spring. • Waterfall. • Raised chute. • Stream. • Pond.	Exploratory. Sensory stimulation. Social skills. Environmental education.	Child-programmed, self-programmed, high programming potential.	Water depth. Edge details. Pond surface, observable from a distance.	Glass in water. Water quality. Filtration system. Daily check. Wild life mgt. for pond.	Access at various points and at various heights. variety of water experiences at varying levels of accessibility. Quiet to active play across ages.	Chlorination. Natural system most important design element for play.
Stage Area • Platform. • Adobe Bldg. • Lawn. • Storage.	Dramatic, social skills. Community place.	High programming potential.		Lawn mowing.	Stage access with ramp 1:10 over 15'. Access over lawn difficult.	Electrical wiring in adobe building.

FLOOD PARK PLAY AREA PLAN CHECKLIST

SETTING TYPE	PLANNING CRITERIA					
	Play Value	Program Potential	Safety	Mgt/Maint.	Access/Integration	Issues
Table Games • Seating. • Vegetation. • Surfacing.	Intergenerational. Problem solving. Social skills.	Self programmed.	Loose parts. Hard nonslip surface.	Loose parts.	Loose seats for wheel– chair access, pedestal base on tables.	Check out games in ranger area.
Outdoor Kitchen • Sinks. • Counter.	Support area for barbecue.			Keeping it clean.	Sink and counter height.	
Family Picnic • Tables. • Grills.	Support area. Social skills.	Family programmed.	Grill area.	Keeping it clean.	Loose benches for wheelchair access at any point. Grills with place to hold platters.	Loose benches.
Restrooms • Men. • Women.	Support area.		Observable.	Keeping them clean.	Fully accessible.	Prebuilt modular systems.
Planting • Trees. • Shrubs. • Flowers.	Environmental education. Play props. Fantasy play.	Child programmed. High programming potential.	Observable. Nontoxic, nonallergenic.	Pruning, leaf pick up, protection for new vegetation.	Branch overhang height. Ability to get into and near vege– tation.	

PART D :

Programming and Management

23. PLAY PROGRAMMING

This chapter provides an overview of play programming for integration of all children.

Play opportunities should provide challenging experiences for all children in safe, healthy, stimulating, and accessible environments. Creating a fully integrated community recreation program is difficult, but not impossible to achieve if the public agency makes a commitment to implement such a program.

23.1   Case Study Program

From 1980 to 1989, PLAE, Inc., of Berkeley, California, developed a prototype program as an action-research effort to discover how to integrate children with disabilities in a program serving over 2000 children, one-third with developmental, physical, emotional, or learning disabilities. The ages of the children ranged from six to sixteen. Several conclusions were reached as a result of this experience (Iacofano et al., 1985):

a.   The greater the range of outdoor settings the wider the assortment of programmed activities that can be supported.

b.   A broad range of activities allows more children of different ages and ability levels to participate at the same time.

c.   A programmatic base in the community arts, instead of sports, offers many opportunities for participation by all children.

d.   A thematic approach to workshop activities, in combination with skilled play leadership, provides a structure which allows children to work together through dramatic play. It also helps adults relate positively to the program and to better understand its value.

e.   The "play value" of play settings is highly dependent on how they are programmed and managed, especially for the integration of children with and without disabilities.

23.2   Play Programming Criteria for All Children

Based on the above findings, PLAE has developed a management model for providing direct community recreation services to all children. The model takes into consideration the range of settings, the program of activities, play leadership, and the physical setting.

a.   **Environmental Diversity.** A variety of physical settings must be provided to support varied programming and to accommodate different leader abilities and skills.

b.   **Environmental Control.** Both children and staff must have control over their environment. Lockable storage, use of restroom facilities, large trash receptacles, electricity, and water are necessary.

c.   **Defensible Space.** For leaders to feel free enough to take risks and be adventurous in programming, the environment must be easily supervised. Play leaders need to see who is entering or leaving the activity area and be able to locate children easily. However, this does not mean that the environment must be totally open or without walls, buffers, and other subdivisions.

d.   **Adaptability/Flexibility.** Programs must remain open to changing situations and the individual needs of participants within a structural framework.

e.   **Arts-based Programming.** Programming that is based in the arts provides a context for innovation, creativity, and discovery of one's relationship to the world.

f.   **Choice of activities.** A variety of activities are required to engage and capture children's imaginations:

1)   Activities that make everyone a star.

2)   Trust-building activities.

3)   Risk-taking activities.

4)   Activities that promote sharing and cooperation.

5)   Activities that allow for creative expression.

6)   Activities that are fun!

7)   Group problem solving.

8)   Construction activities.

9)   Activities that are "larger than life."

g.   **Dramatic Play.** Dramatic play stimulates imagination and creativity. The conscious incorporation of dramatic play into a program supports and nourishes children's natural abilities.

h.   **Spontaneity.** Providing play props, loose parts, and a variety of scrap materials that can be transformed into something else allows children to take an activity initiated by the play leader and expand on it. For example, with simple building materials, children can create structures around which elaborate fantasy dramas may unfold.

i.   **Product.** Products are an important part of the play experience They show accomplishment. Products can be ends in themselves or they can become parts of a larger group project, such as a circus performance.

j.   **Cooperation.** A team approach to projects helps children work together. By assigning individual responsibility for parts of a project, children have an individual accomplishment which leads to a group product. A balance is struck between encouraging the development of self-potential and fostering community awareness and positive social interaction.

k.   **A Creative Atmosphere.** The play environment is a place to experiment, take risks, and make mistakes.

l.   **Play Leadership.** Play leaders and animators are the backbone of any play program. They are highly skilled professionals trained in the use of creative arts and physical settings to create play events that are stimulating and challenging for a wide variety of children. Animators create a context for fantasy and dramatic play by introducing activity scores, scripts, props, and loose parts that help involve children and facilitate use of the environment to its fullest potential.

Animators can provide a positive role model for all children, demonstrating qualities such as autonomy, practical skills, cooperation, flexibility, willingness to listen, and the desire to change and grow.

m.   **Openness.** Integration of all children is promoted as disabled children and non-disabled children are involved in the same program. Accommodations for children with a variety of disabilities should be present or readily available by adapting a tool or an activity on the spot.

n. **Empowerment.** Play programs can empower children to utilize their full capabilities and to learn how to participate in the making of decisions that affect them.

o. **Behavior Management.** An organized program structure is important to children's safe play experiences. Positive limits can be set and children can participate in solving problems and taking responsibility for their own behavior.

p. **Communication.** Staff that works well together and communicates openly contributes to making an environment where children feel safe. Children benefit from seeing positive interactions between staff.

q. **Parent/Staff Interaction.** A healthy relationship between parents and staff is essential for supporting child development.

r. **Setting, Program and Leadership.** Physical environment, program and leadership must be managed as a system: the environment sets the stage and context in which structured yet flexible program activities can be executed and brought to life by creative play leaders. This interaction of physical setting, program and leadership is the heart of the management model.

24. RISK MANAGEMENT STRATEGIES

This chapter is a revised and updated version of a paper that originally appeared in Children's Environments Quarterly *(Moreland et al., 1985).*

Safety, security, and liability have become major factors in determining the quality of children's environments and play programs. Swings and suspended nets are being eliminated from some playgrounds. Thickly planted areas, typically used by children for hide-and-seek games, for exploration of nature and other creative activities, are being omitted from the design of new play spaces to permit higher visibility for adult supervisors. Installed playground equipment has come under intense scrutiny and design standards have been called for by consumer agencies and federal, state, and local governments.

Rising insurance rates have forced many play and recreational programs out of business while others have been curtailed. Recent concerns about potential child abuse in child care programs have focused attention on the qualifications and experience of program staff. When children with special needs are enrolled in a program, special safety concerns create even more anxiety for those responsible.

24.1   Who is Responsible?

Given this growing plethora of pressures on organized play, one may seriously ask whether professionally run programs are going to be possible at all in the future. The outcome lies clearly in the hands of those directly involved: public and private programming agencies, play equipment manufacturers, designers, equipment specifiers and the insurance industry.

In the forefront are the public agencies responsible for both programs and settings. Their ability to engage in successful risk management will largely determine whether quality play programming has a future; or whether it will be overcome by the growing number and size of liability suits; or whether it will simply fade away, by default, as creative staff become disenchanted with the many bureaucratic rules, regulations and conservative attitudes endemic of risky situations.

24.2   What is Risk Management?

Where does the risk management concept come from? It is a relatively new subject, even on the broader frontiers of management practice. It is an excellent example of contemporary philosophy of management as both science and art. The key assumption is that any life worth living is a risky business. One cannot learn except by taking risks: "Nothing ventured, nothing gained," the saying goes. However, the other critical assumption is that risk is not the same as danger or hazard.

The objective of proper risk management is to ensure that hurt, injury or accident is **prevented**; not to eliminate risk, but to reduce the potential for negative consequences to acceptable levels. Accidents cannot be eliminated entirely. Tragedies do occur. The natural environment, human relations, life itself, are to some degree, by their very nature, unpredictable. Chance (conception and birth is the obvious example) and truly "unforeseen circumstances" will always be present. Risk management is a strategy of "reasonable means" to prevent tragedy while allowing risk.

24.3   The Criterion of Reasonableness

What constitutes reasonableness is the crucial judgement: getting hit by a car is a common cause of serious injury and death among children, yet even the most modest suggestions for control (low speed limits, diverters, necked crossings, cul-de-sacs, speed bumps, etc.) are usually met with howls of protest by adult drivers who evidently feel them to be quite unreasonable suggestions in relation to saving a few children's lives (Appleyard, 1981). Like other social issues, they do not strike home except at a personal level. A highly visible campaign in the Netherlands to control residential traffic was started by a journalist whose own child had been killed by a car. The campaign was successful because, in this case, people were eventually **persuaded** that the traffic control proposals were reasonable.

24.4   Risk Management is both Art and Science

This is where the **art** of risk management comes in: the preparation of convincing arguments, the use of telling examples, the implementation of effective community/public relations. These strategies must stimulate all concerned to be involved in helping to define "reasonableness," Once defined, they must be made operational as management objectives and properly communicated back to the community.

The **science** of risk management also enters the picture, providing descriptive facts and figures of accidents and incidents, where they occur and under what circumstances (information that is still pitifully sparse).

24.5   Risk Management in Practice

Successful programs for children with and without disabilities depend on a complex environment which offers diverse opportunities for stimulating and challenging play (Goltsman, Moore & Iacofano, 1982). Paradoxically, the elements of a complex environment carry greater inherent risks, both real and perceived. A manipulative environment gives children and program leaders objects which can be used for creative play activities but which may be especially difficult to control safely (Beckwith, 1985), particularly when such items are introduced spontaneously. Desirable environmental and programmatic elements from a child development perspective appear to be in direct opposition to safety and liability concerns. The purpose of risk management is to mitigate this apparent conflict. A proactive approach depends primarily on the **prevention** of incidents which jeopardize the safety and security of the child. Key strategies are as follows:

a.   **Reporting Incidents.** For incident reporting and management purposes, four types of situations in which safety and security problems (incidents) may arise have been defined:

1)   **Child-to-Self:** Situations in which the individual child experiences an accident through interaction with the environment. Examples include falling down while running, and falling from a tree or wall.

2)   **Child-to-Child:** Situations in which two of more children provoke harm or injury to one another. Examples include fighting, accidents during games, and the pressuring of children by peers into risky behaviors.

3)   **Adult-to-Child:** Situations in which the health and safety of a child are jeopardized by actions taken or not taken by an adult in charge. Examples include physical or sexual child abuse and accidents due to negligence.

4)   **Outside Influences to Child:** Situations in which factors enter from outside the play environment to affect the safety and security of the child. Examples include unauthorized persons entering the environment, litter and pollution and roaming animals.

b.   **Incident Data Analysis.** An evaluation process should be developed to determine where accidents occur and if they are environmentally related. Questions should be asked about where the accident occurred, who was involved, the time of day, the nature of the injury and what actions were taken after the accident.

c.   **Shared Environmental Control.** Control over the physical environment is essential to the safety and security of children. Because program settings are often on public park or school property, use of the site must be negotiated and relationships with other programmed activities must be maintained. By inviting the involvement of others, potentially difficult or dangerous interactions are minimized and the situation is used to build up community support.

d.   **"Defensible" Program Space.** To provide further for the safety of children during program events, a more decentralized use of the site is required. "Play stations" can be established with individual play leaders at each station to supervise smaller groups of children. In this sense, the territory occupied by the program can be defined and monitored more naturally (Newman, 1972).

e.   **Shared Site Maintenance.** Maintaining the program site to eliminate potential hazards to children should be the joint responsibility of the programming organization and the community. In complex settings, a finer, more subtle approach to routine maintenance is often required than that normally provided for conventional equipment settings. Willing play leaders who understand how the environment functions as program space can support a nonjanitorial approach to maintenance and even engage users in the process.

Children can participate in occasional "Trash Pickup Contests"—essentially games where children work cooperatively to gather bottles, cans, paper and other litter.

f.   **Supervision.** Effective supervision of children's outdoor play activities is the key to both safety and the maximization of play opportunities.

Supervision goes beyond the passive overseeing of activities to include provision of activities which stimulate the imagination, promote the integration of all children and extend the learning experiences inspired by children's play. Play leaders must serve as positive role models. They should be recruited from a variety of cultures and abilities/disabilities to help children appreciate cultural diversity. The following are specific safety considerations:

1)   Staff should be trained in Red Cross first aid and CPR techniques as well as site safety procedures.

2)   The site should be prepared to facilitate rapid emergency response. A telephone, emergency transportation procedures, and first aid supplies should be readily available.

3) Staff should be trained in promoting positive play experiences. This will minimize the chance of children engaging in high risk activities due to boredom.

4) An adequate staff-to-child ratio is necessary. Staff-to-participant ratios vary in different programs. An ideal ratio is 1:5. A workshop of twenty-five children typically has three adult supervisors and at least two teenage aides. Additional aides may be hired, depending on the types of disabilities represented in the group. Higher ratios produce benefits that tend to outweigh the costs: parents feel more secure and satisfied and the staff feels more capable of providing adequate security.

g. **First Aid Preparedness.**

1) Children should receive adequate instruction regarding rules. These rules should be periodically reviewed.

2) Parents should receive a copy of rules. Leaders should meet with parents of participating children and explain common sports hazards and methods of preventing accidents. Parents should be instructed to review these accident prevention measures with their children at home.

3) Emergency procedures should be developed for dealing with both major and minor accidents during program participation. Important considerations include:

- Parent's release form for emergency treatment;
- First aid procedures;
- Location of first aid equipment;
- Cardiopulmonary resuscitation;
- Location of nearest telephone;
- Location of nearest hospital emergency room;
- Transportation to the emergency facility;
- Procedure for notification of parents; and
- Maintenance of a file of phone numbers where parents and other individuals (who parents may designate as alternative contacts), may be reached. These procedures should be reviewed and updated on an annual basis.

4) A copy of the emergency procedures manual should be maintained on the site at all times.

5) The site should be prepared in order to provide a rapid emergency response. Access to a nearby telephone should be maintained at all times. Emergency numbers (ambulance, hospital emergency room and poison control center) should be posted in a visible place near the telephone.

6) First aid supplies should be available, including ice or "instant ice packs."

7) A procedure should be developed for periodically checking and replenishing first aid supplies. Maintaining a list of supplies which are included in the first aid kit can facilitate this process.

8) Adequate staffing should be maintained to ensure supervision of remaining children if one leader must accompany a child to an emergency treatment center or provide first aid on site.

9) Provide staff training. All staff should complete an American Red Cross certified first aid course.

10) At least one staff member certified by the American Red Cross in cardiopulmonary resuscitation (CPR) should be present on-site at all times. Other staff should know the staff members who are certified in CPR.

11) Under no circumstances should an untrained staff member attempt CPR; serious injury can result.

12) In-service training on emergency procedures should be required of all staff on an annual basis.

13) All staff should receive a copy of the emergency procedures manual and be encouraged to review it periodically.

h.   **Training.** Play leadership training for both staff and aides is essential for providing safe yet challenging play activities. Play leaders need to learn how to give appropriate directions and avoid the kind of pitfalls that can lead to accidents.

On-the-job training can take place through "apprenticeships" of prospective play leaders with trained staff. Trainees can learn proper use of potentially hazardous materials such as fire, ropes, hammers and saws in situations involving children.

Play leadership seminars can teach staff about the programming organization, its policies and goals. Trainees become aware of potential site hazards, learn procedures for managing accidents, learn how to handle behavior problems and how to include children in cooperative play activities.

i.   **Built-in Risk Taking**. Built-in risk taking within program activities provides a safe yet challenging experience for children. Recognizing that children like to climb on things that are potentially dangerous, safe programs of activity can be designed. In the PLAE workshop "Treasure Island," for example (*Treasure Island PLAE Score*, 1986), children "escape from the shipwreck to the life raft (climbing net)." Workshop leaders and aides are on hand to assist. To add to the perceived challenge (but not to the risk), the sand pit under the net is flooded with a few inches of water. "Shark fins" (cutout cardboard props) stick out menacingly (but not dangerously) from the water beneath the net.

Children love to jump off walls, rope swings, rooftops and other challenging places. In Treasure Island, blindfolded "pirates" jump off a plank positioned over a sand pit made safe with layers of foam rubber. Thus, children are provided with a heightened experience of jumping and risk taking.

Insuring the safety and security of children is easier if they participate in programmed activities. Play leaders must provide direction as well as supervision. Children are more actively engaged in programmed activities if they are cooperatively structured. Working and playing with play partners, in teams and in small or large groups, keep children actively engaged and less exposed to unforeseen risks.

j.   **Programming for Spontaneous Play.** To maintain high quality play programs, spontaneous (potentially hazardous) play must be integrated into programmed activities. In this way, children can have fun and seek challenge, while play leaders direct and supervise their activities.

Recognizing that children like to wade into ponds, jettison pieces of wood across water surfaces and build bridges, similar activities are programmed in the "Treasure Island" PLAE workshop. Play leaders help children collect empty plastic milk cartons to increase flotation. Together they construct more substantial, safe "rafts" that serve the same purpose and allow all children to participate.

Children's behavior can be directed appropriately to reduce risks to acceptable levels while not defeating children's creative play. To achieve this requires sensitive, carefully trained play leaders. They must be flexible enough to allow spontaneous play activities to be safely incorporated into the program theme, thereby supporting the goal of child integration.

k.   **Community-Based Management.** Parents, children and community members should be involved in the planning, design and operation of settings and programs. Parents of program participants can serve on the Board of Directors. Routinely solicited evaluations from both children and parents can provide comments and suggestions for incorporation into future programming. Community needs assessments can be conducted before new programs or services are implemented.

l.   **Community Involvement.** As the population served by a newly integrated program expands, efforts to involve families in a participatory way must also grow. Parent-child workshops can be sponsored, free events can be held in parks for families and other opportunities for increased family participation in the program development can be proposed, such as picnics where parents, children and play leaders can meet.

Radio shows and community slide presentations can build a solid foundation of mutual respect and support. Over the years, an extended "program family" can evolve that includes all former participants. Hundreds of families can be touched so that parents and children approach the play leaders easily with suggestions and criticisms as well as praise. Whenever concerns arise, the personal relationships which have developed among the participants and staff provide a basis for working out difficulties.

m.   **Multilevel Communication Between Parents and Leaders.** The safety and security of children is strongly supported by community based management. Parent board members can help develop a rapport with parents of children in the program, seeking their input and feedback. This makes parents feel more secure about the risks their children may take.

Program descriptions can be made available to parents in advance so that problems their children might have can be anticipated. Parental feedback can also be solicited through post-program evaluations to help identify concerns.

Program registration forms should require parents to provide information on their child's special needs: the need for extra attention because of shyness, assistance in eating because of an orthopedic disability, medication requirements, etc. These forms should also provide information about the adults authorized to pick up the child, whether the child will walk home, emergency and doctor phone numbers, parent's wishes when minor scrapes occur, and so on. In cases of unusual need, additional aides may be called in to supplement workshop staff.

Parents should also receive a complete description of the program setting and risk management policies. They should be apprised of accident policies which can be adjusted in individual cases. Parents should be informed about the staff's level of supervision, the staff's experience and qualifications, and the level of safety and security the program realistically can provide. The purpose of these efforts is to make sure parents are fully aware of the risks and allow them to make properly informed choices on behalf of their children. The aim should be to minimize the anxiety of parents so that they can go about their business without fretting about their children's welfare.

Communication is the crucial link in providing a children's program that parents feel comfortable with. Professional leadership training helps staff learn the language to use when describing the program to others, how to communicate effectively with parents and how to respond to parent requests and desires. The end result is that parents understand the risks and opportunities their children face. They appreciate the goal of providing a stimulating play environment and feel equipped to share in the responsibility for their children's well-being.

n. **New Risk Management Models.** There is no such thing as a completely safe play environment. Children will naturally seek out potentially hazardous physical challenges. Instead of removing all hazards, thus creating sterile and unstimulating play spaces, careful programming can lead to safe activities that satisfy children's need for enjoyment and challenge. This suggests the need for new models of supervised programming that can be incorporated into public recreational environments so that risk can be more sensitively balanced with creative play.

Communication is the key to effective risk management. Everyone connected with the program—staff, parents, children, administrators, community members—must share ultimate responsibility for child safety and security. Opportunities for families and community members to participate in the management of programs must be provided. In this way, when incidents occur, they can be managed from a base of preparedness and mutual understanding.

The greatest challenge being faced by providers of children's play and learning environments is not just to avoid major lawsuits for broken bones or astronomical insurance premiums; it is the responsibility for raising a generation of young people who have the opportunity to play in healthy and stimulating surroundings.

24.6   Taking Action

The *Play For All Guidelines* were developed to meet the challenge of balancing safety with child development objectives. Since the *Play For All* conference at Stanford, many inquiries have been received requesting assistance in applying the guidelines to local communities.

The following is a process which has been developed by *Play For All* staff to assist parks and recreation departments, schools and child care agencies in applying the guidelines:

a.   **Develop a Safety First Policy.** The development of a safety first policy is a proactive approach to providing healthy, safe and developmentally appropriate outdoor play environments. It involves a consciously applied set of strategies designed to:

1)   Mitigate the known and perceived safety hazards in an environment and in organized programs.

2)   Prevent harm and injury.

3)   Establish a process for handling and documenting incidents that occur.

4)   Share responsibility for safety and security of children with their families.

b.   **Create a Site Master Plan Based on the PFA Guidelines.** After initiating a safety first program, every site should be analyzed for its appropriateness as a children's play and learning environment. This is an important task in the construction of new playgrounds or the rehabilitation of existing ones. A thorough inventory of the characteristics of each site should include, but not be limited to: location; site function, natural features and utilities; human and cultural features; existing equipment; and social and geographical setting within the community.

A site master plan should be developed. The master planning process should involve administrators, staff, maintenance personnel, risk managers, parents and children in setting goals for the site and developing a program of activities to meet those goals. The master plan can then be designed to support selected activities. Consideration should also be given to ensure that all children's play environments are accessible to children with disabilities. A phased development plan can be created to prioritize improvements to allow strategic improvements to be made as funds become available.

The following steps might be taken to develop a positive response to safety:

1) **Task Force.** Create a task force to oversee the project. Members of the task force should include business managers, site personnel, maintenance staff and community members.

2) **Budget.** Determine how much money is needed:

- Assess the amount of money being spent on legal action related to play environment injuries.
- If there are no accidents, find out the direct costs of managing the site.
- As a starting point, take the above information to the local insurance pool or risk manager and ask for 5% of their exposure to begin the process of upgrading the play environment.

3) **Master Plan.** No matter how small, create a master plan for the site. This master plan should involve task force members in establishing goals and a list of priority site improvements.

4) **Site Evaluation.** Using the goals and activities identified in the master plan, evaluate the existing site.

- How do the existing equipment settings and other settings support the goals and activities identified in the master plan?
- Is the site and its equipment safe, accessible, and well maintained?
- Do they support the desired play behavior? (Use a safety checklist as a guide.)

5) **Current Equipment Usage.** Using the site evaluation information as documentation, decide what needs to be removed, replaced or adapted.

6) **Phased Improvement Plan.** In most situations, all the desired site improvements cannot be afforded at one time.

- Create a phased improvement plan to guide purchase and maintenance decisions and to help community groups decide on projects to support through fund-raising, gift donations or, when appropriate, new settings.
- Create a set of guidelines and procedures for the design, purchase, installation, and maintenance of the site.

7) **Document the Process.** A clear record of the process and decisions made will help future users evaluate current needs in light of previous decisions.

c.   **Share Responsibility and Risk.** Since no play environment is completely safe, parents must be involved in sharing the responsibility of operating a play environment or program which can promote healthy child development. Providing opportunities for parent involvement in policy development, maintenance of the environment and program planning and implementation creates a sense of parent ownership.

Everyone connected with a play environment—staff, parents, children, administrators, and community members—must ultimately share responsibility for child safety and security. Real opportunities for families and community members to participate in the management of programs and environments must be provided. In this way, when incidents occur, they can be managed from a base of mutual understanding.

Children will naturally seek out physical challenges that can be hazardous. Rather than creating sterile and inappropriate outdoor play spaces, careful design, programming, maintenance and supervision can lead to safe activities that children both enjoy and find challenging.

This responsibility can be best met through the development of local safety first policies, creating site master plans to guide future play area development and involving parents and community members in sharing the risk and responsibility for play programs and environments.

APPENDICES

A. ABOUT DISABILITY AND INTEGRATION

The editors wish to thank the Bay Area Outreach Program (BORP) for permission to include this edited selection from *We Can do It: A Training Manual for Integrating Disabled People into Recreation Programs.*

A.1   Mainstreaming/Integration (Fitzgerald, 1982)

Mainstreaming is sometimes used as another word for *integration.* Even though the two terms have been used interchangeably they mean different things. Mainstreaming connotes the placing of a few "different" people (a disabled, racial, or sexual minority) into a regular program or activity, thereby implying that the other "regular" people have more power or authority. Integration implies that both groups have equal status and are moving toward a common point of reference. Even though mainstream is more commonly used in education and government circles, a word with more positive connotations can help affect more positive change.

Integration is a dynamic process with the individual progressing through a continuum of various stages from the segregated experience at one end to the totally integrated experience at the other. Not all people with disabilities are ready to be integrated; some need support services which can prepare them for the next stage on the continuum. Progression through these various stages permits people with and without disabilities to have increasingly greater opportunities for social interaction at a pace that is appropriate for each individual.

A.1.1 Integrated Recreation

Not many years ago, everyday activities such as school, employment, and recreation were unavailable to people with disabilities. They had separate schools, sheltered workshops, and segregated recreational facilities. In fact, many people with disabilities were institutionalized and kept out of sight from the able-bodied community. During the early 1970's, Wolf Wolfensberger introduced a concept called "normalization"—introducing people with disabilities to a more "normal" environment. This represented a change from the prevailing attitudes towards people with disabilities.

Although normalization applies to all aspects of one's life, when applied to recreation, it created a new strategy for recreators with disabilities. In addition, change was brought about by federal and state legislation mandating that a continuum of services be given in the "Least Restrictive Environment" to children with disabilities.

Budget cuts in community and social services played an important factor too. Many community agencies had to pool their resources in order to stay open. When organizations which had provided recreation to people with disabilities were cut back or closed, city and university recreation programs were asked to provide services. It was found that offering integrated recreation activities in existing programs was very cost effective. All of these factors led to the development of integrated recreation.

A.2   Legislative History

There have been a great number of Federal laws which have implications for recreational opportunities for people with disabilities. The most recent and far-reaching has been the Americans With Disabilities Act. Following are brief descriptions of major landmarks in the legislative history of accessibility rights in the United States:

a.   **Vocational Rehabilitation Act of 1963.** Funds for training and research in recreation for the ill and handicapped were included in the 1963 revision of the Vocational Rehabilitation Act of 1954. This was the first Federal action recognizing the importance of recreation services for people with disabilities. Following this action, several colleges and universities received funds to implement training programs at the graduate level in "recreation for handicapped individuals," providing a foundation for the growth and development of therapeutic recreation.

b.   **The Architectural Barriers Act of 1968 (Public Law 90-480).** This was the first federal law requiring facility access for the physically disabled, stating that "any building or facility constructed in whole or in part by federal funds must be made accessible and usable by the physically handicapped." The impact of the Architectural Barriers Act, although fairly limited in its scope (affecting only federally funded construction or remodeling), has been profound. It provided the legislative mandate for development of accessibility standards and the legal foundation for future accessibility efforts.

c.   **The Uniform Federal Accessibility Standards (Federal Standard 795).** The Uniform Federal Accessibility Standards (UFAS) define the standards for design, construction and alteration of buildings to meet the requirements of the Architectural Barriers Act. UFAS is based on the Minimum Guidelines and Requirements for Accessible Design (MGRAD), which were developed by the Architectural and Transportation Barriers Compliance Board to provide direction to federal agencies that oversee federally owned, leased, or financed buildings. UFAS is the title of the standards actually adopted by those agencies. Recreational and civic buildings and sites that require public access, or that might serve as a place of employment for a person with disabilities, are among the facilities addressed in these standards. UFAS does not address program accessibility issues (except as they relate to physical access).

d. **Rehabilitation Act of 1973 (Public Law 93-112).** This document is a comprehensive revision of the 1963 Vocational Rehabilitation Act, removing emphasis from "vocational" rehabilitation and focusing on total rehabilitation of all disabled persons. Several features of this legislation that impact recreation include:

1) **Title II - Research and Training.** This title continues authorization of funds for training of recreation professionals to work with disabled persons and research in this area.

2) **Title III. Section 304 - Special Projects and Demonstrations.** This section authorized grants for "Operating programs (including renovation and construction of facilities, where appropriate) to demonstrate methods of making recreational activities fully accessible to handicapped individuals."

3) **Title V. Section 504 - Rehabilitation Act of 1973 (Public Law 93-112 as amended by PL-516 and PL 95-602).** "No otherwise qualified handicapped individual in the United States . . . shall, solely by reason of handicap, be excluded from the participation in, be denied the benefits of, or be subjected to discrimination under any program or activity receiving Federal financial assistance."

While the Architectural Barriers Act demands *physical access* in programs and facilities, Section 504 requires barrier-free *programming* for physically disabled persons. Barrier-free programming includes making the program available in alternative locations when the site itself cannot be made accessible. It also addresses access to programs related to people with sensory impairments.

e. **Rehabilitation Act Amendment of 1974 (Public Law 93-516).** This legislation authorized the planning and implementation of the White House Conference on Handicapped Individuals which was held in May 1977. Recreation was one of sixteen major areas of concerns addressed. Recommendations for increased Federal funding, better accessibility in parks, monuments and recreation programs, more consumer involvement in planning, program implementation and employment evolved from conference sessions.

f.   **Education of All Handicapped Children Act, 1975 (Public Law 94-142).** This law amends Public Law 90-380, greatly expanding educational opportunities for children with disabilities. PL 94-142 requires a free, appropriate education for all children. The emphasis in the rule is the word "appropriate," and specific guidelines are given for what is considered appropriate education. An individualized education plan is required for each child, which includes evaluation of their present educational performance, establishing specific educational goals, a statement of services to be provided to reach these goals, and a continuum of placements in "the least restrictive environment." Recreation as a related service is included in the law. The definition of recreation as it pertains to this rule includes assessment of leisure functioning, therapeutic recreation, recreation in schools and communities, and leisure education. This law began to promote leisure and recreation as a significant aspect in the total education of children with disabilities.

g.   **Fair Housing Amendments Act.** This Act was signed in September 1988 and became effective on March 12, 1989. It is intended to strengthen enforcement of Fair Housing requirements and to extend civil rights protections for families with children and persons with disabilities. It has three broad purposes in relation to people with disabilities: 1) to end segregation of the housing available to people who have disabilities; 2) to give people with disabilities greater opportunity to choose where they want to live; and 3) to assure that reasonable accommodations be made to the individual needs of people with disabilities in securing and using housing. Effectively, the Fair Housing Amendments Act has increased and broadened the housing market to families with children and people with disabilities. Thus, the need for accessible and usable outdoor play settings and related recreational spaces is increasing so as to serve the full range of families, including those with parents or children with disabilities.

h.   **Americans With Disabilities Act of 1990 (Public Law 101-336).** The Americans With Disabilities Act (ADA) is a comprehensive law prohibiting discrimination against people with disabilities in employment, public transportation, telecommunications and public accommodations, including recreation facilities and programs. It extends to persons with disabilities similar comprehensive civil rights protections provided to persons on the basis of race, sex, national origin, and religion under the Civil Rights Act of 1964. In regard to physical accessibility, ADA extends the intent of the Architectural Barriers Act to cover all public facilities regardless of federal funding, including facilities such as restaurants, hospitals, movie theaters, medical and law offices and retail stores. The sections of the

Act that address these issues are Title II (Public Services and Public Transportation) and Title III (Public Accommodations and Services).

Implementation of ADA is being accomplished through a new set of standards called the "ADA Accessibility Guidelines for Buildings and Facilities." These guidelines use UFAS as their model, expanding as needed to address the additional facilities and issues covered under ADA.

i.   **State Laws.** In some states, building codes have been adopted that go above and beyond the requirements set forth in UFAS and the ADA Guidelines. In these states, Federal codes must be supplemented by the State code when checking sites for accessibility. The rule to follow in cases of inconsistency or overlap between the State code and Federal codes is that the most stringent standard applies. In states where no specific building code addressing accessibility issues has been adopted, UFAS and the ADA Guidelines are the applicable standards.

A.3   Descriptions of Disabilities

A.3.1 Sight Disabilities

There are many kinds of visual disabilities, each with a wide range of ability and limitation. Someone who is described as legally blind may be able to read large print and move about without mobility aids in many or all situations. They may also be able to perceive light and darkness and perhaps some colors. However, someone else who may also be legally blind may not have any of these skills.

There are some conditions where the individual's vision may vary from day to day, depending on fatigue and other factors.

It is impossible to generalize visual disabilities into one problem with one solution. People with congenital visual disabilities (disabilities present from birth) may have skills in reading braille and tactile orientation aids. However, people who have lost their sight later in life usually have visual memories of color and scale, and concepts such as reflections, that people who have been blind since birth do not have.

The process of aging also affects visual perception. Both visual acuity and opacity are affected. Visual acuity influences how we perceive objects at a distance, and opacity of the lens determines the way light is transmitted, affecting perception of colors and textures.

Generally, older people perceive almost 20 percent less keenly than those with normal vision. Colors often blend together and closely related textures cannot be discerned.

Glare is a major problem for many people, particularly older people. Do not confuse the term "glare" with "light level." Low light levels cast heavy shadows, making it difficult for many people with low vision to perceive hazards such as stairs, changes in floor surface, etc. Glare usually results when too much light bounces off light colored walls and floors, making it difficult and uncomfortable to navigate a long corridor or around a room.

Many children with sight disabilities have been overprotected by parents, friends, and teachers; as a result, they may not have had the opportunity to explore their environment during early childhood. These children need to explore as much of their environment as possible to build concepts that their peers acquire through sight.

Children who are blind or have severe sight disabilities may lack skills in body control, balance, coordination, and physical abilities. Poor posture is another characteristic of many people with severe sight disabilities. They may develop faulty carriage because of the inability to orient their posture to their surroundings. They have a tendency to lean forward with their arms outstretched to avoid hitting objects. Some blind children are very tense, walking rigidly with their heads tilted backward.

Early detection of blindness or sight disability is essential for treatment and education of children. The main objectives of treatment are to restore or improve sight and to prevent further deterioration of vision.

Education of children with visual disabilities may take place in a mainstream setting, a special classroom, or a special school. With a totally blind child, auditory instruction and reading by touch using the braille system are emphasized. Children with partial vision may attend regular school, providing the teacher is trained to meet their special needs. Parents also receive training to better meet the needs of their child with a visual disability.

As adults, the greatest emphasis in rehabilitation is independent mobility training (skills in moving about and in coping with environmental factors). Following World War II, the Veteran's Administration began to train blinded veterans in the use of the white cane system. This system developed after observing that for various reasons many blind people could not, or did not wish to, adjust their lives to using guide dogs.

It is important to note that many blind adults do not read Braille. In fact, less than 10 percent of the people who are blind or who have severe visual disabilities are able to read Braille. Many adults choose to get written information transcribed onto audio cassettes and listen to the material.

A.3.2 Hearing Disabilities

People with hearing disabilities are unable to respond normally to sound in most social situations. There are two main classifications of hearing disabilities, each with subdivisions.

a.   Hard of Hearing:

1)   Mild. People with a mild hearing loss learn speech by ear and are able to function almost normally in group and individual conversations. These people may have difficulty discerning singular and plural forms of words and in hearing subtle tone changes.

2)   Marginal. People with marginal hearing disabilities usually have difficulty understanding speech from a distance of more than a few feet and in following group conversation.

3)   Moderate. People with moderate hearing disabilities have enough hearing to learn language and speech with amplification of sound through a hearing aid when the auditory sense is aided by visual information.

b.   Deaf:

1)   Severe. People with severe hearing disabilities have trainable residual hearing with amplification of sound through one or two hearing aids. Their language and speech do not develop spontaneously so they must learn communication through specialized techniques.

2)   Profound. People with profound hearing disabilities cannot learn to understand language and speech by ear alone, even with amplification of sound. Sign language or lip reading is usually needed for communication.

The time at which hearing loss occurs in a person's life has a profound affect on the development of communication and social skills. Congenital disabilities (disabilities present at birth) are often caused by certain contagious diseases such as rubella, mumps and influenza during the mother's pregnancy. Acquired hearing disabilities may develop any time during one's life after certain childhood diseases, injuries, ear infections, etc.

A.3.3 Developmental Disabilities

In people described as developmentally disabled, learning ability develops slower than average. Reasoning and judgement capabilities may also develop at a slower pace. For most people with developmental disabilities, it is not the ability to learn that is missing, but the speed and ease with which things are learned that is lessened.

The range of capabilities in people with developmental disabilities is probably greater than in any other disablility group. It is also the group about which the general public has the most apprehension and misconceptions.

People with developmental disabilities are often overprotected and discouraged from exploring the world or interacting with others. Often, they are limited to programs that are designed "especially for their needs," and allowed to socialize only with "their own kind." After finishing a specialized education program as a child or young adult, many may spend their adult years in inactivity.

Fortunately, the practice of institutionalizing people with developmental disabilities is changing. With more appropriate training and education, many people learn to become independent citizens, managing their own homes or apartments and money. Many are able to obtain and hold a non-skilled or semi-skilled job.

Many people with developmental disabilities have problems with coordination, balance, agility, strength, body awareness, and self image. These problems are often the result of inactivity and lack of opportunity to participate in group activities.

People with mild to moderate developmental disabilities will usually not behave very differently from their peers. They may be interested in things that we perceive to be more appropriate for younger people and some social skills may be below their expected age level.

While the learning skills of a person with developmental disabilities may be more concrete, more repetitive, and perhaps less focused than many of their peers, their emotional life, sense of humor, and sensitivity to others may be more sophisticated than expected.

A.3.4 Emotional Disabilities

There are many situations or behaviors that may lead us to label someone as having an emotional disability. These behaviors may develop as part of an individual's "coping strategy" to survive in their environment. People with emotional disabilities have adapted methods to interact with their surroundings with a "fight for survival approach."

Someone may simply have a lifestyle and needs that are different from the prevailing "norm." Others may have a variety of behavior problems and may act them out, may become aggressive and perhaps harmful to themselves and/or others. Still others may be people whose lives are filled with extreme fears, withdrawal, depression, anxiety, and stresses. Some people have developed problems as a result of alcohol and drug abuse.

Conditions that may be labeled as autistic, schizophrenic, psychotic, and other severe disabilities may appear to give people a "lack of contact with the real world," and an inability to relate to others. These people may have severe language disabilities, a strong need for predictability in their daily lives and repetitive behaviors.

Sometimes the greatest barriers in working with a group that has been labeled as having an emotional disability are the fears and expectations other people have about their behavior. These fears and expectations may affect the approach and design of programs. Knowing the cause or definition behind a label does not improve our services or skills. What is important to remember is that people with emotional disabilities are just like any other group.

A.3.5 Epilepsy

Epilepsy means seizure, but not all convulsive seizures are due to epilepsy. Seizures are classified by variations in severity, duration, frequency, and warning of impending attacks.

a. **Grand Mal.** This is easily recognized by rigidity, loss of consciousness, and falling. Biting of the tongue may occur from strong contraction of the jaw muscles. Jerking, twisting, involuntary cries, and complete amnesia are also characteristic of this type of seizure. The seizure itself may only last a few minutes, but the deep sleep that follows may last several hours. Upon waking from a grand mal seizure, the person may experience weakness, mental dullness, or headaches.

b. **Petite Mal.** This is a short lapse of unconsciousness followed by immediate recovery. The eyes blink or roll and fix upon some object, and fine muscular twitchings may be unnoticed except by the epileptic.

c. **Psychomotor Attack.** This condition is characterized by sudden strange behavior in which there is consciousness without apparent recall. The person experiencing this type of rare attack may go out of the room without reason, may have a sudden temper tantrum, or appear to act out a bad dream. During the seizure the person is apt to be injurious to others. Most often these types of attacks are associated with psychosis.

An epileptic person may participate in activities designed for the general population provided the person is supervised by a leader who is considerate of the person's special needs and trained to effectively meet those needs. An epileptic's seizure threshold seems to be lower when experiencing emotional upsets, bodily discomfort, or low blood sugar due to hunger. Many studies indicate, however, that lying around and constantly resting seem to spark emotional upsets. An epileptic should get a reasonable amount of physical and mental activity. It has been shown that seizures rarely occur when the person is alert and active.

A.3.6 Mobility Disabilities

The following descriptions list conditions that may affect an individual's mobility and independence within the environment.

a.   **People Who Use Wheelchairs for Mobility.** Wheelchairs allow people with many disabling conditions to have mobility that they might otherwise not have, or would find greatly reduced. Congenital disabilities, accidents, and illness can all leave parts of our bodies in different stages of weakness, paralysis, or absence. Paralysis may not only affect motor control of certain parts of our body, but may also affect responses to external stimuli, such as touch, temperature, pain, and sometimes even awareness of body position.

Some environmental concerns of people who use wheelchairs include obvious things such as ramped entrances and elevators instead of stairs, adequate parking in convenient areas, level walks with firm surfaces, and wide aisles in stores and classrooms. Not only are accessible toilet facilities a must, but so is the availability of drinking water. Due to immobility, it is imperative that large amounts of water be consumed.

Many people with upper and lower limb impairments, or with reduced stamina, use electrically powered wheelchairs for mobility. Uneven surfaces, such as cobblestones, can cause a moving chair to jolt and the fine control required to operate an electrical wheelchair may become erratic or even stop. Uneven surfaces can also aggravate extreme pain in some people.

Many people with mobility disabilities also have faulty internal thermostats and are unable to adjust their body temperature needs to meet external demands. In hot weather they may not be able to perspire freely, and thus may suffer heat stroke at a relatively low temperature. In some conditions pain and/or muscle and joint flexibility may be affected by cold and dampness. Thus, people with mobility limitations need opportunities to escape from uncomfortable climatic conditions, which may become life threatening for some.

b.   **People Who Have Difficulty in Walking.** People who have difficulty in walking may (or may not) walk with aids such as crutches, a cane, a walker, braces, artificial limbs, or even holding onto a friend's arm. Reduced agility, speed of movement, difficulty in balance, reduced endurance, or even a combination of these may contribute to impaired mobility. Energy reserves are often used faster than average. A person who walks with difficulty may be required to spend their energy in trying to keep their balance or otherwise meet challenges of the environment as it confronts their disability.

Some environmental elements of concern to people with walking difficulties include uneven walking surfaces, walks interrupted with raised or uneven expansion joints, slippery surfaces such as highly polished floors or wet shower rooms, walks filled with debris, areas that collect standing water, sand and/or ice, etc.

People who wear leg braces or artificial limbs may find stairs with square nosings a great hazard. Their toe may get caught by the nosing, making it difficult to pass from one level to the next and possibly causing them to fall.

Handrails on both sides of stairs and ramps are particularly helpful to people with walking difficulty. Handrails are needed on both sides, as someone may be stronger on one side over the other, and not everyone is "right-handed." Often people who may be using a wheelchair will use handrails along the ramp as an assist up the incline.

Heavy doors are often a problem for everyone, but people who use crutches, canes, or walkers may have another problem. The door may close too quickly and trap the crutch or tip below the bottom of the door.

c.   **People With Upper Limb Impairments.** While we do not normally think of someone with "two good legs" having a mobility problem, the environment requires extensive and complex upper body manipulative skills and strength for people to function independently.

Environmental concerns of people with upper limb disabilities include styles of knobs, buttons, and handles to operate doors, drinking fountains, coin operated vending machines, telephones, elevator controls, the weight of exterior doors, etc.

People with upper limb disabilities may also have some difficulty with balance, especially when climbing stairs or walking up inclines. Handrails along both sides of the risers will be helpful in providing support when the individual leans against them.

d.   **People With Less Than Average Agility, Stamina, and Slower Reaction Time.** Many people have multiple health problems which may include cardiovascular and cardiopulmonary diseases, hypertension, and degenerative conditions of aging. Pregnant women and young children may also have difficulty with limited agility, stamina, and slower than average reaction times.

There are many environmental elements that require people to make quick decisions and/or to be strong and agile. Such elements include revolving doors, escalators, street crossings, boarding buses and street cars, etc. Not only do elderly people have difficulty with these facilities, but most children are also impeded.

A.3.7 Some Common Physical Disabilities

a.   **Cerebral Palsy.** Cerebral palsy is a neurological disorder resulting from damage to the brain before, during, or after birth. Control of the muscles is lost or impaired, ranging in degree from mild to severe. Four general groups of cerebral palsy are spastic, athetoid, ataxic, and rigid. Persons with cerebral palsy (CP) may fall into more than one of these categories.

b.   **Spinal Cord Injuries.** Spinal cord injuries are generally caused by trauma rather than congenitally. Diving and motorcycle accidents are the most frequent causes of trauma, followed by auto accidents and falls.

Depending on the level of injury, a person is either a quadraplegic (quad meaning four) where all limbs are impaired or paralyzed, or a paraplegic (para meaning two) where both legs are affected. When the cord is damaged or severed, sensory and motor nerves are not able to send impulses below the level of the injury. Some of the nerves that are damaged relate to loss of bladder and bowel control.

c. **Poliomylitis.** This is a disease which affects motor cells in the spinal cord, which in turn destroys the nerve impulses in certain muscles. Residual effects of polio are varied. If nerves are not completely destroyed there will usually be a certain amount of recovery. Some persons will have mild effects of the disease while others can become quadraplegics.

d. **Stroke.** This is destruction of brain substance resulting from a rupture of a cerebral blood vessel, an occlusion of a cerebral blood vessel or vascular insufficiency. Hemiplegia, speech disturbance and perceptual disorders are specific symptoms. These vary depending on the severity and area of brain injury.

e. **Multiple Sclerosis.** This is a slowly progressive disease of the central nervous system characterized by partial paralysis involving one or more limbs, visual disturbances, or heaviness of the limbs. It is primarily a disease of young adults.

f. **Arthritis.** Joints of the body are inflamed and may become enlarged and painful to move, causing a loss of range of motion and mobility.

g. **Spina Bifida.** A congenital malformation of the spinal column in which some portion of the vertebra fails to form over the spinal cord (thus leaving it exposed). This can be corrected with surgery. Spinal cord involvement may occur producing varying degrees of neurological impairment affecting strength and movement of the legs as well as bowel and bladder control.

h. **Muscular Dystrophy.** Muscular dystrophy is a chronic, progressive disease of the muscles manifested by the gradual weakening of the voluntary muscles. Muscular dystrophy (MD) itself is not fatal. However, eventually all of the voluntary muscles become involved and are unable to perform their functions in respiration and circulation.

A.3.8 Amputees

Individuals who have lost a limb(s) or part of a limb are included in this group. A large number of amputations are a result of automobile, machinery, or explosion accidents. Certain diseases like diabetes also cause many amputations. Some terms used to describe the location of the amputation are:

*   Unilateral - one arm or leg
*   Bilateral - two arms or legs
*   Double - one arm and one leg
*   Multiple - more than two limbs

A person who loses an arm or leg experiences not only physical loss but psychological damage as well, as is true of most people with physical disabilities. The person must rearrange thinking and place added value on those things that previously may have been of little concern or value.

A.3.9 Disfigurement

Disfigurement can result from a number of causes, including birth defects, burns, and accidental injury. An important factor to remember is that the degree of disfigurement does not indicate the degree of difficulty that an individual may have in adapting to his or her disability. Often an individual with a "minor" disfigurement has a more difficult adjustment than an individual whose disability appears more severe.

B. ORGANIZATIONS AND INSTITUTIONS INVOLVED IN PLAY FOR ALL

The following is a list of organizations and institutions involved in *Play For All* who continue to lend support to the program in many ways.

Access California, Oakland Social Services Dept., Oakland, CA

Adaptive Environments Center, Boston, MA

Airspace U.S.A., Asheville, NC

American Alliance for Health, Physical Education, Recreation and Dance (AAHPERD), Reston, VA

American Association for Leisure & Recreation, Reston, VA

American Foundation for the Blind, Inc., New York, NY

American Hotel & Motel Association, New York, NY

American Occupational Therapy Association, Rockville, MD

American Society for Deaf Children, Silver Spring, MD

American Society of Landscape Architects, Washington, DC

Association for Play Therapy, Yonkers, NY

Balsam America Sports Facilities, Inc., Houston, TX

Barrier Free Environments, Inc., Raleigh, NC

Bay area Outreach Recreation Program, Berkeley, CA

Beckwith Associates, Forestville, CA

BigToys, Tacoma, WA

Bing Nursery School, Stanford University, CA

Brazoria County Park Commission, Angleton, TX

Breakfall Inc., Milwaukee, WI

Bureau of Engineering, City of San Francisco, CA

Bureau of Parks and Recreation, Portland, OR

California Parks and Recreation Society, Sacramento, CA

Callander Associates, San Mateo, CA

Cam-Turf, Spring, TX

Center for Childcare Alternatives, Ltd, Washington, DC

Center for Human Environments, New York, NY

Center for Human Policy, Syracuse, NY

Center for Independent Living, Berkeley, CA

CHILDESIGN, Inc., New York, NY

Childhood City Network, New York, NY

Children's Environments Quarterly, New York, NY

Children's Playgrounds, Inc., Cambridge, MA

Children's World, Golden, CO

College of Social and Behavioral Sciences, University of Texas, San Antonio, TX

Community Development Dept., City of Buffalo, NY

Community Playgrounds, Novato, CA

Community Services Department, City of Escondido, CA

Community Services Department, City of Byran, TX

Community Services Department, City of Fremont, CA

Consumer Product Safety Commission (CPSC), Bethesda, MD

Curriculum in Recreation Administration, University of North Carolina, Chapel Hill, NC

Cypress Enterprises, Inc., San Jose, CA

Daly City Parks and Recreation, Daly City, CA

Denver Parks and Recreation, City of Denver, CO

Dept. of Architecture, New York State University, Buffalo, NY

Dept. of Architecture, University of California, Berkeley, CA

Dept. of Architecture, University of Florida, Gainesville, FL

Dept. of Art, Southwest Texas State University, San Marcos, TX

Dept. of Community Development, City of Buffalo, NY

Dept. of Environmental Design, University of California, Davis, CA

Dept. of Environmental Management, County of San Mateo, Redwood City, CA

Dept. of Education, University of Texas, Austin, TX

Dept. of Environmental Psychology, City University of New York, NY

Dept. of Landscape Architecture, University of California, Berkeley, CA

Dept. of Parks, City of Redding, CA

Dept. of Parks and Marina, City of Berkeley, CA

Dept. of Parks and Recreation, City of Austin, TX

Dept. of Parks and Recreation, City of Bloomington, IN

Dept. of Parks and Recreation, City of Dallas, TX

Dept. of Parks and Recreation, City of Escondido, CA

Dept. of Parks and Recreation, City of Lafayette, CA

Dept. of Parks and Recreation, City of Napa, CA

Dept. of Parks and Recreation, City of San Francisco, CA

Dept. of Parks and Recreation, City of San Ramon, CA

Dept. of Parks and Recreation, City of Santa Cruz, CA

Dept. of Parks and Recreation, City of Seattle, WA

Dept. of Parks and Recreation, City of Sunnyvale, CA

Dept. of Physical Education, University of Southern Florida, Gainsville, FL

Dept. of Recreation, City of Dublin, CA

Dept. of Recreation, City of Folsom, CA

Dept. of Recreation, City of Kentwood, MI

Dept. of Recreation, City of Plano, TX

Dept. of Recreation, City of Scottsdale, AZ

Dept. of Recreation, City of Washington, DC

Dept. of Recreation and Leisure Studies, San Francisco State University, San Francisco, CA

Dept. of Recreation and Parks, City of Baltimore, MD

Disabled Children's Computer Group, Richmond, CA

Diversified Recreation, Little Rock, AR

Division of Environmental Planning and Management, University of California, Davis, CA

Division of Parks, City of Anaheim, CA

Division of Physical Education, North Texas State University, Denton, TX

East Bay Regional Parks District, Oakland, CA

Elaine Day LaTourelle & Associates, Seattle, WA

Environmental Design Dept., Wheelock College, Cambridge, MA

Environmental Design Research Association (EDRA), Washington, DC

Federal Home Loan Bank, Washington, DC

FPE Group, Lafayette, CA

HAGS PLAY, Sweden

Handicapped Adventure Play Association, United Kingdom

Hayward Area Recreation & Park District, Hayward, CA

Henn, Etzel and Mellon, San Francisco, CA

Human Services and Parks Commission, Culver City, CA

Industrial Design Magazine, New York, NY

International Association for the Study of People and Their Physical Surroundings, London, England

International Association of the Child's Right to Play, (IPA), Stockholm, Sweden

Iron Mountain Forge, Farmington, MO

John Carrol University, Cleveland, OH

Kinder-Care Learning Center, Inc., Montgomery, AL

King County Natural Resources and Parks Division, Mercer Island, WA

Kompan, Inc,. Windsor Locks, CT

Lafayette Community Center, City of Lafayette, CA

Landscape Architecture Magazine, Washington, DC

Landscape Structures, Inc./Mexico Forge, Delano, MN

Let's Play to Grow, Washington, D.C.

Lisle Park District, City of Lisle, IL

Log Rhythms Playground Specialists Inc., Boulder, CO

Los Angeles Department of Recreation and Parks, City of Los Angeles, CA

Mafer Children's Hospital, Brisbane, Australia

Massachusetts Architectural Barriers Compliance Board, Boston, MA

Matrix Design Consortium, Canyon Lake, TX

Metropolitan Dade County Park & Recreation Dept., Miami, FL

Moore Iacofano Goltsman, Berkeley, CA

Naperville Park District, Naperville, IL

National Association for Children with Autism, Washington, DC

National Community Education Association

National Endowment for the Arts, Washington, DC

National Easter Seal Society, Washington, D.C.

National Playing Fields Association, London, England

National Safety Council, Chicago, IL

National Theraputic Recreation Society, Washington, D.C.

New Orleans Parkway and Park Commission, New Orleans, LA

New York City Department of Parks and Recreation, NY

North Bakersfield Recreation & Park Dist., Bakersfield, CA

Northern Suburban Special Recreation Association, Highland Park, IL

Office of State Architect, Access Compliance Section, Sacramento, CA

Pacific Early Childhood Institute, Daly City, CA

Pacific Oaks College, Topanga, CA

Pacific Playground, Inc., Tacoma, WA

Palo Alto Recreation Department, City of Palo Alto, CA

Parks, Beaches & Recreation Dept., City of Pacifica, CA

Parks and Recreation Dept., City of Gilroy, CA

Pentes Design Inc., Charlotte, NC

PLAE, Inc., Berkeley, CA

Play Works, Milwaukee, WI

Playcatering Ltd., Baltimore, MD

Playground Clearinghouse, Phoenixsville, PA

Playground Review Committee, Escondido, CA

Playscapes Children's Environments, Madison, WI

Playworld Systems, New Berlin, PA

Program on Urban Studies, Stanford University, Stanford, CA

Public Works Department, Division of Architectural Engineering, City of San Jose, CA

Recreation Center for the Handicapped, San Francisco, CA

Recreation Environments Co., Annapolis, MD

Recreation Plus, Aurora, CO

Reese Industries, Inc., Prospect Heights, IL

Ross Recreation Equipment, Novato, CA

San Diego County Office of Education, San Diego, CA

San Francisco Foundation, San Francisco, CA

School of Architecture and Urban Planning, University of Wisconsin, Milwaukee, WI

School of Design, North Carolina State University, Raleigh, NC

School of Design, University of Washington, Seattle, WA

School of Health, Physical Education and Recreation, University of Northern Iowa, Cedar Falls, IA

Summit Supply Corporation of Colorado, Durango, CO

Super Tots, Washington, DC

The Markfield Project, London, England

Tiger Hug Toys, Denver, CO

United Cerebral Palsy Association, Washington, DC

United States Association for the Child's Right to Play, Austin, TX

United States Consumer Product Safety Commission, Seattle, WA

Universal Play Systems, Inc., New Rochelle, NY

University of Texas, San Antonio, TX

Vagelatos Associates Landscape Architecture Ltd., Vancouver, B.C.

Walt Rankin and Assoc., La Mesa, CA

Wellesley College, Center for Research on Women, Wellesley, MA

Whole Access, Redwood City, CA

World Leisure and Recreation Association, Canada

World Rehabilitation Fund, Inc., New York, NY

Wooden Environments, Inc., Speonk, NY

BIBLIOGRAPHY

SELECTED BIBLIOGRAPHY

Below are listed works consulted in the preparation of this document. Where appropriate, in support of specific points, they are cited in the text. The following organizational abbreviations are used:

AEC (Adaptive Environments Center), Boston, MA

ANSI (American National Standards Institute), Washington, DC

BFE (Barrier Free Environments, Incorporated), Raleigh, NC

CAH (Center for Accessible Housing), North Carolina State University, Raleigh, NC

CCCY (Canadian Council on Children and Youth), Ottowa, Canada

CMHC (Canadian Central Mortgage and Housing Corporation), Ottowa, Canada

CPSC (Consumer Product Safety Commission), Bethesda, MD

FPC (Fair Play for Children), London, U.K.

HAPA (Handicapped Adventure Playground Association), London, U.K.

HUD (U.S. Department of Housing and Urban Development), Washington, DC

IPA (International Association for the Child's Right to Play) Stockholm, Sweden

NCBFE (National Center for a Barrier-Free Environment), no longer in existence

NPFA (National Playing Fields Association), London, U.K.

PLAE (Playing and Learning in Adaptable Environments, Inc.), Berkeley, CA

Abernethy, W.D. (n.d.). *Playgrounds.* London: NPFA.

———— (n.d.). *Playleadership.* London: NPFA.

Adams, E. (1990). *Learning Through Landscapes: A Report on the Use, Design, Management and Development of School Grounds.* London: Learning Through Landscapes Trust (Technology House, Victoria Road, Winchester Hants, SO23 7DU, U.K.).

Adaptive Environments Center (1980). Environments for All Children. *Access Information Bulletin.* Washington, DC: NCBFE.

Allen, Lady, of Hurtwood (1968). *Planning for Play.* Cambridge, MA: MIT Press.

Allison, L. (1975). *The Reasons for Seasons.* Canada: Little, Brown and Company.

Andel, J. van (1986). Physical Changes in an Elementary Schoolyard. *Children's Environments Quarterly* 3(3), 40–51.

Andrews, J.S. (1981). Negligence: As It Applies to a Recreation Leader. *Australian Parks and Recreation.* 22:3, 15–17.

ANSI (1980). A117.1

Appleyard, D. (1981). *Livable Streets.* Berkeley, CA: U.C. Press.

ASTM (1991). F1292. Standard Specification for Impact-Attenuation of Surface Systems Under and Around Playground Equipment.

Balmforth, N. & Nelson, W. (1978). *Jubilee Street.* London: British Broadcasting Corporation.

Barrier Free Environments, Inc. (1980). Doors and Entrances. *Access Information Bulletin.* Washington, DC: NCBFE.

Beamish, A. (1980). Child–Pedestrian Safety in Residential Environments. Ottawa: CMHC.

Beckwith, J. (1988). Playground equipment: a designer's perspective. In L.D. Bruya (Ed.). *Play Spaces for Children: A New Beginning.* Reston, VA: American Alliance for Health, Physical Education, Recreation and Dance.

——— (1985a). Play environments for all children. *Journal of Physical Education, Recreation and Dance.* May/June, 10–35.

——— (1985b). Equipment selection criteria for modern playgrounds. In J.L. Frost and S. Sunderlin (Eds.). *When Children Play.* Wheaton, MD: Association for Children Education International.

——— (1983a). Further thoughts on falling. *ProData.* 1(2), 3.

——— (1983b). Playgrounds for the twenty-first century. *Cities & Villages.* 21(5).

——— (1982). It's Time for Creative Play. *Parks and Recreation.* September, 1982.

——— (1979a). You can build a playground. *American School & University.* January, 1979.

——— (1979b). *Playground Planning and Fundraising Guide for Schoolyard Bigtoys.* Tacoma, WA: Northwest Design Products, Inc.

Bengtsson, A. (1972). *Adventure Playgrounds.* London: Crosby Lockwood.

——— (1970). *Environmental Planning for Children's Play.* New York: Praeger.

Benk, H. (1986/87). Playground Injuries. *Australian Parks and Recreation.* 23(2), 14–17.

Björklid, P. (1984–85). Environmental Diversity on Housing Estates as a Factor in Child Development. *Children's Environments Quarterly.* 1(4), 7–13.

——— (1986). A Developmental – Ecological Approach to Child–Environment Interaction. Stockholm: Stockholm Institute of Education.

Blakely, K. (Ed.) (1985). Safety in Outdoor Play. Special issue of *Children's Environments Quarterly.* 2(4), Winter 1985.

Blue, G.F. (1986). The Value of Pets in Children's Lives. *Childhood Education.* 63:2, 85–90.

Boehm, E. (1980). Youth Farms. In Wilkinson, P.F. (Ed). *Innovation in Play Environments.* London: Croom Helm.

Boyce, W.T., Sobolewski, S., Sprunger, L., & Schaefer, C. (1984). Playground Equipment Injuries in a Large, Urban School District. *American Journal of Public Health.* 74:9, 984–6.

Bowers, L. (1988). Playground Design: A Scientific Approach. In L.D. Bruya (Ed.). *Play Spaces for Children: A New Beginning.* Reston, VA: American Alliance for Health, Physical Education, Recreation and Dance.

——— (1979). Towards a Science of Playground Design: Priniciples of Design for Play Centers for All Children. In J. Levey (Ed.). *Leisure Today: Play;* from *Journal of Physical Education, Recreation and Dance.* October, 1979.

——— (1977). Play Learning Centers for Pre-School Handicapped Children. *U.S.O.E. Research and Demonstration Project Report.* Tampa, FL: College of Education, University of South Florida.

Brink, S. (1980). Design Criteria for the Development of Sheltered Play Spaces in Medium to High Density Housing Projects. Ottawa: CMHC.

——— (n.d.). Environmental Safety and the Prevention of Childhood Accidents. Ottawa: CMHC.

British Standard Institute. (1979). BS5696 Play Equipment Intended for Permanent Installation Outdoors. London: BSI.

Broadway, C. (1979). *Animals and Adventure Playgrounds: A Guide for Play Leaders and their Managements*. Leicester: Highfields Adventure Playground Association (76 Hartington Road, Leicester).

Brower, S. (1977). *The Design of Neighborhood Parks*. Baltimore, MD: Department of Planning.

——— (1977). *Streetfronts and Backyards*. Baltimore, MD: Department of Planning.

Bruner, J.S. & Sherwood, V. (1976). Peekaboo and the Learning of Rule Structures. In J.S. Bruner, A. Jolly & K. Sylva (Eds.). *Play: Its Role in Play and Evolution*. New York: Basic Books, Inc., Publishers.

Bruya, L.D. (Ed.) (1988). *Play Spaces for Children: A New Beginning*. Reston, VA: American Alliance for Health, Physical Education, Recreation and Dance.

——— & Langendorfer, S.J. (Eds.) (1988). *Where Our Children Play: Elementary School Playground Equipment*. Reston, VA: American Alliance for Health, Physical Education, Recreation and Dance.

——— (1985a). Design characteristics used in playgrounds for children. In J.L. Frost & S. Sunderlin (Eds.). *When Children Play*. Wheaton, MD: Association for Childhood Education International.

——— (1985b). The Effect of Play Structure format differences on the play behavior of children. In J.L. Frost & S. Sunderlin (Eds.). *When Children Play*. Wheaton, MD: Association for Childhood Education International.

——— & Beckwith, J. (1985). Due Process: Reducing exposure to liability suits and the management of risk associated with children's play areas. *Children's Environments Quarterly*. 2(4).

———, Carter, C.S. & Fowler, C.L. (1983). Position effects as an indicator of play routes on a play structure. Presented at the International Conference on Play and Play Environments, June 29 - July 1, 1983. Austin, TX.

———, Robbins, R. & Fowler, C.L. (1983a). Play patterns exhibited by three, four and five year old children when playing on a contemporary tire swing. Presented at the Inernational Conference on Play and Play Environments, June 29 - July 1, 1983. Austin, TX.

———, Robbins, R. & Fowler, C.L. (1983b). Preferred use of parts of the play structure by three, four and five year old children. Presented at the Inernational Conference on Play and Play Environments, June 29 - July 1, 1983. Austin, TX.

———, Sullivan, M. & Fowler, C.L. (1979). Safety on the horizontal ladder: An intermediate catch system. In C. Gabbard (Ed.). *Texas A&M Conference on Motor Development and Movement Experience of Children*. College Station, TX: Texas A&M Press.

Bunin, N., Jasperse, D., & Cooper, S. (1980). *A Guide to Designing Accessible Outdoor Recreation Facilities*. Washington, DC: U.S. Dept. of the Interior, Heritage, Recreation and Conservation Service (Lake Central Regional Office, Ann Arbor, MI).

Campbell, E., Bruya, L.D. & Fowler, C.L. (1983). The suspension bridge as a part of a larger play structure and its use rate by children. Presented at the International Conference on Play & Play Environments. Austin, TX.

Canadian Council on Children and Youth (1980). *Play Space Guidelines*. Ottawa: CCCY.

———— (1980). *Play Leadership Training*. Ottawa: CCCY.

Cangemi, P. (1987). Correspondence.

Cary, J. (1978). *How to Create Interiors for the Disabled: A Guidebook for Family & Friends*. New York: Pantheon Books.

Center for Accessible Housing (CAH) (1992). *Accessibility Standards for Children's Environments*. Final Technical Report to the Architectural Transportation and Architectural Barriers Compliance Board (Contract #QA90003001).

Central Mortgage and Housing Corporation (1979). *Play Opportunities for School-Aged Children, 6–14 Years of Age*. Ottawa: CMHC.

———— (1978). *Play Spaces for Preschoolers*. Ottawa: CMHC.

———— (1977). *Creative Playground Information Information Kit*. Ottawa: CMHC.

Chawla, L. (Ed.) (1990). Special Places, special issue of *Children's Environments Quarterly*, 7(4).

A Child's Garden (1980). San Francisco: Chevron Chemical Company (Public Affairs Department, Box 3744, San Francisco, CA 94119).

Childhood City Newsletter (1980). Participation 1. No. 22.

———— (1981). Participation 2: Survey of Projects, Programs and Organizations. No. 23.

———— (1982–83). Participation 3: Techniques. 9(4)/10(1).

Children's Environments Quarterly (1984). Children and Animals. 1(3).

Chilton, T. (1985). *Children's Play in Newcastle-Upon-Tyne*. Birmingham, U.K.: Play Board.

City Farmer. Bristol, U.K.: National Federation of City Farms (The Old Vicarage, 66 Fraser St., Windmill Hill, Bedminster, Bristol BS3 4LY, U.K.).

Collard, R.R. (1979). Exploration and play. In B. Sutton-Smith (Ed.). *Play and Learning*. New York: Garner Press.

Consumer Product Safety Council (CPSC) (1981) *A Handbook for Public Playground Safety. Vol I: General Guidelines for New and Existing Playgrounds. Vol II: Technical Guidelines for Equipment and Surfacing*. Washington, DC: CPSC.

———— (1990) *Playground Surfacing*. Washington, DC: U.S. Government Printing Office.

———— (1991) *Handbook for Public Playground Safety*. Washington, DC: U.S. Government Printing Office.

Cooper Marcus, C. (1974). Children's Play Behavior in Low-Rise, Inner-City Housing Developments. In Robin C. Moore (Ed.). *Man-Environment Interactions, Vol 12: Childhood City*. Washington, DC: EDRA.

Cooper Marcus, C. (1986). Design Guidelines: A Bridge Between Research and Decision-Making. In Ittelson, W., Asai, M. & Ker, M. (Eds.). *Cross-Cultural Research in Environment and Behavior. Proceedings of the Second United States–Japan Seminar*. Tucson, AZ: University of Arizona.

———— & Sarkissian, W. (1986). *Housing as if People Mattered: Site Guidelines for Medium Density Family Housing*. Berkeley, CA: U.C. Press

Cox, D., McMaster, I. & Obuch, J. (1990). *Grounds for Learning: A Practical Guide to Schoolground Use and Development.* Surrey Hills, Victoria: Dellasta. Available from Natural Resources Conservation League, 593 Springvale Road, Springvale South, Victoria, Australia.

Coyle, T. (1980). *Incentives as an Aid for Improving the Quality of the Family Housing Environment: A Position Paper.* Ottawa: CMHC

Cunningham, C. (1984). Planning for Small Natural Areas: a Case for Kids. *Proceedings.* Symposium on Small Natural Areas: the Conservation and Management Trust of New South Wales, Australia.

——— (1987). The Geography of Children's Play: Australian Case Studies. Paper presented to 56th ANZAAS Conference and 14th New Zealand Geography Conference, Palmerston North, New Zealand, January 1987.

Department of Education and Science (1990). *The Outdoor Classroom: Educational Use, Landscape Design and Management of School Grounds.* Building Bulletin 71. London: Her Majesty's Stationary Office.

DIN7926 (FRG norms) Parts 1–5 (1985). Playground Equipment for Children; Concepts, Safety Requirements, Testing. Linford Wood, Milton Keynes: British Standards Institution (Technical Help for Exporters). Issued by Deutsche Institut für Normung (DIN), Postfach 110, D-1000 Berlin 30, FRG.

Duncan, J., Calasha, G., Mulholland, M.E. & Townsend, A. (1977). Environmental Modifications for the Visually Impaired: A Handbook. *Visual Impairment and Blindness.* December, 1977. 444–452.

Eikos Group (1980). *Children's Perceptions of Play Environments.* Ottawa: CMHC.

Ellis, M.J. & Scholtz, G.J.L. (1978). *Activity and Play of Children.* Englewood Cliffs, NJ: Prentice-Hall.

Eriksen, A. (1985). *Playground Design.* New York: Van Nostrand Reinhold.

Esbensen, S.B. (1979). An International Inventory and Comparative Study of Legislation and Guidelines for Children's Play Spaces in the Residential Environment. Ottawa: CMHC.

Fair Play for Children (n.d.). *Safety Checklist.* London: FPC and NPFA.

——— (1976). *Training for Leadership.* London: FPC.

Federal Register, July 26, 1991. Part III: Nondiscrimination on the Basis of Disability by Public Accommodations and in Commercial Facilities; Final Rule. Washington, DC: Department of Justice, Office of the Attorney General.

Fernie, D.E. (1985). The promotion of play in the indoor play environment. In J.L. Frost & S. Sunderlin (Eds.). *When Children Play.* Wheaton, MD: Association for Childhood Education International.

Fitzgerald, A. (1982). *We Can Do It: A Training Manual for Integrating Disabled People into Recreation Programs.* Berkeley, CA: Bay Area Outreach Recreation Program.

Franham-Diggory, S. (1972). *Cognitive Processes In Education: A Psychological Preparation For Teaching And Curriculum Development.* New York: Harper & Row.

Freedberg, L. (1983). *America's Poisoned Playgrounds: Children and Toxic Chemicals.* Oakland: Youth News.

Frost, J.L. & Klein, B.L. (1983). *Children's Play and Playgrounds.* Austin, TX: Playscapes International.

——— & Campbell, S.D. (1985). Equipment choices of primary-age children on conventional and creative playgrounds. In J.L. Frost & S. Sunderlin (Eds.). *When Children Play*. Weaton, MD: Association for Childhood Education International.

——— & Strickland, E. (1985). Equipment choices of young children during free play. In J.L. Frost & S. Sunderlin (Eds.). *When Children Play*. Weaton, MD: Association for Childhood Education International.

——— & Sunderlin, S. (1985). *When Children Play*. Weaton, MD: Association for Childhood Education International.

Gehlbach, R.D. (1986). Children's Play and Self-Education. *Curriculum Inquiry*. 16:2, 203–13.

Gold, S.M. (1972). Non-use of Urban Parks. *Journal of the American Institute of Planners*, 38 (Nov.), 369–78.

——— (1981). Designing Public Playgrounds for User Safety. *Australian Parks and Recreation*. 22:3, 10–14.

Goltsman, S.M., Moore, R., and Iacofano, D. (1982). Project PLAE: Using Arts and Environment to Promote Integration of All Children With and Without Disabilities. *IPA Newsletter*. 8:2, 2–8.

———, Gilbert, T.A. & Wohlford, S.D. (1992). *The Accessibility Checklist: An Evaluation System for Buildings and Outdoor Settings*. Berkeley, CA: MIG Communications.

Gordon, F. (1985). *The Playleader: Her Role in Scottish Pre-School Playgroups*. Glasgow: Scottish Pre-school Play Association.

Gordon, R. (1972). *The Design of a Pre-School Therapeutic Playground and Outdoor "Learning Laboratory"*. New York: Institute of Rehabilitation Medicine, New York University Medical Center.

Gray, A. (1974). *Learning Through Play*. Aukland, New Zealand: New Zealand Playcentre Association.

Gray, La V. & Brower, S. (1977). *Activities of Children in an Urban Neighborhood*. Baltimore, MD: Dept. of Planning.

Gröning, G. (1986). An Attempt to Improve a School Yard. *Children's Environments Quarterly*. 3(3), 12–19.

Hanan, E. & Lucking, G. (n.d.). *Playgrounds and Play*. Dunedin Playground Advisory Committee and Christchurch Playground Advisory Committee.

Handicapped Adventure Playground Association (1978). *Adventure Playgrounds for Handicapped Children*. London: HAPA.

Harkness, S. & Groom, J. (1976). *Building without Barriers for the Disabled*. NY: Watson-Guptill Publications.

Hart, R. (1979). *Children's Experience of Place*. New York: Irvington.

——— (1987) Children's Participation in Planning and Design: Theory, Research and Practice. In C. Weinstein & T. David (Eds.), *Spaces for Children: The built environment and child development*. New York: Plenum Press.

Herron, R.E. & Sutton-Smith, B. (1971). *Child's Play*. New York: John Wiley & Sons.

Heseltin, P. (1985). *A Review of Playground Surveys*. Birmingham, U.K.: Play Board.

——— & Holborn, J. (1987). *Playgrounds: The Planning, Design and Construction of Play Environments*. New York: Nichols Publishing.

Heusser, C.P. (1986). How Children Use Their Elementary School Playgrounds. *Children's Environments Quarterly*. 3(3): 3–11.

Hewes, J.J. (1974). *Build Your Own Playground!* Boston: Houghton Mifflin Company.

Hill, P. (1979). *Play Opportunities for School-Age Children, 6 to 14 Years of Age.* Ottawa, Ontario: CMHC.

Hogan, P. (1982). *The Nuts and Bolts of Playground Construction.* West Point, NY: Leisure Press.

Hole, V. (1966). *Children's Play on Housing Estates.* London: Her Majesty's Stationary Office.

Iacofano, D., Goltsman, S., McIntyre, S., and Moreland, G. (1985). Project PLAE: Using the Arts and Environment to Promote Integration of All Children. *California Parks and Recreation.* 41:4.

International Association for the Child's Right to Play (1977). *Declaration of the Child's Right to Play.* IPA: Birmingham, UK.

Jeavons, S. (1987). Criteria for Assessment of Play Environments. *Australian Parks and Recreation.* 23(2), 7–13.

Johnston, J. (1990). *Nature Areas for City People.* London: London Ecology Unit (Bedford House, 125 Camden High Street, London NW1 7JR, U.K.).

Kiewel, H.D. (1980). Ramps, Stairs and Floor Treatments. *Access Information Bulletin.* Washington, DC: NCBFE.

King, F. (1980). *Towards a Safer Adventure Playground.* London: NPFA.

Kirkby, M. (1984). *Young Children's Attraction to Refuge in the Landscape: An Opportunity for Dramatic Play.* Landscape Architecture Thesis. Seattle, WA: University of Washington, Center for Planning and Research.

——— (1989). Nature as Refuge. Children and Vegetation, special issue of *Children's Environments Quarterly*, 6(1), 7-12.

Kompan (1984). *Playgrounds and Safety: Comparison Between Various Playground Equipment Standards.* Windsor Locks, CT: Kompan.

Lambert, J. & Pearson, J. (1974). *Adventure Playgrounds.* Harmondsworth, Middlesex, England: Penquin.

Langendorfer, S.J. (1988). Rotating spring rocking and see-saw equipment. In L.D. Bruya & S.J. Langendorfer (Eds.). *Where Our Children Play: Elementary School Playground Equipment.* Reston, VA: American Alliance for Health, Physical Education, Recreation and Dance.

Langley, J.D. (1984). Two Safety Aspects of Public Playground Climbing Equipment. *New Zealand Medical Journal.* 97:404–6.

——— (1982). School Playground Climbing Equipment—Safe or Unsafe. *New Zealand Medical Journal.* 95: 540–2.

———, Silva, P.A. & Williams, S.M. (1981). Primary School Accidents. *New Zealand Medical Journal.* November, 1981. 336–339.

Lawrence, R.J. (1982). Designers' Dilemma: Participatory Design Methods. Bart, P., Alexander, C., & Francescato, G. (Eds). *Knowledge for Design.* Proceedings of the 13th International Conference of the Environmental Design Research Association, College Park, MD.

Lee, B.C. (1990). Estimate of Skin Cancer from Dislodgeable Arsenic on Pressure Treated Wood Playground Equipment. Washington, DC: USCPSC.

Leedy, D.L. (1982). Planning for Wildlife in Cities and Suburbs. *Urban Wildlife.* Washington, DC: Superintendent of Documents, U.S. Government Printing Office.

Le Fevre, D.N. (1983). *Playing for the Fun of It.* Stockholm, Sweden: Vattumannen Bookshop.

Lewis, M. (1979). The social determination of play. In B. Sutton-Smith (Ed.). Play and Learning. New York: Garner Press.

Lifchez, R., Williams, D., Yip, C., Larson, M. & Taylor, J. (1979). *Getting There*. Sacramento, CA: California Dept. of Rehabilitation.

Linberg, L. (1986). *Facility Design for Early Childhood Programs*. Washington, DC: National Association of Young Children.

Los Angeles, City of (1984). Design Standards for Children's Play Areas and Equipment. Los Angeles: Department of Parks and Recreation.

Lynch, K. (1961). *Image of the City*. Cambridge, MA: MIT Press.

——— & Hack, G. (1984, 3rd ed.). *Site Planning*. Cambridge, MA: MIT Press.

Mace, R., Hardie, G. & Place, J. (1990). Accessible Environments: Toward Universal Design. In W.E. Presier, J.C. Vischer & E.T. White (Eds.). *Design Intervention: Toward a More Humane Architecture*. New York: Van Nostrand Reinhold.

Mason, J. (1982). *The Environment of Play*. West Point, NY: Leisure Press.

Massingham, B. (1972). *Gardening for the Handicapped*. Aylesbury, Bucks: Shire Publications, Ltd.

McCracken, J.B. (1990). *Playgrounds Safe and Sound*. Washington, DC: National Association for the Education of Young Children.

McIntyre, S., Goltsman, S.M. & Kline, L. (1989). *Safety First Checklist: The Site Inspection System for Play Equipment*. Berkeley, CA: MIG Communications.

Melvin, J.H. (1980). *Play Spaces to Accommodate Disabled Children*. Ottawa: CMHC.

Miller, J. (1987). The Work of the Play Leader. *Australian Parks and Recreation*, 23(2), 27–32.

Miller, P.L. (1972). *Creative Outdoor Play Areas*. Englewood Cliffs, NJ: Prentice–Hall.

de Monchaux, S. (1981). *Planning with Children in Mind*. (a notebook for local planners and policy makers.) Sydney: New South Wales Department of Environment and Planning.

Moore, G.T., Cohen, U., Oertel, J. & van Ryzin, L. (1979). *Designing Environments for Handicapped Children*. New York: Educational Facilities Laboratories.

Moore, R.C. & Wong, H.H. (in press). *Another Way of Learning: Child Development in Natural Settings*. Berkeley, CA: MIG Communications.

Moore, R.C. (1989a). Before and After Asphalt: Diversity as a Measure of Ecological Quality in Children's Play Environments. In Bloch, M. & Pellegrini, T. (Eds.). *The Ecological Context of Children's Play*. Ablex Publishing.

——— (1989b). Playgrounds at the Crossroads. In Altman, Irwin and Zube, Erwin (Eds). *Public Spaces and Places*. New York: Plenum.

——— (1989c). Plants as Play Props. In Children and Vegetation, special issue of *Children's Environments Quarterly*, 6(1), 3-6.

——— (1987). "Like Diamonds Melting: Children's Play and Learning in Aquatic Settings." *Children's Environments Quarterly*, 4(2), 11-18.

———— (1986a). The Power of Nature: Orientations of Girls and Boys Toward Biotic and Abiotic Settings on a Reconstructed Schoolyard. *Children's Environments Quarterly*. 3(3), 52–69.

———— (1986b). *Childhood's Domain: Play and Place in Child Development*. Berkeley, CA: MIG Communications.

———— (1984). "Animals on the Environmental Yard." *Children's Environments Quarterly*, 1(3), 43-51, Fall 1984.

———— (1980). Learning from the Yard: Generating Relevant Urban Childhood Places. In Wilkinson, P.F. (Ed.). *Play in Human Settlements*. London: Croom Helm.

———— (1978a). A WEY to Design. *Journal of Architectural Education*. XXXI(4), 27–30.

———— (1978b). Meanings and Measures of Child/Environment Quality: Some Findings from the Environmental Yard. In Rogers, W.E. & Ittelson, W.H. (Eds.). *New Directions in Environmental Design Research*. Washington, DC: Environmental Design Research Association.

———— (1976). The Environmental Design of Children–Environment Relations. In *Children, Nature and the Urban Environment*. Proceedings of a Symposium–Fair. Darby, PA: U.S. Forest Experiment Station (Publication #19028).

———— (1975). The Place of Adventure Play in Urban Planning for Children's Leisure. In *Adventure Playgrounds and Children's Creativity*. Proceedings of the 6th World Congress of the International Association for the Child's Right to Play in Milan, Italy. Birmingham, UK: IPA.

———— (1974a). Open Space Learning Place. In Coates, G. *Alternative Learning Environments*. Stroudsburg, PA: Dowden, Hutchinson and Ross.

———— (1974b). Patterns of Activity in Time and Space. In Canter, D. & Lee, T. (Eds.). *Psychology and the Built Environment*. London: Architectural Press.

———— (1966). An Experiment in Playground Design. Masters Thesis. Massachusetts Institute of Technology, Department of City and Regional Planning.

———— & Schneekloth, L. (Eds.) (1989). Children and Vegetation, special issue of *Children's Environments Quarterly*, 6(1).

———— & Wochiler, A. (1975). An Assessment of a Redeveloped School Yard Based on Drawings Made by Child Users. In Moore, R.C. (Ed.). *Man–Environment Interactions, Vol 12: Childhood City*. Washington, DC: EDRA.

———— & Young, D. (1978). Childhood Outdoors: Toward a Social Ecology of the Landscape. In Altman, I. & Wohlwill, J. (Eds.). *Children and the Environment*. New York: Plenum Press.

Moreland, G., McIntyre, S., Iacofano, D., Goltsman, S. (1985). The Risky Business of Children's Play: Balancing Safety and Challenge in Programs and Environments for All Children. *Children's Environments Quarterly*. 2(4), 24–28.

Mount, C. (1985). Boy injured on slide gets $9.5 million. *Chicago Tribune*, January 15, 1985, pp. 1-sec. 1, 1-sec. 2.

National Playing Fields Association (1986). *Grass Seed Mixtures for Children's Play Areas*. London: NPFA.

———— (1985). *Kick-About Areas*. London: NPFA (1st ed. 1977).

———— (1983). *Playground Management for Local Councils*. London: NPFA.

———— (1980). *Towards a Safer Adventure Playground*. London: NPFA.

———— (1978). *Play Mounds*. London: NPFA.

―――― (1977). *Hard Surfaces for Play Areas.* London: NPFA.

National Safety Council. (1985). *Accident Facts: 1985 Edition.* Chicago: National Safety Council.

Newman, Oscar (1972). *Defensible Space.* New York: MacMillan.

Nordhaus, R.S., Kantrowitz, M. & Siembieda, W.J. (1984). *Accessible Fishing: A Planning Handbook.* Santa Fe, NM: New Mexico Natural Resources Department.

Norén-Björn, E. (1982). *The Impossible Playground.* West Point, NY: Leisure Press.

Orlick, T. (1978). *The Cooperative Sports and Games Book: Challenge Without Competition.* New York: Pantheon.

―――― & Botterill, C. (1975). *Every Kid Can Win.* Chicago: Nelson-Hill.

Osmon, F.L. (1971). *Patterns for Designing Children's Centers.* New York: Educational Facilities Laboratories, Inc.

Ostroff, E. (1978). *Humanizing Environments.* Cambridge, MA: The Word Guild.

Page, J. (1976). All you need is love: An investigation of children, their development and the environment in which they play. Unpublished master's thesis. University of Florida.

Parten, M. (1932). Social participation amoung preschool children. *Journal of Abnormal and Social Psychologyy, 27.*

―――― (1971). Social play amoung preschool children. In R.E. Herron & B. Sutton-Smith (Eds.). *Child's Play.* New York: John Siley & Sons.

Peoples Housing, Inc. (1983). *Retrofitting Public Restrooms for Accessibility.* Sacramento, CA: California Department of Rehabilitation.

Peters, G.A. (1986). Warning Signs and Safety Instructions: Covering all the Bases. *Security and Fire News.* Jan/Feb., 1986.

Playing and Learning in Adaptable Environments (PLAE, Inc.) (1981-1987). Program Documentation. Berkeley, CA.

Play Board (1986). *Learning by Playing.* Birmingham, U.K.: Play Board (in association with Fisher–Price Toys and *Nursery World*).

―――― (1985). Play and Children with Special Needs (information pack). Birmingham, U.K.: Play Board.

―――― (1985). *Play and Playgrounds in Rotterdam – A Research Approach.* Birmingham, UK: Play Board.

―――― (1984). Playdata Sheets: Playground Surfacing (n.d.). Birmingham, U.K.: Play Board.

―――― (n.d.). Playground Surfacing. Birmingham, UK: Play Board.

Preece, J. (n.d.). *Play and Education – South Aston Play Centre.* Birmingham: Play Board.

Pre-School Playgroups Association (n.d.). *Guidelines for Playgroups with a Handicapped Child.* London: PPA.

Quality (1987). *GUIDE-LINE™ signs for playgrounds.* Hillsdale, MI: Quality Industries, Inc.

Ratté, D.J., Morrison, M.L. & Lerner, N.D. (1990). Development of Human Factors Criteria for Playground Equipment Safety. Silver Spring, MD: COMSIS Corporation.

Redl, F. (1959). The impact of game ingredients on children's play behavior. In B. Schaffner (Ed.). *Group Processes: Transactions of the Fourth Conference.* New York: Josiah Macy, Jr., Foundation.

Robinette, G. (1985). *Barrier-Free Site Design: Anyone Can Go Anywhere.* New York: Van Nostrand Reinhold.

Root, J. (1983). *Play Without Pain.* Melbourne: Child Accident Prevention Foundation of Australia.

Ross, W. (1978). *Children's Experimental Workshop.* Washington, DC: U.S. Dept. of the Interior, National Parks Service.

Rothenburg, M., Hayward, D.G & Beasley, R.R. (1974). Playgrounds: For Whom? In Moore, R.C. (Ed.). *Man–Environment Interactions, Vol 12: Childhood City.* Washington, DC: EDRA.

Royal Australian Institute of Parks and Recreation (1981). National Seminar on Playground Design and Safety. RIPPR: Lyneham, A.C.T.

Ruddy, N. (1981). ANSI A117.1 (1980) Survey Checklist. *Access Information Bulletin.* Washington, DC: NCBFE.

Rudolph, N. (1974). *Workyards.* New York: Columbia University, Teachers College Press.

Rutledge, A. & Molnar, D.J. (1986, 2nd ed.). *Anatomy of a Park: The Essentials of Recreation Area Planning and Design.* New York: McGraw Hill.

Sandels, S. (1968). *Children in Traffic.* London: Paul Elek.

Sanoff, H. (1986). Planning Outdoor Play in the Context of Community Politics. *Children's Environments Quarterly.* 3(3), 20–25.

Schicker, L. (1986). *Children, Wildlife and Residential Developments.* (Masters Thesis in Landscape Architecture). Raleigh, NC: School of Design, NCSU.

Schneekloth, L. (1985). *Play Environments for Disabled Children: Design Guidelines.* Unpublished ms.

———— (1978). Schools Council (1974). *Animal Accommodation for Schools.* London: English University Press.

———— (1974). *Environments for Visually Impaired Children: Design Guidelines.* College of Architecture, Virginia Polytechnic Institute and State University, Blacksburg, VA. Unpublished ms.

———— & Day, D. (1980). *Comparison of Environmental Interactions and Motor Activity of Visually Handicapped and Sighted Children.* College of Architecture, Virginia Polytechnic Institute and State University, Blacksburg, VA. Unpublished ms.

Scholtz, G.J.L. & Ellis, M.J. (1975). Repeated exposure to objects and peers in a play setting. *Journal of Experimental Child Psychology,* 19.

The School Outdoor Resource Area. London: Longman.

Scott, A.H. (1980). Play in a Cold Climate. In Wilkinson, P.F. (Ed). *Innovation in Play Environments.* London: Croom Helm.

Seattle, City of (1986). *Guidelines for Play Areas: Recommendations for Planning, Design and Maintenance.* Seattle, WA: Department of Parks and Recreation.

Shaw, L.G. (1980). Design Guidelines for Handicapped Children's Play Environments. In Wilkinson, P.F. (Ed.). *In Celebration of Play.* London: Croom Helm.

————— (1976). The Playground: *The Child's Creative Learning Space* (MH 2073-04A1). Gainesville, FL: Bureau of Research, College of Architecture, University of Florida.

Shier, H. (1984). *Adventure Playgrounds*. London: NPFA.

Shildrick, J. (1986). *Grass Seed Mixtures for Children's Play Areas*. London: NPFA.

Simm, D. (1985). *Damage on Playground Equipment*. London: NPFA.

Standards Association of New Zealand (1986). *NZS 5828: Part 1: General Guidelines for New and Existing Playgrounds – Equipment and Surfacing*. Wellington, New Zealand: Standards Association.

Standels, S. (1968). *Children in Traffic*. London: Paul Elek.

Sullivan, M. (1982). *Feeling Strong, Feeling Free: Movement Exploration for Young Children*. Washington, DC: National Association for the Education of Young Children.

Sutherland, A.T. & Soames, P. (1984). *Adventure Play with Handicapped Children*. London: Souvenir Press.

Sutton, S. (1985). *Learning Through the Built Environment: An Ecological Approach to Child Development*. New York: Irvigton.

————— (1971). The playful modes of knowing. In G. Engstron (Ed.). Play: The Child Strives Toward Self-Realization. Washington, DC: AAHPERD.

————— & Sutton-Smith, S. (1974). *How To Play With Your Children*. New York: Hawthorn Books.

Sweeney, T. (1987). Playgrounds and Head Injuries: A Problem for the School Business Manager. *School Business Affairs*, 53(1), 28–31.

————— (1979). Playground Accidents: A New Perspective. *Trial*. 15(4), 40–44.

Thompsen, C.H. & Borowieka, A. (1980). *Winter and Play*. Ottawa: CMHC.

Thompson, D. (1988). Introduction in Bruya, L.D. & Langendorfer, S.J. (Eds.). *Where Our Children Play: Elementary School Playground Equipment*. Reston, VA: American Alliance for Health, Physical Education, Recreation and Dance.

————— & Bowers, L. (Eds.) (1989). *Where Our Children Play: Community Park Playground Equipment*. Reston, VA: American Alliance for Health, Physical Education, Recreation and Dance.

Turner, M. (1983). *Play Education and the Arts*. London: NPFA.

U.K. Department of the Environment (1973). *Children at Play*. London: HMSO.

U.S. Army (1992). Standard Designs for Toddler Play Areas. Huntsville, AL: U.S. Army.

U.S. Consumer Product Safety Council. (1981) *A Handbook for Public Playground Safety. Vol I: General Guidelines for New and Existing Playgrounds. Vol II: Technical Guidelines for Equipment and Surfacing*. Washington, DC: CPSC.

U.S. Department of Housing and Urban Development (1978). *A Playground for All Children: Resource Book*. Washington, DC: Superintendent of Documents.

Van Alstyne, D. (1932). Play behavior and choice of play materials of preschool children. Chicago: Unversity of Chicago Press.

Wade, M.C. & Ellis, M.J. (1971). Measurement of free range activity in children as modified by social and environmental complexity. *The American Journal of Clinical Nutrition*, 24.

Watkins, B. (1980). Play Environments in Arid Lands. In Wilkinson, P.F. (Ed.). *Innovation in Play Environments*. London: Croom Helm.

Westland, C. & Knight, J. (1982). *Playing Living Learning: A Worldwide Perspective on Children's Play*. State College, PA: Venture Publishing.

Wilkinson, P.F. & Lockhart, R.S. (1980). Safety in Children's Formal Play Environments. In Wilkinson, P.F. (Ed.). *Innovation in Play Environments*. London: Croom Helm.

———, Lockhart, R.S. & Luhtanen (1980). The Winter Use of Playgrounds. In Wilkinson, P.F. (Ed.). *Innovation in Play Environments*. London: Croom Helm.

Wortham, S.C. & Frost, J.L. (Eds.) (1990). *Playgrounds for Young Children: National Survey and Perspectives*. Reston, VA: American Alliance for Health, Physical Education, Recreation and Dance.

Zirpolo, N. (1987). Plan Checking Report, Flood Park Barrier Free Access Design Project, San Mateo County Parks and Recreation Division, Department of Environmental Management, San Mateo County, CA.

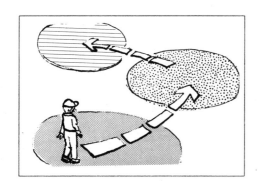

INDEX

A

accessibility
    definition, 32
    definition of "levels," 45
    at drop-off zones, 35
    international sign for, 58
    levels of (Flood Park), 220
    management criteria for, 32
    to manufactured equipment, 78-82
    multipurpose games setting (Flood Park), 216
    to drinking fountains, 188
    to fireplaces and grills, 186
    on ramps, 51
    to sand settings, 165
    in site design, 9-10
    on steps and stairways, 50-1
    survey, 201
    to swings, 98
    to toilets, 190-1
    to water sources, 187
    to watertables, 159
    at worktables, 185

accessible routes, 39-40

adventure playgrounds, 173-4
    see also adventure village

adventure village, 172

age groups
    design for all, 16
    in sand settings, 164
    separation of, 66-7

allergies
    as design criterion, 82

Americans With Disabilities Act
    description of, 250
    in the Second Edition, xiv

amphitheaters, 177-8

amputees, 259-60

animals
    domestic, 25, 147
    habitats, 25, 147-8
    setting design, 145-9

animal settings, **145-9**
    see also animals

appearance
    as design criterion, 77-8
    and vegetation, 137

Architectural Barriers Act of 1968
    (Public Law 90-480), 248

arenas, 177

artificial grass, 116

arthritis, 259

asphalt
    as pathway surface, 46

assumptions about play and
    play settings, xi-xii

ASTM F1292 shock-absorbing surfacing standard, 117

B

balance play events, 100-101

ball play areas, **111-12**
    ball game ideas, 112-13

bark nuggets, 119-20

Barrier Free Access Design Project, **199-226**

behavioral disability
    as design criterion, 81

behavioral goals, 3-4

bicycles
    control of, 80
    in pathway design, 40
    racks, 192

birdlife, 147

birdscaping, 149

bollards
    at entrances, 36

boundaries of play settings, 24

breakaway points, 18

C

campfire circles, 177

cerebral palsy, 258

chain
    in manufactured play equipment, 89

challenge
    definition, 66

change in settings
    in site design, 14

chemical pollutants, 67

child development objectives, 3-4

children's design workshop, 200-201

circulation routes, 23

climbers, 99-100

cognitive delays
    as design criterion, 81

color
    as design criterion, 77

communication
    between parents and play leaders, 240
    in entrance settings, 37

community context
    in site analysis, 7
    see also community needs assessment

community involvement in risk management, 31, 240

community needs assessment, **199-201**
    see also community context in site analysis,
        community involvement, comunity workshop

community workshop, 199-200

compost
    heap as wildlife habitat, 148

concrete
    as pathway surface, 46
    as surfacing material, 116

Consumer Products Safety Commission (CPSC)
    climber requirements, 99-100
    compliance requirements, 71-6
    200 g's attentuation standard, 74, 117
    in the Second Edition, xiv
    rocking/spring-mounted equipment requirements, 103-4
    slide requirements, 91-5
    spinning equipment requirements, 102-3
    structural testing, 86
    swing requirements, 95-8

    upper body event requirements, 101-2
    wood treatment requirements, 87

court games, 111

Critical Height of play equipment
    related to surfacing depth, 117-18

crushed stone
    as pathway surface, 47

curbs
    to pathways, 44, 49

D

decks, 177

decision-making opportunities, 3

decomposed granite
    as pathway surface, 47
    as surfacing material, 116

defensible space
    in play programming, 230
    in risk management, 30, 236
    in site design, 13

design programming, 5

design workshop (children's), 200-201

detectable warnings, on stairs, 51
    see also warning textures

developmental disabilities
    description of, 254

differentiation of settings
    as design criterion, 71
    in site design, 22-4

disabilities
    descriptions of, 251-60

disfigurement, 260

diversity and clarity
    in site design, 11

documentation
    checklist for manufactured play equipment, 105-6
    in risk management, 31

domestic animals, 25, 147

drainage
    and equipment installation, 84

dramatic play
    opportunities, 4
    in play programming, 231
    setting (Flood Park), 210

dress-up clothes, 171

drinking fountains, 188

drop-off zones, 35-6

E

edges
    around equipment areas, 84-6

"edge effect," 24

Education of All Handicapped Children
    Act of 1975 (Public Law 94-142), 250

emotional disabilities
    description of, 254-5

enclosure, **60-3**
    of gathering, meeting and working places, 181
    for manufactured play equipment, 74-6
    of sand settings, 163
    variety with vegetation, 134
    see also fences

entrapment, 71-2

entrances, **34-7**
    communication function of, 37
    plan (Flood Park), 206-7

Environmental Yard, the, xiii

epilepsy
    description of, 255-6

equipment
    see manufactured equipment

electrical services, 192

erosion control
    and vegetation, 138

existing conditions
    in site analysis, 5-7

F

Fair Housing Amendments Act, 250

farmyard animals, 147

faucets, 187

fences, **60-3**
    degree of protection, 62
    design considerations, 61
    see also enclosures

field houses, 195

finishes
    in manufactured play equipment, 90

fireplaces, 186

first aid preparedness, 237-8

fish, 147

flexibility
    in site design, 12

Flood Park (case study), **199-226**

found objects, 169-70
    as gathering, meeting and working places, 182

fountains
    see water settings

fragrance garden play station, 218

G

games
    multipurpose accessible setting (Flood Park), 216
    court, 111

garden settings, **142-44**

gates, 43

gathering, meeting and working places, **179-92**
    design principles, 180-2
    importance of, 180
    plan (Flood Park), 214
    types of, 182-4

gazebos, 177

graduated challenge in site design, 11-12

grass
    artificial grass, 116
    as ground cover, 115-16
    as pathway surface, 47

ground covers, **114-217**
    see also surfacing

gravel
    as pathway surface, 48
grills, 186
group program spaces, 177
guidelines in action, **199-226**

H

handrails
    of pathways, 49
    of ramps, 53
    of stairways, 50-1
hard-surfaced play areas, 111
    see also mutlipurpose game settings
hardware
    in manufactured play equipment, 89-90
hazard
    definition, 66
hearing disabilities
    as design criterion, 81
    description of, 253
Hogan, Paul, 123
hollow blocks, 172
hose-filled temporary ponds, 154

I

identity (visual)
    of gathering, meeting and working places, 182
incidents, reporting and data analysis, 235
indoor-outdoor relationships, 26
infant play setting
    plan (Flood Park), 107, 209
inflatables, 104
    as props, 171
insects
    as play resources, 147
integration, 247-60
interpretive play equipment, 104
installation of manufactured equipment, 83-4

L

landforms, **128-31**
    "hill" and "hill circle," 129
    see also topography
landmarks, 19
large muscle activity
    as a design criterion, 69
Laurel Town Hall play station, 219
learning opportunities, 3
letter specifications for signs, 57-8
levels of accessibility
    definitions, 45
lighting, 192
linkage and flow
    as a design criterion, 70
loose parts, 170

M

mainstreaming
    see integration
maintenance
    and risk management, 82-3, 236
    of vegetation, 140-1
management
    criteria for play settings, **29-33**
    definition, 32
    of manipulative settings, 175
manipulable settings
    in site design, 14
    and vegetation, 135-36
    see also manipulative settings, play props
manipulative settings, 166-75
    management, 175
    natural settings as, 174-5
    types of, 169
    value of, 168
    see also manipulable settings, play props
manufactured play equipment settings, **64-109**
    design criteria for, 66-82
    plan (Flood Park), 208
    purchase documents, 107-09

master plan, 201
  Flood Park, 201, 203
  as risk management strategy, 243
materials
  in manufactured play equipment, 86-9
Max G Surface Resiliency Tester, 123
meadow, multipurpose setting
  plan (Flood Park), 213
meeting places
  see gathering, meeting and working places
metal
  in manufactured play equipment, 88
microclimate
  in designing gathering, meeting and working places, 181
  modified by vegetation, 134
  in site design, 14-15
modularity, 86
modular play props, 171-2
motor challenge
  as a design criterion, 70
motor disabilities
  design requirements, 79
  description of, 256-8
  enclosure requirements, 76
motor skill opportunities, 3
movement activity
  as a design criterion, 69
multiple disabilities
  as a design criterion, 82
multiple sclerosis, 259
multipurpose game settings, **110-13**
  meadow (Flood Park), 213
multisensory stimulation
  cues, 20-1
  fragrance garden play station, 218
  in site design, 14
muscular dystrophy, 259

N

National Federation of City Farms, 144
natural ground covers, 115-16
natural settings
  as manipulative settings, 174-5
  see also vegetation, water settings
nonambulatory
  as a design criterion, 79-80
nonclimable enclosure height, 74-6
nonslip (slip resistent, antiskid)
  surfaces, 44

O

oak circle play station, 219
open-endedness of settings in site design, 14
outdoor room play station, 219
outdoor storage
  box, 195
  compounds, 195
  cupboard, 194

P

pathways, **38-53**
  accessible routes, 39
  activity, 41
  choice of route, 41
  components of, 49
  design development, 53
  dimensions, 39
  Flood Park, 220
  surface treatments, 43, 46-8, 220
  treatment definitions, 48
pavers
  as pathway surface, 46, 47
pea gravel
  as surfacing material, 121-2
permanence of settings
  in site design, 14
physical disabilities
  description of, 258-9

picnic settings
    multiuse plan (Flood Park), 215
    see also picnic tables

picnic tables, 178
    as work tables, 185
    see also picnic settings

planning criteria for settings (Flood Park), 222-6

plants
    child-plant interaction, 137
    design of child-plant interactions, 139
    impact of plants on users, 137-8
    impact of users on plants, 138-9
    people-plant interaction, 25
    see also vegetation

plastics
    in manufactured play equipment, 88-9

play equipment
    see also manufactured play equipment settings

play events, 91-104

play leadership
    in adventure playgrounds, 173-4
    definition, 29
    in play programming, 231
    training for risk management, 238

play options
    as a design criterion, 68
    extended by vegetation, 134

play props, 166-75
    purpose-made, 171
    see also manipulative settings

play programming, **229-32**

play setting
    definition, 33
    evaluation (Flood Park), 222-26

play stations (Flood Park), **217-19**

play value
    definition, 29
    in manufactured equipment design, 68-71

poliomylitis, 259

ponds
    see water settings

pond life, 147

pools
    see water settings

programming potential
    definition, 29

protrusions, 72

R

ramps, **51-3**

Rehabilitation Act of 1973
    (Public Law 93-112), 249

Rehabilitation Act Amendment of 1974
    (Public Law 93-516), 249

retainers
    for manufactured equipment, 84-6
    see also edges

retreats, 18

risk management, 30-1
    definition, 233-34
    new models of, 241
    site improvement process, 242-4
    strategies, **233-44**

risk taking
    in play programming, 239

rocking equipment, 103-4

rope
    in manufactured play equipment, 89

rubber surfacing materials, 122-3

running, 111

S

safe challenge
    in site design, 10

safety
    definition, 30
    inspection programs, 82-3
    safety first policy, 242
    site improvement process, 242-4

safety inspection programs, 82-3

sand
  as pathway surface, 48
  as surfacing material, 121-2
  see also sand settings
sand settings, 160-5
  design principles, 162-4
  plan (Flood Park) 199, 211-12
  playability criteria, 161
  raised sand area, 164
  sand depth, 161
  sand pit, 164
  sand table, 165
  see also sand
scale
  as design criterion, 78
  in site design, 21
seasonal variation
  marked by vegetation, 134
Schools Council, 149
seating, 184
sensory cues, 205
sensory variety
  as design criterion, 68
  with vegetation, 134-5
  see also multisensory stimulation
sequoia grove play station, 219
shared environmental control, 30
shared site maintenance in risk management, 30
shelters
  in pathway design, 42
  in site design, 15
sight as sensory cue, 21
sight disabilities
  description of, 251-2
  design requirements, 78-9
signage, **54-9**
  guidelines for readability, 56-8
  international access symbol, 58
  program information, 59

signs
  design considerations, 56-8
  international access, 58
  warning, 76
  see also signage
site analysis, **5-8**
site design criteria, **9-26**
slides, 91-5
slope
  of pathways (Flood Park), 220
smell as sensory cue, 21
social development opportunities, 4
social spaces
  design of variety of, 16-17
  design with vegetation, 136
social interaction
  in site design, 16
soil (untreated)
  as pathway surface, 48
sound
  as sensory cue, 20
  sound waves play station, 209
spatial complexity, 68
  see also spatial experience
spatial experience
  design variety of, 17-18
spatial orientation, 19
special population design requirements, 78-82
spina bifida, 259
spinal cord injuries, 258
spinning equipment, 102-3
sports areas, **111-12**
spring-mounted equipment, 103-4
staff ratios in risk management, 31
stages, 177
stage settings, **176-8**
  plan (Flood Park), 213
  types, 177-8
stairways (and steps), **50-51**

"standard of care," 71

steps (and stairways), **50-51**

storage settings, **193-5**
    function of, 194

stroke, 259

structural considerations
    in manufactured equipment, 86

sun clock play station, 218

supervision
    in site design, 13
    in risk management, 236-7

surface treatments for pathways, 43-4

surfacing materials, 117-23

surfacing matrix, 124-7

surfacing standards, 117
    ASTM F1292, 117
    depth and Critical Height, 117-18
    surfacing matrix, 124-7

Swedish blocks, 165-66

swings, 95-8

synthetic surfacing materials, 122-3

T

tables (work), 185
    see also picnic tables

tactile warnings in pathway design, 44-5

"Tarzan ropes," 98

telephones
    outdoors, 189-90

terraces, 177

testing
    manufactured play equipment, 86

theme
    as a design criterion, 77

toilets, 190-1

topography, **128-31**
    and drainage, 130
    surface slopes, 130
    see also landforms

touch as sensory cue, 21

toys
    small manufactured, 170
    toy play in sand settings, 163
    wheeled, 173

transition zones
    around equipment, 86

trash receptacles, 189

trees, **132-41**
    as design feature, 134-7
    climability, 141
    see also vegetation

trip hazards, 85-6

turf, 115-16

U

Undefined places
    as play settings, 24-5

Uniform Federal Accessibility Standards
    description of, 248
    in the Second Edition, xiv

upper body play events, 101-2

use analysis, 201

V

Vegetation, **132-41**
    for craft and culinary activities, 136
    protection techniques, 62
    in sand settings, 163
    see also trees

verandas, 177

visible completion points, 18-19

visual identity
    as design criterion, 77
    in site design, 19

Vocational Rehabilitation Act of 1963, 248

W

waiting zones, 36

walking tour (assessment method), 200

warning textures
    on pathways, 44-5

waterfalls
    see water settings

water places
    as wildlife habitats, 149
    see also water settings

water settings, **150-9**
    aeration of, 158
    design criteria, 154-5
    on handicapped adventure playgrounds, 152
    plan (Flood Park), 212
    pools, fountains, cascades, sprays, 157
    recirculation design, 156
    types of, 153-4
    water tables, 159

weather watch play station, 218

wheeled toys
    and pathway design, 41-2

wildlife habitats, 25, 136

wood
    in manufactured play equipment, 86-7
    wood pile as wildlife habitat, 148

wood chips
    as pathway surface, 48
    pile as wildlife habitat, 148
    as surfacing material, 120

wood decking
    as pathway surface, 47

working places
    see gathering, meeting and working places